The Rise of the Staffordshire Potteries

Origins of Industry

THE RISE OF THE STAFFORDSHIRE POTTERIES

by John Thomas, Ph.D

WITH A PREFACE BY G. D. H. COLE

Adams & Dart

First published 1971 by Adams & Dart, 40 Gay Street, Bath, Somerset
S.B.N. 239.00063.3 The text is set in 'Monotype' Caslon
Printed in Great Britain by R & R Clark Ltd, Edinburgh

Contents

ACKNOWLEDGEMENTS

I would like to express my thanks to the many individuals and institutions who have helped me in my research for this book. Three direct descendants of Josiah Wedgwood, the founder of Etruria – the late Hon. Josiah Wedgwood, the late Tom Wedgwood and Sir John Wedgwood – gave me access to the valuable Wedgwood archives that were then housed in the old Etruria, whilst the late Lord Wedgwood of Barlaston kindly placed at my disposal his private collection of Wedgwoodiana.

As a member of the National Pottery Council from 1925–1939 I had many close personal contacts with leading potters, among them the late Percy W. L. Adams, and several Directors of other leading pottery firms, including Spode and Copeland, Minton's, the Tuscan Pottery, Henry Richards Tiles and Twyfords Sanitary Pottery.

Important Trade Union documents of the nineteenth century were made available to me by my friend the late Arthur Hollins, M.P.

I would like to thank the following Public Libraries for their assistance: Stoke on Trent City Library; William Salt Library, Stafford, for giving me special facilities to study their valuable collection of ceramic documents; the Birmingham City Reference Library for allowing me to examine and copy the original archives of Boulton and Watt. I would also like to thank the Public Record Office in London for allowing me to transcribe valuable Home Office records relating to riots and disturbances in the potteries.

I am deeply indebted to the late Professor R. H. Towney and to H. L. Beales, of the London School of Economics, for their help and encouragement while I was preparing my researches for publication. My wife was of great assistance in the copying of original documents and contemporary maps.

Finally, I would like to express my gratitude to the present Directors of the firm of Wedgwood Ltd, and to the Chairman of Richards Tiles Ltd, for their generous financial assistance which enabled me to undertake the research incorporated in this volume.

J. T.

PUBLISHER'S NOTE

The Preface by the late Professor Cole was written before the last war as a contribution to Dr. Thomas's thesis, and has not since been revised.

List of Illustrations

Preface

The history of the industries of Great Britain is still to a great extent unwritten, though gradually the monographs dealing with particular trades and manufactures in particular stages of their development are accumulating. Of not one even of the greatest industries is there yet a satisfactory connected history covering all its phases; and on most of the manufactures of the second rank there is very little indeed embodying the results of careful, scholarly research. Yet it is impossible to build up a clear account of the general course of economic evolution except on the basis of detailed accounts of the growth of indivdual trades or industries. Easy as it is to generalize about the successive stages of the rise of capitalist production, such generalizations are apt to be very misleading unless they are the outcome of a careful and balanced comparison of the actual course of evolution in many industries, both great and small. In fact, generalizations about the development of British Capitalism were until recently based for the most part too largely upon the known facts about the growth of the textile trades, and above all the Lancashire cotton trade; and even now, when the parallel rise of the coal and iron industries has been more fully studied, far too little use is made of the abundant materials relating to smaller manufactures that have been less written about by scholars intent on both eliciting and interpreting the fundamental facts. Among our great industries, engineering and building are still without even a single historian for a large part of their development; and most histories that do exist for lesser industries are either scrappy and superficial, and largely second-hand, or already long out of date.

It is not difficult to understand why this situation persists. The writing of the history of an industry is an exacting business, bound to consume a prodigious amount of time and involve endless trouble, if it is to be completely done. It is entirely unremunerative – in the sense that, even if the book in which the writer embodies his results sells well, within the limits possible for a book of this order, the remuneration cannot conceivably amount to payment for the toil and trouble of writing it, even at the most unskilled labourer's rate of wages. The author will, indeed, be most exceptionally fortunate if he succeeds in recovering his bare out-of-pocket expenses. Nor is this all. The work of writing an industry's history is not suitable for ordinary research students who have recently taken their degrees and are in search of subjects for doctoral theses. It demands too much background, too much technical knowledge of processes and organization, and too much and too expensive travelling about, reproduction of scarce documents and so forth. It cannot be done at all in the two, or at most three, years which the ordinary post-graduate research worker can assign to the preparation of his thesis.

So the task, as no one cares to finance it so as to make possible the doing of it by senior, qualified research workers, remains mostly unaccomplished. The greater credit is due to Dr. John Thomas, who, in the interstices of a busy life as Resident Tutor in the Potteries under Oxford University and the Workers' Educational Association, has managed to execute a thoroughly creditable history of the potters' trade during the most interesting phases of its development.

Dr. Thomas had, indeed, two advantages in setting out upon his formidable task. The first was that a great deal has been written already about the pottery trade, though not in the shape of a connected economic history. The second was that the high degree of localization of the trade in the north of Staffordshire made the discovery of the essential materials less difficult than it would have been in the case of a more widely dispersed branch of manufacture. There were many potteries in other parts of England; but throughout the period of which Dr. Thomas writes Stoke-on-Trent and its immediate neighbours have been pre-eminently 'The Potteries', and their history the history of the pottery trades.

On the first of these two points, however, a reservation needs to be made. Much has been written about pottery; but by far the greater part of it has been rather about the ceramic art than about pottery as an industry; and those writers who have dealt with the economics of the subject have for the most part approached it in the spirit rather of biographers than of economic historians. Consequently, while there were many books for Dr. Thomas to consult, none of them covered anything like the same ground as he attempts to cover in this volume; nor could he hope to find most of the materials he needed in the already published records. He had to go back throughout to original sources – to the business archives of such firms as Wedgwoods, Spodes and Mintons, and to that invaluable storehouse – the Boulton and Watt papers and correspondence, not to mention a host of lesser authorities.

I think it will be generally agreed that Dr. Thomas has done his work well, and that his book throws a large amount of new light both on the evolution of the pottery trades and on the general development of the 'Industrial Revolution' in the eighteenth and early nineteenth centuries. In particular, it is valuable to have corrected for us the common misconception that the industry of the Five Towns was barely touched till nearly the middle of the nineteenth century by mechanisation. Dr. Thomas, I think, fully proves his point that, on the contrary, the pottery trades under Wedgwood's influence were affected both early and to a great extent by the advent of mechanical processes based on steam power. It is valuable also to have the evidence about the early use of coal in the industry so completely marshalled – for on a few matters is there so much misunderstanding as about the use of coal in manufacture during the earlier phases of the 'Industrial Revolution'. Finally, it is of special value to have the story of labour and Trade Unionism among the potters re-told in the light of the real facts about the development of productive technique.

With these few prefatory words, I can safely leave the reader to Dr. Thomas's expert guidance through the complex story of the pottery trades. If I may add a wish, it is that his book may encourage other teachers whose regular work brings them in to close contact with some interesting industry or industrial area to bestow upon other trades a skill and energy comparable with that which is shown here. Especially, as an old tutor and officer of the Workers' Educational Association, I hope it may stimulate other WEA and extra-mural tutors to follow Dr. Thomas's admirable example.

G. D. H. COLE

PART I

FROM PEASANT POTWORKS
TO POTTERY FACTORY

CHAPTER I

The Peasant Pottery Stage

'The Potteries', that concentration of factory towns within a space of little over 20 square miles in North Staffordshire, was one of the notable products of the Industrial Revolution.

The first outlines of the area can be seen taking shape between 1710 and 1715 in a list of 47 potworks of that period, in Burslem, Hanley and other places left by Josiah Wedgwood, the great pioneer, in his manuscript collection.[1]

But, 30 years earlier, when Robert Plot was making a topographical survey of Staffordshire, its industries and arts, there is no mention or sign of such a district. Only Burslem, marked on Plot's map as a 'mercat towne' along with Newcastle-under-Lyme and Uttoxeter, is dignified with the title 'pottery towne'.

'The greatest pottery they have in this County is carreyed on at Burslem near Newcastle-under-Lyme, where for making their several sorts of pots, they have as many sorts of clay, which they dig around the Towne, all within half a mile distance, the best being found near the coale.'

Potting, in Plot's day, then, was very much a 'peasant' industry or craft carried out on a small scale by members of the potter's family. (A view to be later expressed by J. C. Wedgwood, a descendant of Josiah, in his study of the industry in the seventeenth century.)[2]

These craftsmen made butter pots for farmers to sell their produce in at markets and fairs, and Plot has much to say about the link between the production of butter and the necessary earthenware containers.

But the whole craft was not devoted to 'utility ware'. Plot describes the 'ornamental' ware made by using some different coloured clay ('slip') or by mixing in two minerals, either lead or manganese. This slip-ware was porous and Plot describes how later on it was lead glazed before being fired in the potter's oven.

How the ovens were fired he does not say, though he mentions 'pit-coal' in use at brickworks, a clamp of 16,000 bricks, taking '7 tunns of coal'.

[1] Now in Etruria Museum   [2] *Staffordshire Pottery and Its History*

'In 24 hours an Oven of Pots will be burnt [i.e. fired] then they let the fire goe out by degrees, which in 10 hours more will be perfectly done, and then they draw them for sale which is chiefly to the poor Cratemen, *who carry them at their backs all over the Country*'. Whether the 'poor cratemen' earn little or are to be pitied as human packhorses, Plot does not say. But they sold their 'flatware' or plates and 'hollow ware', jugs, mugs and cups to housewives and the butter pots went for sale to fairs and market towns.

Plot says little of the state of traffic or wider transport links except that Amblecot clay is 'sent as far as London, sometimes by waggon and sometimes by land to Beaudley and so down the Severn to Bristol'.

In Plot's survey, then, it is a rural craft without 'Potteries' or known potters. But changes were already underway, even as his work was published. Plot himself mentions no potters by name (though he mentions Charles Riggs, a tobacco-pipe maker and a Thomas Wood tilemaker – both of Newcastle-under-Lyme). The local historian Simeon Shaw takes up the story from 1686 and carries it forward to 1730 in his *History of the Staffordshire Potteries*. This work, published in 1829, concentrates on the industry and is full of the names of the potters, the men who were helping bring about the vital changes by their experiments with materials and techniques.

'About 1685, Mr. Thomas Miles of Shelton mixed with the whitish clay found in Shelton some of the fine sand from Baddeley Hedge and produced a rude kind of White Stone Ware. Another person of the same name of Miles Bank, Hanley, produced the Brown Stone Ware of that day, by mixing the same kind of sand with the Can Marl obtained from the coal pits.'

By 1690, says Shaw, 'Crouch-ware' was being made in Burslem, using common brick clay and fine sand from Mole Cob (Mow Cop today). Some used Can Marl and sand, while others used the dark grey clay from the coal pits together with sand for the body. Then a potter named Astbury, who together with Twyford, another former pottery worker, set up on his own in Shelton, began to experiment with clays from outside Staffordshire.

'Astbury very soon began to employ the pipe clay from Biddeford. The pipe clay was levigated until only the finest particles were suspended in the water, forming a substance like cream'. Astbury 'tried this clay and the Shelton marl for his white ware with such success that he soon rejected the native clays entirely'.

As a shrewd chemist, Simeon Shaw gives us the difference between these 'native clays' and the 'Biddeford' or as it was later called 'Chester' clay. 'The native clays are all metalliferous, each having a portion of oxide of iron, the clays from Devon or Dorset have all their impurities extracted before they are vended to the purchases. They possess every property required for their designed purpose, being extremely white when fired'.

Shaw credits Atsbury with the introduction of an ingredient from outside the area: 'He first employed the flint (after it had been calcined and pounded in a mortar) in a mixture with water to a thick pulp, as a wash or dip, which he applied to give a coating to the vessels, some time before he introduced it along with the clay in the body of his ware'.

Others were at work improving the ingredients. David Elers, who employed Astbury, before he set up on his own, was a renowned innovator, though there was dispute over his claim to some of the improvements.

Writing to Thomas Bentley, the Liverpool merchant who became his partner, Josiah Wedgwood says one of Eler's improvements was 'the refining of our common red clay by sifting, etc., and making it into Tea and Coffee ware in imitation of the Chinese Red.'

The 'sifting etc.' meant that the clay was washed, sieved, ground, blunged, and later weathered before it was thrown on the wheel. This improved 'body' allowed the potter, after throwing the clay on the wheel, to improve its outward appearance by turning it on the lathe. According to Shaw, Astbury was 'put to work a treadle lathe' by Elers. The lathe was then something new, but Shaw thinks there is 'no evidence to show that the Elers were the first to utilise it'.

As Plot had reported, the pots would be glazed before firing. In Plot's account they were lead-glazed. Shaw says that Crouch ware was sometimes glazed with lead or later with salt. The idea of glazing with salt came in from outside, but there is disagreement over who brought it in. Josiah Wedgwood has no doubt that 'glazing with salt, by casting it amongst the ware, whilst it is red hot, came to us from Germany'. But 'whether Mr. Elers was the person to whom we are indebted for the improvement, I do not know'. Neither David Elers, nor John Philip, another potter, introduced salt-glazing to North Staffordshire, states Shaw, categorically. But J. C. Wedgwood in his *Staffordshire Pottery and Its History* takes the other side: 'We may assume that Mr. Elers did in fact introduce the salt glaze into North Staffordshire'.

Throughout this period of new techniques, new materials, the number of potbanks grew. But still, to judge from Wedgwood's list covering 1710–15, they were all small units.

Not one had a total output valued at more than £6 a week. The average output of the 40 potworks is quoted at £3. 10s. a week. The estimated output of all the 40 is given as only £139. 10s. in one week. Wedgwood states the master of the

RSP B

potworks drew 10s. a week as his profit, in addition to 6s. for his labour as master potter. As to the number of workers engaged at the potworks, they never exceeded six. Many of the workers were members of the master-potter's family or relatives by marriage. The potworks was a family concern, with a domestic touch about it. There was a certain degree of specialization in the potworks. The master-potter and his journeyman could be experts as slipmakers, throwers or turners, as well as able to 'stouk' (i.e. as handlers or makers of spouts). Boys started work as apprentices for a period of seven years from 14 to 21, at which age they received 4s. a week till they were considered 'full journeymen' receiving 6s. a week for a further term of five years. Then they could become master potters. Shaw quotes an apprentice indenture of Aron Wood, who was apprenticed to Dr. Thomas Wedgwood, one of Josiah Wedgwood's relatives.

During these early decades of the eighteenth century, there was little change in the ornamentation of pottery wares, except for 'the ornamentation with tea branch in relief', referred to in Wedgwood's letters to Bentley. The newer Elers and post-Elers teapots sold for 12s. to 24s. a piece, according to Shaw. Coffee and tea drinking had begun to be fashionable in the houses of the rich in London, and in the houses of gentry outside London. In the capital, new clubs and coffee houses flourished where tea, coffee and chocolate drinks were popular. All this naturally meant a new demand for earthenware teapots, coffee jugs, mugs and cups and saucers.

Transport serving the expanding potworks had changed little from that described by Robert Plot. Josiah Wedgwood has left us some notes relating to the transport of coal and clay to potworks.

Clay, 2 cart loads,   at   2s. = 4s.
Coals, 48 horses loads, at   2d. = 8s.
Carriage of   do.   at 1½d. = 6s.

Then in a footnote Wedgwood adds: 'Only one horse and one mule left in Hanley. No carts scarcely in the country. Coal carried on men's backs'.

But this state of affairs could not remain. To cope with the expanding market for their pots, the master potters needed to expand production, develop techniques, develop a transport network to carry their goods. As we shall see in the following chapters, they were to do just this and potter-industrialists, like Josiah Wedgwood, were to play a leading part.

CHAPTER 2

Craft into Industry

A sketch map published in 1750 shows Burslem as a rural place, with 150 or so householders – a nest of potworks, some public houses with village lanes ending in pleasant meadows, barnfields and crofts – Velvet Croft, Hole Croft, Kin Croft, Birch Croft, Oxley Croft, and, of course, glebe lands attached to the church. To the south a belt of countryside separates Burslem from Hanley and to the North from Tunstall. The maypole on the village green is a symbol of Burslem's truly rural character even in 1750.

This map was based on a list of potters drafted in 1750 by Enoch Wood, himself a potter. Compared with the list drafted by Josiah Wedgwood, to cover the years 1710–15, there are few changes – some potters have dropped out, because of death, the closing of a potworks or a takeover. This was Burslem, described by Josiah Wedgwood as 'the principal pottery in North Staffordshire', Burslem at the time when the slow change over from the master craftsman stage to that of the pottery factory was beginning.

A symbol of that change is marked on the 1750 map – a windmill on 'The Jenkins', a hillock or plot of land originally owned probably by a man named Jenkins.

Like other windmills which have survived to this day at Hilderstone and Werrington, close to the modern Potteries, the windmill on 'The Jenkins' was used to grind corn, where there was no water to drive a water-wheel. But, perhaps a decade or two before 1750 (date of the map) the windmill on The Jenkins was adapted to another purpose – one nothing to do with direct agricultural needs, but everything to do with an embryo industry.

It was adapted to crush flints for mixing with the local clays to improve the pottery ware. Benson's method of crushing flints in water had been patented in 1726. A great demand for crushed or powdered flint, as an ingredient in the actual body of the clay or as a glaze for the 'biscuit' ware, soon had local mill-wrights adapting the mechanism of the wind-driven corn mill to do the harder task of crushing and pounding flint stones.

Eliza Meteyard, in *The Life of Josiah Wedgwood*, writes: 'Two millwrights — J. Gallimore of Millfield-gate, Lane End, and Joseph Bourne of Bemersley — were the first to adapt the ordinary [corn] mill machinery of the district to this new process, or who built mills entirely for this purpose.'

Samuel Smiles, too, in the section on James Brindley in his *Lives of the Engineers* records that the now famous millwright came to settle in the Potteries and 'hired a millwright's shop, belonging to T. and J. Wedgwood, and was employed to work on this windmill on 'The Jenkins'.

Miss Meteyard gives further details:

In January 1756 T. Wedgwood of the Churchyard seems to have let or sold to his distant cousins John and Thomas Wedgwood of the Big House a part of his inherited estate at Brownhills, known as the Great Oldfield or Jenkins, on which to erect a windmill, of greater power than any yet known in the district, for grinding calcined flints. The site or its immediate neighbourhood, as it was the highest ground in or immediately about Burslem, appears to have been long previously occupied by a (wind) mill.

Brindley was called in, and, Miss Meteyard tells us, he:

. . . busied himself with what he had previously termed "a new invention". . . . Its construction involved some peculiarities, as within its walls a well was sunk for the supply of water to the grinding vats and its sails and gearing were unusually large and powerful. On the first day the mill was set in motion, to the consternation of everybody and most so of the engineer, the sails were blown off during the high wind. But Brindley was not one to be disheartened by small mischance . . . and at once he set to, to repair the mischief done. At length, one of the most valuable mills of that day in or about Burslem was completed, and the Messrs. Wedgwood were the owners of a property, which preserved its utility long after they had passed away.

Smiles' account corroborates Miss Meteyard's story of Brindley's connection with this windmill on The Jenkins, and its adaptation for grinding flints for the potters. Simeon Shaw unfortunately makes no reference to this Brindley Jenkins Windmill episode, and its adaptation for flint grinding. Probably, when Shaw wrote his *History of the Staffordshire Potteries*, the windmill was derelict and already obsolete. As Smiles puts it in his life of Brindley: 'Wind and water had heretofore been almost the exclusive agents employed for the purpose. But far-seeing philosophers and ingenious mechanics had for centuries been feeling their way towards the far greater power derived from the pent-up force of vaporised water, and engines had actually been contrived which rendered it probable that the problem would ere long be solved and a motive agent invented which should be easily controllable and independent alike of wind, tides and waterfalls'.

How that agent — steam power — was introduced into the Potteries, we shall see in Chapters 4 and 5. But in the days of the adaptation of the Jenkins wind-mill, that revolutionary change was still some three decades away, and the potworks in and around Burslem were only slowly beginning their transformation into factories.

In 1750 then, the potworks belong to one master craftsman, aided by members of his family or near relatives. There is not evidence yet of partnerships between family potters, the only possibility of joint ownership being between brothers, like Thomas and John Mitchell, the Cartlich Brothers, the Woods, the Wedgwood or Adams families. But some sense of the changes impending can be gained by moving forward half a century.

Another map of the Potteries was published in *The Staffordshire Directory* of 1800 by T. Allbutt of Hanley. A comparison of this map with that of 1750, reveals that great changes had taken place during these five decades. First, the isolation of Burslem is beginning to disappear. As Burslem itself grows and Cobridge expands, the rural belts between Burslem and Hanley and Burslem and Newcastle-under-Lyme are gradually being industrialized. Hanley itself expands in the fork marked by the Cauldon Canal and the Grand Trunk Canal. Then from Stoke Lane in a straight line almost through Stoke-upon-Trent, on through Lower Lane and Lane Delph (today known as Fenton) on to Longton, we get a growing cluster of potworks. At the top of the map from Burslem via Brownhills, potworks extend towards Tunstall, the northernmost town of the six which today make up the industrial region called 'The Potteries', and the civic unit 'The City of Stoke-on-Trent'.

By 1800 even 'the pottery of Burslem' of Wedgwood's note of 1710–1715 had become the modern ceramic hub of 'The Potteries'. More, this 1800 map and list show that the potworks had increased from 50 in 1710 to 124. But there was a qualitative change, which neither maps nor statistics alone can depict. But there are several contemporary writers who help one to visualize the changes, during the five decades ending in 1800 and a little beyond. Arthur Young in his *Six Months Tour Through the North of England*, in 1769: 'I viewed the Staffordshire Potteries at Burslem and the neighbouring villages, which have of late been carried on with such amazing success. There are 300 houses, which are calculated to employ on an average 20 hands each or 6,000 on the whole, but if all the variety of people that work in what may be called the preparation for the employment of the immediate manufactories, the total number cannot be much short of 10,000 and it is increasing every day.'

John Aikin gives a picture of the Potteries in *Thirty Miles Around Manchester*, with a good deal of space devoted to Wedgwood's influence there. In fact, J. C. Wedgwood in his *Staffordshire Pottery and its History* suggests that this section of Aikin's book was written by Alexander Chisholm, Secretary to Wedgwood in 1795. Aikin describes a string of villages 'something more than 7 miles, a considerable part of which by joining together, strikes the traveller as but one town, although under different names'. W. Tunnicliff's *Topographical Survey of the Counties of Staffordshire, Cheshire and Lancashire*, published in 1787, was plagiarized later by mumerous writers of views, guides and directories of the Potteries, with varying tables of freights etc.

THE MANUFACTORIES

There is one noticeable feature in all books referring to the local industries from 1780 onwards. The term 'potworks' of Plot's days and early eighteenth century is replaced by the term 'manufactory'. Aikin refers to the 'manufacture', not 'potworks' in 1795. In 1817 Pitt in his *History of Staffordshire* uses such phrases as 'first-rate manufactories'. 'Manufactory' is the term used for a pottery in the Report of the Government Inquiry into Children employed in Manufactories (1816). In fact, the first question put to Josiah Wedgwood II in this Inquiry was, 'You are engaged in an extensive manufactory in the Potteries?' He replied, 'I am.' Simeon Shaw in his *History* (1829) refers to all the pottery establishments as 'manufactories'. Ward in his *History of Stoke-upon-Trent* (1838) also uses this term.

Government official documents published from 1833 onwards class the pottery establishments, definitely, as '*factories*', though 'The 1841 Census Reports on Population' resorts to the 'Pottery China and Earthenware Manufacture'. With the large number of employees and degree of concentration of works in large establishments, the term 'factory' would have been more appropriate. Clive Day in his survey *Distribution of Industrial Occupations 1841–1861* states, 'The largest single industry with a national distribution outside the textiles and metals was pottery, employing some 23,000, nearly two-thirds of the total number of workers were concentrated in the single county of Staffordshire'. Fong in his survey of the pottery industry, *Triumph of the Factory System*, refers to the pottery establishments as 'factories'. He based his authority mainly on the practice of Factory Commissioners from 1833 onwards, and especially in the Census Report of 1844.

In his evidence to the 1816 Commission of Inquiry, Josiah Wedgwood II argued that his pottery at Etruria and others in Staffordshire were 'manufactories' that were 'scattered [houses] and only two storeys in height', in contrast with textile 'factories' in which 'machinery supplies the power'. This 1816 Inquiry was a device of Sir Robert Peel to convert some opponents to his new Bill, endeavouring to extend the operations of the First Factory Act of 1802 entitled

'The Factory Health and Morals Act', which applied to textile factories only. Wedgwood in his evidence on his own behalf, as well as for his fellow potters, resisted the Bill on three grounds. First, the size and structure of the manufactory with its scattered workshops of only two storeys. Secondly, the question of concentration of numbers of employees in one large unit or distributed in several workshops. And thirdly, the scale on which power-driven machinery was used in the manufactory. In 1816 Wedgwood said he employed 387 workers. It is true many of these were modellers, designers and artists, who from the nature of their work could be housed in scattered houses of only 'two storeys in height'. But it is certain that many other ceramic operations were carried out by larger groups, housed in a workshop much larger than a house of two storeys. There would be found even in Etruria, some concentration of employees. As the business grew, these smaller workshops naturally would be extended or even rebuilt. The more the pottery production increased, the greater became the need to install steam-engines, as we have recorded earlier.

Josiah Wedgwood, when cross-examined at the Commission and asked, 'Your manufactory does not employ much force?', replied frankly: 'I employ a steam-engine for grinding the materials and some of the lathes are turned by the steam-engine'. From 1816 onwards the pottery establishments kept on increasing in size, and added to the number of steam-engines used, not only to drive grinding and mixing mills, but to drive other machines – throwers' wheels, turners' lathes, jiggers, jollies and other pottery machinery (see Chapter 5). In 1833, Enoch Wood's pottery was recorded in the 1833 Factory Report as employing 1,100 hands. It was not until 1867 that the potteries were declared 'factories' by statute.

A potworks might confine itself to making just 'pots', plain glazed earthenware, requiring no separate 'shop' or decorating works to ornament it. It might remain a small 'potworks' purchasing its clay, ready mixed flints and other materials from a larger pottery. Some potters with small potworks even purchased their crates or packing casks from a large pottery and thus had no crate-shop. Even today many potters buy their colours ready mixed from colour merchants, and some even buy their clays and flints ready mixed from some potters' mill distant from the actual pottery.

The very term 'workshop' or 'workroom' persists today, even in some of the largest pottery establishments. For example, in the Spode-Copelands factory there is a 'sagger-workshop' in quite a separate part of the premises, just as it was in the days of the founder, Josiah Spode. The actual sagger-makers are *not* on the pay-roll of the factory. They are contract workers on their own.

Sagger-making has been a family craft and these workers can trace their ancestry back to sagger makers who worked for Josiah Spode.

By courtesy of the late P. W. L. Adams, F.S.A., a direct descendant of the founder of Adams' Pottery at Tunstall, I was able to see the account books of his ancestors from 1800 to 1827. There I found accounts showing Sam and Thomas Cartledge being supplied by Adams on various dates, with 40 lbs. of composition for 2s. sometimes 90 lbs., but never more than 1 cwt. in any one week.

Then in 1808, John and Ralph Hall regularly bought 10 cwts. of composition per month for £3. Adams, who was a local landowner and colliery proprietor, sold coals for the Hall brothers to fire their kiln. They paid £86. 4s. 9d. to Adams for coal and marl on 27 November 1807. In this valuable collection of accounts, I found sales to small potters by Adams of supplies of ground glaze, ground fritt for glazes, mixed colours, coals, sand, Cornwall stone, blue clay and composition.

It is very difficult to know accurately the number of potter workers before Arthur Young's estimate in 1769, when he toured the Potteries. Still, from Wedgwood's list of potworks for 1710–1715, a provisional estimate can be made. There were 47 potworks in this list. Taking this number in round figures, say that in 50 small potworks there were employed an average of 6 men, with 4 apprentices or boys. This would make a total of, say 500 employed in all the potworks in the Burslem area. Moving on to 1769, and Arthur Young's estimate. He writes of 300 houses in the potteries, engaged as potworks. He estimates an average of 20 employees per 'house', i.e. workroom, giving in all about 6,000 employees. This may be an overestimate, so let us say, that in 1769 there were 5,000 employees.

At a Committee of the House of Commons in 1785 Wedgwood stated that there were between 15,000 and 20,000 employed in the pottery industry. Here he was speaking on behalf of all the pottery industry of Britain – those in the out-potteries of London, Liverpool, Bristol, Derby and Worcester as well as those in his native county. One can be sure that Wedgwood, the tactician and strategist, would quote the higher figure of 20,000 so as to win his case for his fellow-potters in his fight in the House of Commons Committee. So let us assume that the lower figure of 15,000 is a safer estimate.

How many of this 15,000 actually worked in the Potteries? Figures for potters in the trade unions of the Pottery Workers show that about 75 per cent. of the pottery employees are in Staffordshire. This is over 10 per cent. more than the figures given in the 1841 census. So in 1785 the percentage of pottery employees would be 15 per cent. or perhaps 30 per cent. less than in 1841. On this basis, I would conclude that in 1785, there were between 5,000 and 7,500 pottery workers employed in the Potteries. This would tally very well as an increase on the Arthur Young estimate of 6,000 in 1769.

John Boyle in his *Journal of the Royal Statistical Society* 1839 gives statistics relating to the employees in 130 factories during the 1835 potters' strike.:

78 on strike with 19,160 employees idle.
52 not on strike with 940 employees working.
130 factories employ 20,100 employees when not on strike

Boyle's figures may be taken as fairly accurate, for he was then an active member of the Chamber of Commerce in the Potteries. Perhaps we could whittle his estimate with safety down to 20,000.

The 1841 census of occupation for the Potteries gives a figure of 15,158 for employees in pottery and earthenware factories. This total includes only establishments employing over 100. In the smaller pottery works, it is safe to say that a few thousand employees were engaged, but not included in the census returns. So I would add a minimum of 5,000 to the census returns, making at least 20,000 employed.

Summarizing the estimates for this period:

ESTIMATED NUMBER OF POTTERY EMPLOYEES IN THE POTTERIES

Date	Number of Employees
1710–15	500
1785	15,000
1835	20,000
1841	20,000–23,000
1850	25,000

The expansion of the pottery industry is reflected, not only in the above table, but also in the statistics of the censuses of population. These naturally show a greater rate of expansion than in the number of pottery workers, for the expansion of the pottery establishments would attract into North Staffordshire Potteries families from the out-potteries, and families ministering to the consumer and other needs of the more numerous pottery employees. The increasing application of steam-driven machinery from 1835 to 1850 increased the number of women and girls employed on these machine processes. Here are the census returns:

Years	Estimated Population
1801	42,514
1811	56,292
1821	68,567
1831	84,039
1841	107,257
1851	130,258

CAPTAINS OF INDUSTRY

With the development of the industry, and transition to factories, occurs the rise of captains of industry choosing business associates – in contrast to the earlier master potters, who worked alongside their journeymen and apprentices.

Though Josiah Wedgwood had been apprenticed to his brother Thomas, who had inherited his potworks from his father, he was not taken on as a partner with Thomas. Josiah started on his own as a master potter at Cliff Bank in Stoke, with a practical potter named Thomas Alders as his partner, in or about 1752, along with a John Harrison, who had acquired an interest in Alders' small pottery. Rhead states that Wedgwood supplied only £20 as capital, a sum he had inherited from his father. Harrison contributed the rest of the capital, while Josiah provided the master potter's technical skill. This partnership did not last long. In 1754 Wedgwood entered into partnership with Thomas Whieldon of Fenton Low, a potter of distinction, who had built up a good business. This Whieldon-Wedgwood partnership ended in 1759, and Wedgwood started a pottery on his own by renting the Ivy House Works for £10 a year from his prosperous relatives, John and Thomas Wedgwood of 'The Big House' in Burslem. Later in 1762, Wedgwood moved to the Brick House Pot-bank, still in Burslem, at a rental of £21 a year. Here he installed his cousin Thomas Wedgwood, as the manager of his 'useful' wares. In 1766 Josiah made Thomas Wedgwood his partner at the Bell 'useful' wares pottery in the Brick House.

In the same year, Josiah Wedgwood suggested to Thomas Bentley, a successful cultured merchant of Liverpool, that he should join him as a partner in the new pottery he had decided to build at a spot between Hanley and Newcastle-under-Lyme. This later became the world famous Etruria Pottery. Bentley accepted the proposal and became a partner at Etruria in 1769, and continued until his death in 1780. Wedgwood paid £3,000 for the Bridge House Estate to accommodate his new factory, and new house Etruria Hall for his family, as he had married his cousin Sarah, the daughter of Richard Wedgwood, a cheese factor of Spen Green.

After Thomas Bentley's death Wedgwood made his nephew Thomas Byerley his partner. After the death of Wedgwood Senior, the younger Josiah continued with Byerley as partner. On Byerley's death the firm was known as 'Josiah Wedgwood' till 1823, when Josiah Wedgwood II made his son a partner, and the firm was called 'Josiah Wedgwood and Son'. Other sons of Josiah Wedgwood III became partners in 1827, and the firm was called 'Josiah Wedgwood and Sons' till 1895, when the qualification 'Ltd' was added.

Josiah Spode I started as an apprentice with Thomas Whieldon. After his term of apprenticeship, Spode worked as a journeyman with Whieldon until 1762, when he became works manager with Turner and Banks at their Stoke pottery. John Turner in 1770 dissolved his partnership with Banks, to start his own pottery at Lane End. So in 1770, Spode took over the Stoke pottery, as a master potter with Tomlinson, a local solicitor, supplying the capital. Spode was ambitious and entered into partnership with a Thomas Mountford, who owned a potworks in Shelton – about a mile from his Stoke pottery. These two partnerships lasted only seven years, and in 1776, Spode purchased his Stoke pottery outright and soon introduced his son Josiah into the pottery, putting him in charge of his London warehouse in association with William Copeland, a capable merchant in the tea business. After his father's death, Josiah Junior took his son Josiah Spode III into partnership, along with Copeland. The firm then traded as 'Spode, Son and Copeland'.

Here the parallel development with Wedgwood ceases. After the death of Spode II, his son Josiah Spode III took very little interest in the potworks. This may have been the result of an accident at the factory which deprived him of his left arm. Probably another factor was that he had married the heiress to a large fortune in the coal and iron business around Stoke. In 1829, Spode's widow and her son, Josiah IV, left the potteries, severing all connection with the firm, and in 1833, the son of William Copeland, Alderman W. T. Copeland, acquired the pottery and took a Mr. Spencer Garrett as partner. The firm then was called 'Copeland and Garrett (late Spode)'. In 1847 Garrett retired, and the firm was known till 1867 as 'Copeland (late Spode)'. In 1867, Copeland took his four sons into partnership and the firm was then called 'W. T. Copeland and Sons Ltd.'

Within a stone's throw of this Copeland (Spode) pottery is that of Thomas Minton, once employed by Josiah Spode as an engraver. Thomas Minton came to Stoke in 1789 as an engraver of willow and other patterns for Josiah Spode I. In 1793, when promoted as master engraver, Minton decided to set up a pottery of his own. He chose a site opposite a stone china factory owned by Joseph Poulson, who was once a manager at Spode's pottery. The new potworks was completed by 1796 and consisted, according to Llewellyn Jewitt, of 'one Bisque and one glost oven, with slip house for preparing the clay and only such other buildings and appliances as were necessary to make good working commencement'. Following the example of John Turner and Banks, who appointed a practical potter, like Spode, to manage their pottery, Minton the engraver made Joseph Poulson the manager of his new factory. For 18 weeks' work Poulson was paid £18. 18s. 0d. But later in 1797, Minton made Poulson his partner. The firm was known till 1803 as 'Minton and Poulson'.

As the demand for his wares increased, so he needed to expand and enlarge his factory. Thus Minton followed the example of Wedgwood and Spode. He took as a partner with capital and business experience, a Mr. William Pownall, hailing from Liverpool, the city where Wedgwood had found his merchant partner Bentley. The firm then became 'Minton, Poulson and Pownall'. Poulson died in 1808, and with Pownall retired, Thomas Minton was left as sole proprietor. The firm was then titled 'Thomas Minton' from 1809 to 1817. In 1817, Minton took his two sons into partnership, and the firm became known as 'Thomas Minton and Sons'. This name was retained till 1823, when Minton's eldest son Thomas Webb Minton left the pottery to enter the Church. His second son Herbert stayed with his father as partner, and from 1823 till 1836, they traded successively as 'Thomas Minton', 'Thomas Minton and Co.', and 'Minton and Co.', as revealed by a perusal of their business head-bills in their archives made available through the courtesy of one of their present directors.

In 1828 Herbert withdrew from the partnership and Thomas Minton once more had the business to himself, until his death in 1836. Herbert Minton came back to the business in 1836, and took active control with John Boyle as his partner till 1841, and the firm was called 'Minton and Boyle'. Boyle after leaving Minton's firm, became a partner with Godfrey Wedgwood at Etruria in 1843 till 1845. Herbert Minton, after Boyle's withdrawal, carried on the pottery under the title of 'Herbert Minton and Co.' till 1858. On the death of Herbert Minton in 1858, his widow's nephew Michael Daintry Hollins, and his sister's son Colin Minton Campbell carried on the firm under the title 'Mintons'. Then in 1883 the present title 'Mintons Ltd' was adopted, as it was made into a private company.

Potters were often helped in the development of the business by their wives. Jewitt writes that, 'By his marriage Josiah Wedgwood received an accession to his fortune in the dowry of his wife. This fortune I have heard it stated amounted in the end to no less than £20,000.' Jewitt rightly comments 'a magnificent sum in those days and of incalculable use to a rising energetic and judicious manufacturer'. In addition to helping Wedgwood with capital to purchase the Etruria estate, and enabling him to extend his pottery business, his wife, on Wedgwood's own evidence, was an active participant in his Etrurean experiments. In a letter on 19 February 1765, Wedgwood wrote to his brother John:

'I have just begun a course of experiments for a white body and glaze, which promises well. Sally [i.e. his wife] is my chief helpmate in this, as well as in other things, and that she may not be hurried by having too many irons in the fire, as the phrase goes, I have ordered the spinning wheel into the lumber room. She hath learnt my characters at least to write them, but can scarcely read them at present.' In a letter to Bentley in January 1786, Wedgwood goes further: 'I speak from experience in female taste, without which I should have made but a poor figure amongst the Potts, not one of which of any consequence is finished without the approbation of my Sally.' This 'family' character of the Wedgwood firm has been conspicuous to this day. But there are other examples. Probably Spode was able to draw on financial resources from his wife's haberdashery business to purchase in 1776 the vacant pottery premises of Turner and Banks. From records made available, through the courtesy of Mr. John Campbell, the veteran Director of Minton's, I examined account books of wages paid from 1797–1798. As from 6 March 1797, there are regular weekly wages paid to Mrs. Thomas Minton of £1. 15s. 6d. These are increased in February 1798 to £2. 2s., and later to £2. 12s. 6d. In April, this is raised to £2. 19s. 6d., and on 12 May to £3. 3s. The final entry is on 3 September 1798 for £3. 12s. 8d. In another manuscript, Mr. Herbert Minton gives credit to Mrs. Webb, mother of Thomas Minton's wife: 'After his marriage his mother-in-law (Mrs. Webb) lived with them, and was a great help to him in his business, keeping his books and accounts and, in fact, the financial manager of the concern. She received and paid the money, and superintended the entire office arrangements, thus leaving Mr. Minton at liberty to devote his whole time to the manufactory and to the engraving'. There is an entry on 21 October 1797, 'By Mr. M. per Mrs. Webb £2. 14s. 9d'.

Even more distant relatives were brought into the business, but however tenaciously the founders of a pottery tried to keep control within the family circle, there is ample evidence that when business required it, they and their successors went outside it. Wedgwood soon found a need to expand the market for his wares and this brought him into direct and personal contact with Thomas Bentley, of Liverpool, a cultured successful merchant. Fortunately, in the Wedgwood archives, there is almost a complete set of Wedgwood's letters to Bentley, though so far, unfortunately, copies of Bentley's correspondence with Wedgwood have never been traced. In an undated letter, which Lady Farrer in Volume II of her Wedgwood-Bentley correspondence places between 28 April and 20 May 1767, Wedgwood writes, 'I never think but new improvements crowd in upon me and almost overwhelm my patience, so much do I long to be engaged in that delightful employment, which I have every day fuller assurance of making as profitable to the purse – as it must be pleasing to the mind – but you know what sort of a partner it required. Either resolve quickly to join me yourself, or find me out another kindred spirit.'

Bentley replied to this invitation on 15 May and Wedgwood wrote again on 20 May: 'Your most acceptable letter of the 15th. gave me the highest pleasure in setting before me a nearer prospect than I have yet had of a union, that I have long coveted and which I do not doubt will be lasting, delightful and beneficial to us both. As to the time and manner of leaving Liverpool, make it the most agreeable to yourself in every respect and it will be perfectly so to me.' Bentley must have hesitated over acceptance for Wedgwood's next letter shows him answering some of Bentley's points:

I have read your letter many times over and find several of the objections to our nearer approach may be surmounted. The first is 'your total ignorance of the business'. That I deny, as friend Tristram to St. Paul – You have taste, the best foundation for our intended concern. The difficulty of your leaving your business in Liverpool, I cannot obviate. The money objection is obviated to my hand, and I doubt not in a way that will be agreeable to us both. But the leaving your friends and giving up a thousand agreeable connections and pleasures in Liverpool, for which you can have no compensations in kind, this staggers my hopes more than everything else put together . . . . Can you exchange the frequent opportunities of seeing and conversing with your learned and ingenious friends, which your present situation affords you, besides ten thousand other elegancies and enjoyments of a town life – to employ yourself amongst mechanics, dirt and smoke? If this prospect does not frighten you, I have some hopes, and if you think you could really fall in love with and make a mistress of this new business, as I have done of mine, I should have little or no doubt of your success.

Bentley yielded to Wedgwood's persuasion. He came first to Etruria, and then later found his proper niche in the London showroom, and at the enamel works at Chelsea. Because of Bentley's scientific knowledge in the matter of machinery and raw materials, Wedgwood found him most useful at the point of production at Etruria. As a man of culture and refinement Bentley was an asset in interpreting the taste and needs of the aristocracy and royalty, as patrons of pottery wares. Further, his ready pen was always at hand to support Wedgwood's many projects. His knowledge of Parliamentary procedure in both Houses helped Wedgwood, not only in his canal schemes for the Potteries, but in the fight over clay supplies against Champion and his supporters (see Chapter 3). Wedgwood and Bentley were more than twin souls engaged as partners in business. They had the same love of art, they were both generous and public spirited. There are few such intimate partnerships and Wedgwood felt deeply the untimely loss of his friend in 1780.

There was a short-lived partnership with a William Storer, an inventor of metal ornament of Norwich, signed in 1775. Bentley and Wedgwood contributed £1,000 as capital, and £1,000 in shares allocated to Storer for his stock-in-trade, moulds and designs. Storer failed to fulfil his promises, so the partnership was cancelled. After Bentley's death Wedgwood never associated in partnership with anyone outside his family and close relatives.

William Copeland, a native of North Staffordshire and a successful tea merchant in London, with a good continental connection, became an agent for Spode in London. As the productions of the Spode pottery became better known and output increased, Spode decided to open showrooms in London, first in Fore Street, Cripplegate, with Copeland in charge. Later, Josiah Spode Junior joined Copeland as salesman in a larger showroom in Portugal Street, in Lincoln Inn Fields. The sales in 1793 in the London showroom totalled £9,485. Three years later, when business profits reached £13,000, Spode gave Copeland a gift of £1,000. Later Josiah Spode II took his own son as a partner, and also made Copeland a partner in 1824. This partnership with Josiah Spode II proved so lucrative, that after his death, the descendant of Copeland, Alderman W. T. Copeland, was able to purchase the sole control of the business from the Spode family on their deciding to leave the Potteries. W. T. Copeland followed Spode's precedent by making his London Agent Mr. Spencer Garrett a partner from 1833, till Garrett's death in 1847.

Like Wedgwood, Minton chose as partner a Liverpool merchant, William Pownall, who trained one of Minton's sons to be an expert salesman. When Pownall died, the control of Minton's firm reverted to the members of the Minton family – father, sons, grandsons or his nephews.

The extant records, including records of accounts, correspondence and memoranda in the archives of various firms, give a fairly accurate picture of the various functions performed by the founders of the pottery firms and their partners. The policy to be adopted in the hiring, renting or purchasing a site for the pottery or the question of alteration and extension of the pottery premises was one for decision by the founder of the firm himself or sometimes in consultation with his partners, if any. Whieldon, the sole owner of his pottery, had entered in his Memorandum book such items as 'To John Wood to sinking cellar 8s. od.' and 'Paid to John Wood for drawing ton trave pilings for thacking (thatching) the oven house 3s. od.' This gives an indication of the small size of his pot-bank at this stage. Spode hired or rented his first pot-bank from Turner and Banks, when Turner vacated it to start a new pottery at Lane End. Wedgwood rented his Burslem pottery from his cousins John and Thomas Wedgwood. He later rented Brick House, Burslem, which he worked till the Etruria works were started. Before Bentley became his partner, Wedgwood wrote: 'I do not intend to make this ware at Burslem, and, am therefore laying out for an agreeable and convenient situation elsewhere . . .' on which he could build a manufactory equal to his increasing trade, where he should have scope for the productive efforts he contemplated, and where he could fittingly enter upon a more organized system of details than hitherto had been possible in his works. In August 1766, Wedgwood informs Bentley, 'I have now bought the Estate [Ridgway House later called Etruria] I mentioned to you, for which I am to pay £3,000.'

When contemplating opening a London warehouse, Wedgwood asked Bentley's advice even prior to his being made a partner. Wedgwood wrote: 'I have some thoughts of opening a warehouse, not merely a Pattern Room in the City. . . . Pray consider of it as you will soon be a party concerned and advise me what to do.' In a later letter Wedgwood wrote to Bentley 'I spent a great part of the day in search of a room for my repositary. Pall Mall is the best situation in London. It is convenient for the whole of the Great Town, the avenues to it open and everybody comes there some time or other. There is now to be let in this situation an auction room, the whole for £250. . . . What shall I do about it? Your advice would just reach me before I leave. We must have an elegant and convenient showroom with store rooms and some conveniences for 2 servants at least.'

Later, on 25 March 1768, Wedgwood writes Bentley: 'I expect a set of works to be let in a few weeks with a tolerable smart house to them. . . . Cream tyles are much wanted and the consumption will be great for Dairys, Baths, Summer Houses and Temples.'

Wedgwood's business kept expanding, and he searched for more commodious premises for a warehouse, as shown in a letter to Bentley: 'One of the objects was seeking after a house or rather a warehouse, in which I have at last succeeded to my wishes and quite beyond my most sanguine expectations. I have a lease near the bottom of St. Martin's Lane, Charing Cross, which will be quite convenient for Westminster, and within a 12d. ride from St. Paul's Churchyard.' The rising industrial capitalist was free to change his plans if it suited him, as Wedgwood's letter to Bentley on 31 March 1768 shows: 'I have met with another house which pleases me better for situation than that I have taken. It is at the top of St. Martin's Lane [Great Newport Street], a corner house 60 feet long . . . the rent is 100 guineas a year. My friends in Town tell me it is the best situation in all London for my rooms. I am quite at a loss what to determine and you can hardly help me out without seeing the place.'

The Wedgwood-Bentley correspondence has abundant evidence of Wedgwood making decisions about the type of articles he would make, and the prices he would charge for them. He also controlled the policy relating to the merchanting or sale of wares. When showroom sales in London started falling off, he suggested to Bentley – 'a gentle push in foreign markets', or even pushing his wares at the Pump Room in Bath, with circulars distributed among the visitors. Lady Farrer states, 'It is true that Wedgwood was charmed at the effect of the handbills.'

The founders of pottery firms and their partners took a very active part in the furthering of transport schemes for road and canal traffic to assist in the expansion of their production and sale of wares. Wedgwood and Bentley, as protagonists for the Trent and Mersey Canal and its connections with other canals, have had more publicity than their other contemporaries. But they deserve this praise.

Active though the pottery founders were, as their business grew, they had to delegate some of their directive and executive functions to their partners and others. Wedgwood left to his cousin Thomas the managership of the 'useful works' at Burslem, while he himself concentrated on the development of the 'ornamental works' at Etruria. But even here, he entrusted almost entirely the showroom display side in London, and a good deal of the artistic work in London to his partner Bentley. Further, as business increased, Wedgwood had to substitute a paid secretary and amanuensis, to replace the once welcomed voluntary services of his wife, Sally. Meteyard states that 'Wedgwood had no head for accounts, and admitted losing money because of this deficiency'.

Josiah Spode left the managership of his pottery to Poulson, and the control of his London showroom to Copeland, and later jointly with Josiah Spode Junior. The control of the decoration and ornamentation of his wares he left to Thomas Minton, till Minton set up a factory of his own. Minton, similarly deputed the managing of his factory to Poulson, who had left the employ of Spode to join him. Later, Minton employed John Turner, the son of Wedgwood's friend, John Turner Senior, while the sales side was entrusted to Mr. Pownall, who was to train Minton's son as London Salesman.

During the lives of many pottery founders then, specialization and delegation of functions had developed. Some of their successors, during the nineteenth century were not apprenticed nor trained as practical potters, ceramic chemists, nor as ceramic artists and designers. They employed others, who had been trained or had specialized in these functions. The founders, (particularly from 1730 onwards) well into the first half of the nineteenth century, took such an intense personal interest in their business, that they kept control directly on all aspects of production, transport and marketing of their wares, until they could pass on their tasks to their partners or direct descendants in some sphere of economic activity.

RSP C

THE EXPERIMENTERS

Some writers, such as Bowden in his *Industrial Society in England in the Eighteenth Century*, and Mantoux, Moffitt and Redford, have described the eighteenth century as the 'Age of Invention'. A better title for it, as far as the pottery industry is concerned, would be 'The Age of Experiment'. First of all, the 'inventions' were the result of the spirit of practial experiment that was abroad. The inventions did not spring fully fledged from the mind of the inventor but were the result of continuous effort and the conclusion probably of a series of failures, followed ultimately by success.

For earlier writers on 'The Industrial Revolution', the term 'invention' too often connotes merely a mechanical contrivance or machinery. But an invention can be non-mechanical. It may be a new combination of materials, or processes in handling materials that may result in a new and more effective method of production, or a new commodity. A perusal of Woodcroft's list of patents during the eighteenth and early nineteenth centuries proves this. Some more recent writers, such as Bowden, have introduced a new term to replace 'invention'. They use the term 'change of technique' or 'technical changes' discovered. Still 'the age of experiment' is a better term covering both technical changes and mechanical devices. During the eighteenth century certain persons engaged in industry refused to accept on faith certain traditional methods of producing goods. Their ingenuity and curiosity found out new methods of combining raw materials and processes. They observed more keenly. They measured more accurately. They weighed more finely. They reasoned more cogently. The result was that their experiments succeeded and inventions resulted.

A term used increasingly during the eighteenth century was 'engineer'. Though too often then, and since, used to refer to someone closely associated with an 'engine', or a mechanical device or apparatus, in its original meaning it meant an ingenious person, one possessed of ingenuity, one who discovered new methods of operating a process in production or transport. James Brindley was an 'engineer' of canals, because of his 'ingenuity' as a millwright, with experience of water-driven corn mills and windmills. Wedgwood was closely associated with Brindley in his windmill visits to 'The Jenkins' field in Burslem, and later in his Trent and Mersey Canal venture. He wrote to Bentley on 2 January 1765, 'I scarcely know without a good deal of recollection whether I am a landed Gentleman, an Engineer or a Potter, for indeed I am all three and many other characters by turns.'

With their works located between Birmingham and Manchester, two focal hubs of industry, the potters of North Staffordshire were bound to be influenced by what occurred in those cities. Aikin in his book on *A Description of the Country from thirty to forty miles round Manchester* devotes a chapter on 'Wedgwood's Pottery at Etruria'. Wedgwood and many of his fellow potters were quick to incorporate in their works the mechanical steam inventions of Birmingham, and adopt calico-printing devices for transfer printing for decorating their pottery wares.

These industrial experimenters from the North of England, the Potteries, and particularly the Midlands converged in Birmingham, and drawing in people living at Lichfield, congregated and pooled their ideas at what later came to be called the Lunar Society. They arranged their timetable of meetings for lectures, talks, discussions and actual experiments by Dr. Joseph Priestley, by fixing the time of the meetings according to the full moon. This enabled their members travelling on horseback or coach to reach their homes more safely at night, after meetings usually held at the homes of James Watt, Matthew Boulton, Dr. Priestley or some of the wealthier industrialists of the Black Country. Miss Meteyard with her scrupulous regard for truthful representation states, 'Contrary to the generally received notion Wedgwood was not like Priestley, Watt, Boulton, Dr. Withering and others a recognized member of the Lunar Society.' But she adds, 'He was occasionally present at its meetings and probably contributed at intervals subjects for discussion.' She further excuses Wedgwood by saying 'Etruria and Birmingham were too distant for any regular monthly attendance'.

From a truly philosophical or scientific point of view, the most brilliant member of the Lunar Society and the most regular in attendance was Joseph Priestley, to whom Wedgwood had been introduced by Thomas Bentley, while Priestley was still a member of the teaching staff at Warrington Academy, before he moved to Birmingham. Wedgwood from that moment to his death kept up regular correspondence with Priestley, when the scientist left for Leeds, and later, when he moved to Birmingham, and then to London. Letters[1] range from the first letter Wedgwood wrote after the lamented death of Bentley in 1780, to the last letter in 1792, dealing with an appeal for funds for Dr. Priestley after the Birmingham riots, where his laboratory and home were destroyed.

In these letters, Priestley discloses that Wedgwood not only took infinite pains to make suitable retorts and porcelain test tubes for his 'phlogiston' experiments, but further showed his faith in scientific experiments by contributing generously in money to the cost of these experiments in chemistry. In a letter dated 26 June 1781, Priestley wrote to Wedgwood: 'I have not received

[1] *Scientific Letters of Joseph Priestley* edited by H. Carrington Bolton

last parcel of retorts etc., having this day examined those I received last, I find none that I cannot force my breath through and some in great streams, as may be seen when they are plunged in water. You would oblige me therefore if you would order the same molds, and that a fresh parcel may be sent as expeditiously as possible. I know you will not blame my eagerness as I am in the midst of a very interesting course of experiments, the results of which I flatter myself will not be unpleasing to yourself.' Priestley in a later letter states: 'I shall thank you for a few more thermometer pieces along with these retorts. I have had ample experience of your goodness and therefore make no apology for so many wants.' Again, on 9 October 1788, 'I should have written you before this time to acknowledge the continuance of your generous benefactions notwithstanding my wishes to decline it.' This was a reference to Wedgwood's annual gift of £25 towards the cost of Priestley's laboratory experiments. Miss Meteyard states: 'the annual allowance of 25 guineas to Priestley was continued after Wedgwood's death by his son Josiah to the close of Priestley's life. Other sums were occasionally added as extraordinary gifts.'

In July 1791, on hearing the news of the attack by rioters on Priestley's person, home and laboratory, Wedgwood wrote: 'I do not know whether this will find you, but I can no longer forbear to ask you how do you do, after the severe trials you have lately been exposed to, and to console with you in the irreparable loss you have so lately sustained from the brutality or rather, let us hope, the temporary insanity of your late neighbours. You will have occasion for all your philosophy, for all your Christianity to bear up and support your mind, under the aggravating injuries you have received. If you think of anything in which I can serve or comfort you, you will oblige me in pointing the way in which I can do it.'

Josiah Wedgwood and Joseph Priestley were elected Fellows of the Royal Society during the same year in 1783. Before his election, Wedgwood had contributed a paper on 'The Pyrometer or heat measuring instrument' to the Royal Society, reproduced in *The Philosophical Transactions* in May 1782. After his election, he contributed two more papers entitled 'An attempt to compare and combine The Thermometer with the Pyrometer' and a brief paper on 'The Black Wadd of the Derbyshire Mines'. Miss Meteyard rightly points out that 'The subject of his papers was one which in practice had been before Wedgwood his whole life. His many improvements and discoveries, both in relation to bodies, glazes and colours, had greatly depended on the application of specific degrees of heat, and these papers were rather the philosophical embodiment of a long series of *a priori* results, than discoveries in themselves essentially new.'

Wedgwood had noticed that his cousins Thomas and John Wedgwood of the Big House regulated their kiln fires empirically, through changes observed in colour by progressive heat. These were rule-of-thumb methods, found often to be uncertain, and varying with the size, structure or mode of firing the oven. Josiah Wedgwood on the other hand, after long experiments found that the diminution of bulk while firing argillaceous bodies was a more certain and exact measure of heat. He discovered that the diminution in size of the body increased with the degree of heat. Though since 1783 more precise and exact instruments have been produced to measure oven heat, at the time Wedgwood's pyrometer was a great advance on the methods then used by potters. The pyrometer greatly reduced the number of failures in fired wares and increased the proportion of successes, called 'firsts' by the potters. As Smiles points out in his *Life of Wedgwood*, the pyrometer gained him great fame at home and abroad. His paper to the Royal Society was translated into French, Dutch and many other foreign languages.

William Evans' reference to the pyrometer in his *Art and History of Potting* may be merely a chronicle of idle gossip dished up almost 50 years after the publication of Wedgwood's paper. Evans, without a scrap of corroborative contemporary evidence, states: 'This Pyrometer was invented by Thomas Massey, a Bailiff in Mr. Wedgwood's manufactory. . . . He most resolutely declined communicating to Wedgwood the component of his dods [or trial prisms] and was prevented from informing his brothers Richard and William – the real secret died with him'. Then Evans proceeds to add the most amazing statement about Wedgwood – 'He *guessed* at a clay for the purpose and supplied philosophers therewith'. That one word 'guessed' discounts Evans' story, for if anybody never 'guessed', it was Wedgwood. In any mechanism that he invented or improved, or with any raw material he worked upon, he experimented and worked most meticulously. The 'experimenting' and 'tryals' were not whims of the moment with him. When he had mastered the 'body', after excursions into what we call geology today, and patient chemical research, he developed it, as a ceramic artist, to form different wares. Urns, vases, pitchers, cameos, heads, plaques or seals – all were the result of incessant experiment. Writing to Bentley on 5 August 1767 Wedgwood reports: 'I am going on with my experiments upon various earths and clays for different bodyes, and I shall next go upon glazes. Many of my experiments turn out to my wishes and convince me more and more of the extensive capability of our manufacture for further improvements. It is at present comparatively in a rude and uncultivated state, and may easily be polished and brought to a much greater perfection.

Such a revolution, I believe, is at hand and you must assist in and proffit by it.'

On 8 September 1767, he continues: 'Experiments for Porcelain, or at least, a new Earthenware fill up every moment allmost of my time and would take a good deal more if I had it.' Then on 12 October 1767, Wedgwood continues in a further letter, 'My tryals turn out admirably and will enable us to do such things as never were done.'

Wedgwood not only experimented and still went on with his new experiments – he continuously reviewed his results to perfect them: 'I have for some time past been reviewing my experiments and I find such Roots and Seeds as could open and branch out wonderfully, if I could nail myself down to the cultivation of them for a year or two,' he writes Bentley: 'The agate, the green and other coloured glazes have had their day and are certain of a resurrection soon. The cream colour is of a superior class. The black is sterling and will last for ever. These are a few of the roots . . . and I never look back over my books, but I find many more, which I would very gladly bring into action.'

The discovery of a suitable body for the delicate 'heads' or 'portraits' of famous people of the past and present involved a good deal of anxious trials and experiments by Wedgwood in his laboratory. At last his labours were rewarded, as he reports to Bentley on 14 January 1776: 'I believe I can now assure you of a conquest and a very important one for us. No less than the firing our fine Jasper and Onyx with as much certainty as our Black Basaltes. . . . In respect to firing, they were perfect and the two bodies blue and white agree perfectly together and as I manage them now it cannot be otherwise. This new art . . . is completed and brought to perfection.'

Wedgwood's interest in raw materials for his pottery was not confined to his analysis of them in his 'elaboratory', as he called his experimental den. He indulged in field excursions, along with his partner Bentley, as shown in his letter to him on 8 July 1767: 'I have since thought of meeting you at Derby. If you can stay a few days there. . . . I will bring a spare horse with me. We can make Matlock on our way and visit the Lead Mines, which I want much to do, being in the midst of a course of experiments, which I expect must be perfected by the spath fusible, a substance which I cannot at present meet with.'

Neither was his knowledge of the chemical properties of the raw materials used in his pottery dependent only on his own practical observations and experiments. He was a prolific reader of textbooks on chemistry and other scientific books, for which he ordered Bentley to search in the bookshops of London and elsewhere. On one occasion, Meteyard records, Wedgwood wrote to Bentley, 'My wife says I must buy no more books till I build another house.'

After the death of Bentley, Wedgwood appointed as his secretary and chemical assistant Alexander Chisholm. Meteyard gives interesting information about Chisholm and his services to Wedgwood. 'Chisholm had filled a post for 30 years with Dr. Lewis of Kingston-on-Thames, the author of *Commercium Philosophico – Technicum* and other scientific works. In many chemical matters Wedgwood had but to direct Chisholm and the analysis or experiment was laid perfected before him. . . .'

Wedgwood's enthusiasm for his study of chemistry led him to invite a Dr. Warltire, a great admirer and personal friend of Priestley, to deliver a series of lectures on chemistry while a guest at Etruria Hall for several weeks. Writing to Bentley on 17 February 1779, he states, 'Mr. Warltire comes on Saturday next to give us some instruction, and as my neighbours seem determined to receive it only 3 days in the week, it will make it long before I shall have the pleasure of seeing you at Turnham Green. . . . Mr. Warltire opened his lecture on Tuesday with a subscription of about 30 guineas, and I think he will have more. I too am a lecturer in turn.'

Spode, Minton and Adams were not the great experimenters in the scientific sense that Wedgwood was. Wedgwood's contemporaries, and his successors from 1795 onwards, mainly relied on inventions discovered by others, and on patents, which ultimately came on the market. There were exceptions, like John and William Turner, who patented a discovery they made in 1800 for making porcelain. Later in 1813, C. J. Mason of Ironstone fame, patented his process. In both cases Spode-Copeland purchased the patents and produced wares under the rights acquired. In some cases potters waited till the expiry of the period of the patent, and produced wares according to the expired patent formula. After the famous Champion Bill[1] contest a syndicate of potters in North Staffordshire purchased Champion's patent for China making as early as 1780. Minton's, when they turned their attention to the making of tiles, were content to pay royalties to Samuel Wright for permission to produce tiles according to his Patents No. 5890 dated 26 January 1830, and a later patent No. 10,022 dated 23 January 1844. Some potters became joint owners with patentees of certain processes, so as to be able to exploit them. This was the case when Herbert Minton, son of the founder, joined with W. George Turner in a joint-patent dated 22 June 1839, No. 8124. Then again John Ridgway, a famous potter, joined with George Wall in a Patent No. 8339 dated 11 January 1840, and another of the same date, No. 8340.

[1] See Chapter 3

One interesting case of patents being acquired is that of a Potteries banker, T. Kinnersley, Machin and Potts, a Burslem firm of Potters, who had taken patents for mechanically engraving china and earthenware, according to patents No. 6162, 17 September 1831, and No. 6938, 3 December 1835 and while engaged on these patents borrowed £22,307. 9s. 6d. from the banker. The manuscript I discovered in the Spode archives states, 'Kinnersley accepted the Patent rights, plus all the property ovens, kilns, fixtures, utensils, blocks, moulds, copper plates, cylinders, stock-in-trade, earthenware and china stock, mill stock, raw materials, debts, a gig and horse, and other goods, chattels, utensils, articles and effects in respect of debt and a sum of £1,888. 4s. 8d.' As the above document was in the Spode archives, Josiah Spode III and his Copeland partners probably purchased or acquired the patent, for the Kinnersley family were related to the Henshall-Williamson family, to which Mrs. Josiah Spode III belonged.

Just as James Watt had to keep a watchful eye on pirates who trespassed on his engine patents and engineering discoveries and improvements, so the potters had to watch out for pirates, who copied their patent processes or their designs and special wares. Wedgwood only once patented a pottery process, for he found that it did not give him much protection. After a period of years the patent expired, and its contents were made public the moment it was registered. Pursuing breaches of the patent by unscrupulous potters often led to costly and futile litigation. Wedgwood's sole patent, No. 939, dated 16 November 1769, almost led to a costly contest at law between him and a rival potter, Humphrey Palmer. Fortunately for Palmer and for Wedgwood too, the latter was able to settle the issue amicably by granting Palmer the use of the patent for a price to be fixed by an arbitrator. Even after this settlement we find evidence in Wedgwood's correspondence with Bentley that Palmer's piracy of Wedgwood wares went on surreptitiously.

Wedgwood wrote: 'Mr. Pemberton our seal setter I find was at Palmer's before he came here, and was told that Palmer made seals. We may safely take it for granted they will not let us enjoy this business unrivalled. "Wedgwood and Byerley" is rather too much to put on the back of our seals, with the number besides, the small one especially, and I do not know whether we can put any single mark upon them which our neighbours dare not enjoy.' Then later on 3 July 1773 Wedgwood wrote Bentley: 'I write to acquaint you with the certainty of our having a rival in the seals that you may take your measures accordingly, if any alteration is necessary. P——r [Palmer] is determined to follow close at our heels. He has got some set. . . . Should not this spur us on still more to cultivate them and get first to market, wherever we can. We may as well serve everybody as fast as we can, for Palmer will do it if we do not.' Later still, Wedgwood discovered Palmer pirating his black vases. Here again he advised Bentley, 'We must proceed or they will tread on our heels.' This spur of continually improving his wares, of going one better than his rivals is probably one of the main motives behind Wedgwood's continuous experimenting and inventing new processes and wares.

Wedgwood was always ready to learn from others, as is shown in his letter to Bentley on 22 November 1771. 'Mr. Burdett, a Liverpool artist has taught me to edge our dishes and plates by a little machine by which they may do 6 or 8 for 1, and ten times as well, which is no small discovery for us and may help us wonderfully in completing the sets for our friends, the Princes and Nobles abroad.'

Wedgwood, though starting as a potter with only £20 as capital, left a fortune of half a million to be inherited by his sons and other relatives. Josiah Spode, who started with less capital than Wedgwood, left a large factory to his son Josiah, with a dowry of £8,000 to his daughter Ann. Minton, who was only an engraving artist at first with Spode, started a factory on his own with very little capital, and left one of the largest pottery factories in North Staffordshire to his sons.

These three pottery establishments founded in the period 1730–1850 have not only survived, but expanded during this period, and are thriving concerns today in the Potteries. They all merit this comment by Professor Redford in his book *The Economic History of England*, 'The early industrialists needed to possess exceptional organizing capacity'. Redford is also of the opinion that the industrial capitalists between 1760 and 1860 'were more important as organizers than as inventors'.

I shall try to show in the following chapters this organizational ability applied to the solution of the problem of new material supply, the application of power to pottery processes, transport, and the development of the manbit.

CHAPTER 3

The Search for Raw Materials

The first need of the potter was a supply of good clays, that could later be worked on the thrower's wheel, or on the turner's lathe, before the artefact was first fired. Because of the porous character of the first-fired ware, other ingredients were used as a dip to glaze the first-fired ware, called 'biscuit ware'. This glaze was obtained, as noted in Chapter 1, first by the use of lead, and later by the use of salt. The experimenting with flint, calcined as a glaze, was further advanced. The improvements in decoration and ornamentation of the fired wares was mainly due to the vastly improved character of the raw materials.

The Wedgwood correspondence preserved in the Wedgwood archives at Etruria Museum, and orginal leases loaned by Dorset clay proprietors,[1] help trace the various stages in the increase of imported non-native clays into Staffordshire. A letter, dated 1 March 1766, to Bentley, contains the following:

Thank you my dear friend for the very valuable packets, which I have read several times over, that from America I mean, and am much pleased with his account of the clay, as I apprehend it is of the right kind. What occurs to me to write to Gent on that subject is only to desire he would send a sample 50 or 100lb., by the first conveyance and to send 2 or 3 tons, by so many of the first ships which sail from these parts to any of the ports in England. It may be necessary to give him a hint about getting it very clean, and putting it into strong good casks, and to let you know what the price would be per 100 tons. I apprehend the Virginia clay will come cheapest.

In a later letter to Bentley, dated 26 June 1766, Wedgwood writes: 'Please give my compliments to Mr. Vigor [a gentlemen from Fulham] and desire he will send the few pounds of earth he has by him, that I may give it a fair tryal.' Wedgwood was not the only potter trying out this American clay, for he continues his letter to Bentley: 'A brother of the crockery branch called on me and amongst other clays he had been trying experiments upon, shewed me a lump of the very same earth, which surprised me a good deal. I should almost have thought myself robbed if it had not been larger than my pattern [sample.]

[1] W. Pike, Wareham Dorset (loaned to the author by his family)

He told me it had come from South Carolina, but he could make nothing at all of it, and had returned the remainder to his friend again.'

Several months later: 'I am of opinion with you that the Pensacola clay is better worth attention than the Cherokee, and do not think the price extravagant or too high for answer for manufacturing here. If it be equal to the Cherokee, I should be glad to have a ton by way of sample.[1] But some months passed and with no sample arrived, Wedgwood becomes impatient: 'I wish you would see Mr. Vigor and know if he hath done anything towards procuring some of the Cherokee earth he promised me to see, or write to his friend about it, and I think I was to have a letter with his friend's proposals, but have heard nothing from either. Have you sent to Pensacola [in Florida] for a sample of that earth?'[2]

Later, from London, Wedgwood writes Bentley[3] about his efforts to locate where the Cherokee clay was in South Carolina:

I am in search of the town, where the Steatites grows, and I believe I shall learn every particular about it. One Dr. Mitchel has just published a map of North America (price a guinea and a half) which map, I have purchased. I find the town in his map is *Hyoree* and the same in a map in a Committee Room of the House of Commons. The mistake of a letter as the sound is not so very different was easy to make either by Mr. Vigor or myself, and as the situation answers the description he gave me, I am pretty certain it is the place.

In the same letter, Wedgwood asks advice on the proposal to send, as his clay agent, 'Our Mr. Griffiths' brother, who hath resided for many years in North America and is seasoned to South Carolina climate'.

Three days later, Wedgwood sends another letter to Bentley: 'A patent or exclusive property in the Cherokees is business enough of itself to solicit and prosecute in the best manner with not a soul, a congenial and intelligent soul to advise with.' Wedgwood, however, did find a congenial soul, before he left London, as he explains in his continued letter: 'Since I wrote the above, I have had the honour of a long conference with his Grace [the Duke] of Bridgwater on the subject of the Cherokees. I laid the whole case before him without any reserve and found the confidence I had placed in his honour and advice was not disagreeable. He does not think a Patent will stand for an exclusive right to the Cherokees, and advises to send a person over immediately, without applying for grant, patent or anything else.'

Still in London on his clay quest, Wedgwood writes:[4] 'I spent yesterday with two or three gentlemen, who had resided long in South Carolina. I find the earth must be carried near 300 miles by land carriage, which will make it come

[1] Letter to Bentley, 17 November 1766
[2] To Bentley, 18 February 1767
[3] 20 May 1767
[4] To Bentley 27 May 1767

very heavy. I have had a long conference with Mr. Griffiths and am inclined to employ him.'

But, five days later:

New difficulties spring up as I proceed in the business of the Cherokee clay. A grant must pass through the Lords of Trade and Plantations, amongst whom are Fitzherbert, Member for Derby, a Lord something Clare, Member for Bristol, at both which places are China and Pottworks. So I dare not come there.

An intended Patent must be made publick such a time before it can pass, and so many are interested, that their friends or constituents should share the advantages of such a discovery, endless oppositions and difficulties would probably arise from that mode of procedure, and if I did not succeed, I should raise up a whole swarm of competitors.[1]

Before Wedgwood arrived home, he consulted a second peer:

I waited upon Lord Gower on Saturday last, and laid the whole of my difficulties and designs before him. He told me, he had many personal, but no political friends in the Administration, but if I could wait for a change, he should perhaps be able to serve me. I told his Lordship the danger I apprehended from delaying, as several persons had seen the clay. He then told me, that he had got the Attorney General of South Carolina the place he enjoyed. . . . The result was that his Lordship advised me to send immediately to South Carolina and he would put my Agent under the protection of the Attorney General.[2]

Wedgwood agreed to this advice and wrote further: 'I am now preparing matters for Mr. Griffiths to embark as soon as possible. I have agreed for him to sail in the first ship, and am to give him £50 per annum, besides his maintenance.' And on returning home to Etruria: 'Let me tell you that Mr. Griffiths will sail for South Carolina in about a fortnight'.[3] Unfortunately, there is little further mention by Wedgwood of this clay venture in South Carolina. On 9 January 1768 he writes: 'There is a cask of red and yellow clay in London, which I had from Ashton and Hodgson, and shall order it home by sea.' This may refer to a supply of Cherokee clay sent by Griffiths. It may be that Wedgwood finally decided it would be too costly to transport supplies of the clay from South Carolina.

Eliza Meteyard in her *Life of Josiah Wedgwood* (ii, 7–8) suggests that Wedgwood's scientific friends and merchants advised him 'that unless restricted to the manufacture of highly priced porcelain, the difficulties and expense connected with their transit from so remote a region would render them too dear to be available either to importer or potter'. The latest reference to the use of this Cherokee clay by Wedgwood is in a letter, dated 15 December 1777, mentioning its use in the making of jasper vases, which were among Wedgwood's higher-priced products.

[1] To Bentley 1 June 1767   [2] To Bentley 6 June 1767
[3] To Bentley 13 June 1767

While Wedgwood employed Mr. Griffiths in America as his clay agent, his letters reveal him as a persistent experimenter with clays from the south-west of England. He tells Bentley[1] about a correspondence he had had with a Mr. Whitehurst, a learned geologist-engineer, engaged in lead mining in Derby: 'He [Mr. Whitehurst] has set his miners to work to put by for me various samples of earths and clays,' and again two days later: 'I have tried the clay you sent me, which proves a pretty good sort, but is a little inferior to my own, the last cargo of which cost me 16s. per ton, delivered to you in Liverpool. I have clay enough to serve me for my own use near two years, so cannot take any of it for my own use.'

Wedgwood was elated with the results of his clay trials: 'I am going on with my experiments upon various earths and clays for different bodys. . . . Many of my experiments turn out to my wishes, and convince me more and more of the extensive capability of our manufacture for further improvements. It is at present comparatively in a rude and uncultivated state, and may early be polished and brought to much greater perfection. Such a REVOLUTION, I believe, is at hand and you must assist in and proffitt by it.'[2]

Wedgwood also experimented with clays from China: 'I received the Chinese earths our good friend Mr. Moore [the Secretary of the Royal Society of Arts] was so obliging to send me yesterday.' While experimenting in his Etruria laboratory with these various earths and clays, Wedgwood urged his partner Bentley, in London, to keep a watchful eye on any Patent specifications registered regarding the use of various clays.[3]

On 10 June, Count de Lauraguais had registered a patent for the use of clays in china-making. Wedgwood told Bentley on 24 October 1767: 'Count de Lauraguais' Patent limits us. Why sure you have forgot, who we are . . . however, I am very impatient to see a copy of the Count's Patent, that we may know the worst.' William Cookworthy enrolled his patent in 1768, with specifications concerning the use of china clay and china stone from the south-west of England for china manufacture. The first reference to Wedgwood's interest in Cookworthy's patent is in a letter to Bentley, dated 3 April 1773: 'At your leisure, I should be glad to have a copy of Cookworthy's Patent. It may be of consequence to know everything about this Patent before we begin to make white tea ware.' On 6 May 1774, a deed of Assignment from Cookworthy granted his patent rights to Richard Champion, his business partner. On 22 February 1775, Champion petitioned Parliament that the term of the patent right should be

[1] 16 February 1767   [2] To Bentley 5 May 1767
[3] To Bentley 2 January 1772

extended for the further period of 14 years to himself. If the petition were successful, it would lead to a Bill in the House of Commons. The opposition to this Bill organized by Wedgwood on his own behalf, and that of his fellow potters in North Staffordshire, is an historic landmark in the efforts of Wedgwood and the other potters to secure supplies of clay from the south-west counties of England.

The first hint of action by Wedgwood occurs in a letter to Bentley, on 5 March 1775: 'Several gentlemen you know I should have waited upon, respecting our opposition to Mr. Champion's Bill. . . . Sir W. Bagot is in town, pray see him. Likewise our good friends Lords Stafford, Guernsey and some others you may find in the Court Calendar. Do now, my dear friend, get into your chariot and visit these good gentlemen, and solicit their assistance on our great day. It will do you some *good* and your country a *great deal*.'

The Committee of the House of Commons reported on Champion's Petition on 28 April, and Champion's supporters presented a Bill, which came up for its first reading on 10 May. Wedgwood immediately returned to North Staffordshire and rallied opposition to the Bill, on behalf of all the potters. It was presented as a 'Memorial relative to the Petition from Mr. Champion for the extension of a Patent'. The co-operative character of the opposition is revealed by the wording 'Josiah Wedgwood on behalf of himself, and the manufacturers of earthenware in Staffordshire begs leave to represent'. After an acrimonious debate, the Bill was read a third time in the House of Commons. But Wedgwood took the fight further to the House of Lords. He issued three documents, which again emphasize the collective character of the opposition:

(i) Remarks upon Mr. Champion's reply to Mr. Wedgwood's 'Memorial on behalf of himself and the Potters in Staffordshire'.

(ii) A sheet of 'Reasons why the extension of the term of Mr. Cookworthy's Patent by authority of Parliament would be injurious to many landowners, to the manufacturers and to the public'.

(iii) The case of the manufacturers of earthenware in Staffordshire.

Thanks to the support of Lord Gower and some of his fellow peers, an amendment was secured to the Champion Bill. It read, 'Provided that nothing in this Act contained shall be construed to hinder or prevent any potter or potters or any person or persons from making use of any such mixture of raw materials and in such proportions as are described in the specification hereinbefore directed to be enrolled, anything in this Act to the contrary notwithstanding.' This amendment gave Champion a hollow victory with his Act, when passed in the House of Lords. It really took the sting out of the Act as far as the potters were concerned. It is not surprising to find that Champion closed his Bristol china factory in 1778. As we shall see, he later reappeared in the Potteries.

From London, the two potters who had been selected to present the Memorial to the House of Lords on behalf of the Staffordshire potters, Wedgwood and John Turner of Lane End, made a journey direct to the south-west clay regions. Wedgwood recorded his journey in his Journals and in letters to Bentley: 'Mr. Turner and I had a very pleasant journey. . . . We have concluded to set about washing some clay for ourselves and for others, as soon as we can, if they choose to have it. But at the same time to leave the raw clay open to all those, who choose, rather than prepare it for themselves, for I am firmly persuaded that an exclusive company, or rather an exclusive right in the clay in any company or under any regulations whatever, would soon degenerate into a pernicious monopoly.'[1]

Later, Wedgwood writes[2] that he has left Thomas Griffiths, his former South Carolina clay agent, at St. Stephens as his clay agent in Cornwall. He makes quite clear that he wanted clay not solely for himself, but for the whole pottery fraternity. He wrote, 'If I receive any sample of clay and stone, I shall gladly try it and recommend it to the Pottery, if a sufficient quantity can be obtained for the Pottery at large.' These extracts from Wedgwood's correspondence, and many others available, are a convincing answer to those writers, such as Hugh Owen in *Two Centuries of Ceramic Art in Bristol*,[3] who have bitterly criticized Wedgwood for his opposition to Champion's Bill. Owen writes that Wedgwood 'commenced the opposition on his sole account. The simple truth is that Wedgwood, the Prince of English Potters, could brook no rival in his special dominion.' He goes further: 'Wedgwood had not any authority from [North Staffordshire] manufacturers to make representations on their behalf'. How wrong Owen was in this may be judged from this extract from a letter from Wedgwood: 'We had a general meeting of the Potters yesterday at Moretons on the Mill, when we [Wedgwood and John Turner] told them what had been done for their interest in London and Cornwall. They were highly pleased with our negotiations and the generosity with which the Pottery at large had been treated.'[4]

At this meeting of the potters, Wedgwood proposed a public experimental institution on clays. A fortnight later, we find Wedgwood, Turner and Wedgwood's nephew, Tom Byerley, meeting the committee of the North Staffordshire potters to hammer out a drafts cheme for what would be the first chemical or industrial research institute for the pottery industry. Sadly,

[1] 18 June 1775   [2] 3 July 1775
[3] Published 1873   [4] To Bentley 23 June 1775

Wedgwood's scheme came to nothing. It was wrecked on the financial issues, as Wedgwood was to tell Bentley: 'Our experimental work expired in embrio last night. We could not settle the question whether the partners in the Company should pay separately or jointly. I consented to agree to either plan, for I thought myself bound in honour to the gentlemen who patronised our opposition to Champion's Bill, to give the plan a fair trial. . . . 'It seems it cannot be in this way, and having done my duty I am contented, and I shall take my own course quietly, as well as I can, and may perhaps have it in my power to serve the trade some other way.'

As a result of their excursions to Cornwall in 1775, Wedgwood and Turner took a clay lease at Carlogus from a Mr. Carthew, for Growan clay, which Wedgwood thought 'quite perfect and good. The mine rent, 4s. per ton, and the expense of raising it is a trifle.' Although unable to trace this Wedgwood-Turner clay lease of 1775 with Carthew, I have been fortunate in tracing the second clay lease and agreement, between Carthew and Wedgwood. This was signed on 1 November 1782, and refers to the clay pits at Treviscoe in St. Stephen. The term of the lease was for 40 years, and it gives details of clay digging, gins, stables and stone quarrying. It quotes the price of 4s. a ton for the first 100 tons and 3s. a ton for every 100 tons a year produced as a minimum. Incidentally, in this document, there is reference to a previous clay lease granted to a Thomas Phillips, Potter, Staffs., on 26 March 1779 – which is further confirmation that Wedgwood must have won others than John Turner to take leases for china clay and stone in Cornwall.

Wedgwood visited Cornwall a second time in 1782, and concluded an agreement with Carthew to form the first Cornish clay company, a partnership between two parties, Josiah Wedgwood and John Carthew, 'who have agreed to become joint adventurers and traders in the getting and raising of Clay and Stone called Growan Clay and Growan Stone'. This had a joint working capital of £800, £600 of which was subscribed by Wedgwood and the remainder by Carthew. Later, when the partnership was dissolved, Wedgwood paid him out the sum of £318.

Through this clay company Wedgwood supplied his friends and fellow potters with clay and stone. In a letter to Wedgwood his friend James Watt from Birmingham wrote: 'When I had the pleasure of seeing you here you were so kind as to promise to inform me of the prices at which you sold china stone and clay at the mine, at Falmouth and at Liverpool . . . once satisfied in these particulars they will send a vessel to take on board what they want. In the meantime, if you have any at Liverpool they requested you send them two tons

of Growan clay and one ton of Growan stone for the Delft-field Co., Glasgow.'
As this demand for china stone and clay from Staffordshire and other centres
increased, the clay merchants in Cornwall, Devon and Dorset became dis-
satisfied with the prices contained in their clay agreements. Carthew ended his
agreement with Wedgwood, with less than half its period run. This led to
Wedgwood making a third, and his last, visit to Cornwall, as revealed in a
memorandum to his son John on 7 August 1791:

(1) 'I have been 3 days on a little tour of the Clay District [Cornwall], and
have little doubt but we may be served upon better terms than we are at present,
and much better than it seems they intended we should be, for it is firmly
believed by the clay owners that we must have their clay at any price they should
be pleased to set on it.'

(2) 'We have endeavoured to convince them that they are mistaken. How far
we have succeeded I do not know.'

The main features of the 1791 potter's agreement with the clay merchants,
were as follows:

(1) It was signed by four of Wedgwood's own family, by his nephew Thomas
Byerley, his partner, and 12 other North Staffordshire potters and their partners.

(2) The merchants agreed for five years to deliver a minimum of 1,200 tons
of clay yearly for a sum of £120 to Mr. Pike, Clay Merchant, of Chudleigh,
Devon, over and above the mine rent etc. paid by him. For any clay above 1,200
tons, he was to be paid 1s. 6d. per ton. Pike was a partner in the Wedgwood
Clay Company.

(3) Mr. Pike was not to sell any clay to anyone outside the above Clay
Company from the Company pits or any other pits, 'within 10 miles of Purbeck'.
Josiah Wedgwood and partners were not to purchase any clay from any other
persons in Purbeck or within 10 miles.

(4) Mr. Pike was to have an eleventh share in the clay business – there being
10 shares held by the 7 potters named therein.

(5) Among the names of potters who signed this 1791 clay agreement as
partners with Wedgwood were Samuel Hollins, and John and William Turner,
sons of Wedgwood's fellow delegate John Turner (Senior), who accompanied
Wedgwood on his first Cornish clay excursion.

Mention of these three names brings the story back to Richard Champion,
the Bristol potter.

In addition to these three potters, four other North Staffordshire potters,
Anthony Keeling, Jacob Warburton, William Clowes and Charles Bagnall
joined as partners to form the New Hall Porcelain Company that purchased a

RSP D

porcelain manufacture patent from Champion. The formation of this New Hall Porcelain Company in 1781 followed soon after the dramatic closing down of Champion's Bristol pottery in 1778, barely three years after his paper victory in the House of Commons and House of Lords had extended the period of his patent from Cookworthy. When Wedgwood heard of the closure of Champion's china factory, he wrote to Bentley:[1] 'Poor Champion you may have heard is quite demolished. It was never likely to be otherwise, as he had neither professional knowledge, sufficient capital, nor scarcely any acquaintance with the materials he was working upon.' This extract, quoted by his biographer Miss Meteyard in her *Life of Josiah Wedgwood*, has been pounced upon by two writers – Llewellyn Jewitt and Hugh Owen – to attack Wedgwood for his opposition to Champion. Both of these writers have assumed that since Miss Meteyard quotes no later letter from Wedgwood, nothing further had been written by Wedgwood about 'poor Champion'. Hugh Owen caustically comments: 'This letter was never intended to be read by anyone but the partner [Bentley] to whom it was addressed. The publication of it is a challenge to the opinion of posterity not contemplated by the writer.' Since then, no writer has delved further into the private correspondence between Wedgwood and Bentley on this matter.

One searches in vain the pages of the three volumes by Lady Farrer on Wedgwood's correspondence with Bentley or the Biographical Notes of Thomas Bentley for any later letter than that quoted above about Champion's fate. However, by an examination of all the Wedgwood letters in the Etruria Museum archives, I discovered a letter dated 12 November 1780 from Wedgwood to Bentley. It was, in fact, the last letter in Wedgwood's handwriting to his beloved partner Bentley, who died (26 November) a few days after the letter had been despatched.

I give this letter in full for it is a complete answer to all who have attacked and criticized Wedgwood in his opposition to Champion and his patent. Wedgwood wrote:

Amongst other things Mr. Champion of Bristol has taken me up near two days. He is come amongst us to dispose of his secret, his Patent etc. Who would have believed it – he has chosen me for his friend and confidant! I shall not deceive him, for I really feel much for his situation – a wife and eight children, to say nothing of himself to provide for, and out of what I fear will not be thought of much value here, the secret of china making. He tells me he has sunk £15,000 in this gulf and his idea now is to sell the whole art, mistery and patent for £6,000. He is now trying a list of names that I have given him of the most substantial and enterprising Potters amongst us and will acquaint you with the events.

[1] 24 August 1778

Alas, Wedgwood was unable to communicate further with Bentley, because of the latter's death.

There are some definite conclusions to be made, then, on the Wedgwood-Champion controversy.

(a) Wedgwood's letter seals the date of Champion's disposal of his patent to the New Hall Company. Prior to the discovery of this 1780 Wedgwood letter, Jewitt had placed the date of Champion selling his patent 'about two years' after the opposition to his Bill by Wedgwood, and those whom Jewitt calls 'his Confederates' in 1775. This conclusion of Jewitt shows he had relied on Simeon Shaw's account when he wrote, 'Richard Champion Esq., a respectable merchant in Bristol . . . after fully contemplating his scheme was so unsuccessful in obtaining a demand adequate to the expenditure that about 1777 he sold the Patent to a Company in Staffordshire.' This erroneous date was repeated by Wooliscroft and Rhead, in their book on 'Staffordshire Pots and Potters'.[1]

(b) There can be no doubt now that it was through Josiah Wedgwood's personal initiative and sympathy that the introduction of Richard Champion to his own closest friends as potters in North Staffordshire was made possible. Among these were John Turner Senior, Wedgwood's fellow delegate to the House of Commons and in the House of Lords fight against Champion's Bill. Another was Jacob Warburton, who consented to act as an arbitrator for his friend Wedgwood in the notorious case of Humphrey Palmer and his infringement of Wedgwood's Patent for encaustic painting and his unscrupulous copying of Wedgwood's vases. These two good colleagues of Wedgwood soon collected support from their own close friends – Samuel Hollins, Anthony Keeling, William Glowes and Charles Bagnall, to form the syndicate of potters, that registered as the New Hall Company in 1781.

(c) It may be asked, why did Josiah Wedgwood not participate as a partner in this New Hall syndicate? Wedgwood's mind had been made up long before the Champion Patent Bill of 1775, that he would not be interested in the manufacture of porcelain. He reiterated his determination in a letter to Bentley on 6 February 1776, 'I do *not* wish to purchase any English process, and much less the Bone, which I think one of the worst processes for china making.' Further, let it be stated that during Wedgwood's lifetime Etruria produced neither porcelain nor even bone china. In dismissing this Wedgwood-Champion controversy, I would quote from a letter from Wedgwood to his nephew Thomas Byerley on 14 December 1792: 'I shall let my actions speak for me and continue to perform what appears to be my duty to all around me. I shall certainly love

[1] Published 1906

my friends, and if I cannot arrive at the perfection of loving my enemies, I will not injure them, unless in my own defence.'

After the death of his father, Josiah Wedgwood II was most active in the formation of a new potters' clay company. In 1797, he was the spearhead of a new syndicate, consisting of the signatories of the 1791 Potters' Clay Agreement, or their descendants, as well as 12 new additions consisting of wealthy potters such as William Adams and some of his rich relatives – the Breeze family, also potters. The initial capital subscribed was £20 each in 17 shares to be vested in trust with Josiah Wedgwood, 'towards establishing the said joint undertaking'. They declare their object was 'that they should be able to supply themselves with clays, without the interruption of third persons, and with a view to discover new sources of supply and to prevent that necessary material from becoming the subject of monopoly'. This lease shows the agreement is for 21 years. A mine rent of 2s. a ton is to be paid up to a minimum of 1,000 tons (whether gotten or not) plus a rent of £100. All the partners are liable to a bond of indemnity of £500 to Josiah Wedgwood II and his partner Byerley, for the lease agreement entered into by Josiah Wedgwood and W. Dore.

The seven signatories interested in exploiting Champion's Patent at the New Hall Pottery in 1799 enlisted the support of seven other North Staffordshire potters, to enter into an agreement with William Kent, a Yeoman of St. Austell, Cornwall, to allow them to search for and dig and raise 'tin ore, tin stuff, copper ore, lead, lead ore and all other metals and china clay and stone in all that common or waste called Hendra Common'. The purchase price was £170. The new group of seven potters who joined the New Hall Pottery partners included Josiah Wedgwood II, T. Byerley, Anthony and Enoch Keeling, William Adams, Thomas Minton, Joseph Poulson and W. Pownall. A second indenture was signed in 1802, when the Hendra Company agreed to pay three guineas quarterly to Henry Snell (St. Stephens) and Henry Lambe (St. Austell), plus one fourteenth share for liberty to dig, stream for tin etc. A further document discovered in the Wedgwood archives relates to the allotment of shares amongst the partners of the Hendra Company in the sloop 'Hendra' with its stores, cargo etc. This Hendra Company continued to thrive, despite the withdrawal of some members as partners. They purchased land in 1805 at Trelaver, which had been originally bought by Thomas Minton in 1799. In a document discovered amongst the Wedgwood archives, details are given of a clay wharf set up in the Potteries on land 'near the towing on the south west side of the Navigation from the Trent and Mersey, for a term of 18 years at a rental of £21'. In 1821 the Company appears to have too much clay and china stone at Charlestown, and at the wharf at Stoke, as reported in a letter to Josiah Wedgwood II. Later letters reveal that the Company is in arrears with its rent, and reports that Lord Falmouth is encroaching on several acres of the common owned by the Company.

After the death of T. Byerley in 1810, and Thomas Minton in 1836, the most active members appear to have been lost, because Josiah Wedgwood II, after his election to Parliament in 1831, was not actively engaged in the pottery business. Landowners were reluctant to grant clay leases to syndicates of potters, with the difficulties of such loose associations of partners, liable to be removed on changes within the pottery firms themselves. These factors, together with the highly speculative nature of clay mining, explain why this Hendra Company was the last of its kind amongst North Staffordshire potters.

Between 1730 and 1850 the potters, individually and often collectively, did all in their power to secure a regular supply of ball clay, china clay and china stone, as we have seen, from the Far West, south-west England, and from the Midland counties, as well as from Europe. During the Champion Bill opposition Wedgwood wrote to Bentley:[1] 'We have ordered 50 tons of a fine white clay from Bruges in Flanders. So you see a spirit is up amongst us which must have consequences.' The continuous search for new and better supplies of clays and china stone reflected the industrial changes in the quantity as well as the quality of the products that finally emerged from the potters' kiln. This increased productivity led to a chain reaction that affected the later processes of production, as well as changes in transport and methods of distributing and marketing the new pottery wares.

Pottery, when fired (or in the biscuit stage) is porous. In pre-1730 days the fired pottery was coated with a lead glaze or a salt glaze. Both raw materials, lead and salt, were obtainable either in or near Staffordshire. There was one drawback in the use of a lead glaze on pottery table ware: Dr. Percival, Medical Officer of the Health Board of Manchester, spoke and wrote of the dangers of lead poisoning from the use of lead as a glaze on plates, cups, saucers and jugs. He was supported by Dr. Gouldson, Medical Officer of Liverpool. As Wedgwood's famous 'Queen's Ware' was specifically attacked, Wedgwood wrote Bentley on 22 August 1773, 'I will try in earnest to make a glaze without lead, and if I succeed I will certainly advertise it.' Enoch Booth, as early as 1750, had mixed lead glaze with ground flint as a fluid glaze. Gradually, by reducing the lead content and increasing the flint and other raw materials, a satisfactory lead-less glaze was produced. The fluxing raw materials, added to the calcined and

[1] 23 July 1775

ground flints and china clay consisted of ground Cornish stone, tincal, boracic acid, borax, carbonate of soda and potash, carbonate of lime, whiting and felspar. Most of these fluxing materials the potters had to purchase from chemical merchants.

Because flint was an ingredient of the body of some wares, as well as a glazing material, potters used great quantities of it. As they were dependent on supplies of flint-stones (which they crushed and calcined) from the South of England coast around Rye, and from the French coast, they were often at the mercy of merchants who raised their prices for flint. For a time the potters supplemented these coastal supplies by purchasing river-bed flints, called chalk-pit flints. Wedgwood became alarmed at the possibility of a flint monopoly. He wrote to Bentley on 16 June 1777: 'A word or two about these flints. The demand for these stones by the East India Company and the Potters has raised them from 6s. to 12s. for 35 cwts. and they still talk of raising them, so that there is danger of doing mischief by being too urgent in our demands.' Wedgwood followed this up on 1 August 1777:

I have several reasons for interfering in the Flint Stone business.
(1) To prevent a monopoly.
(2) To convince our Committee that Flint Stone may be had from Gainsboro'.
(3) To prevent a shoal of purchasers from raising the price of the article.
For this purpose I promised Mr. Bill a share of what I bought at prime cost. Mr. Byerley and Co. are to have what they want, and some others I have promised to furnish, who were otherwise posting to the chalk pits and would have raised the price of the stones beyond measure. I wish the flints to be bought and paid for by me and to be supplied on my account from Gainsborough, and I shall distribute them. I do not mean to continue in this business myself any longer than I can consign it to other proper persons here. I wish to put it in a proper train to prevent a monopoly or an extravagant advance in the prices of raw materials.

In his next letter to Bentley on 14 August 1777, Wedgwood stated that the steps he had taken had removed the threatened danger of rising prices. No Flint Company of Potters, similar to the Clay Companies of Potters, has been traced in any of the Wedgwood, Minton or Spode archives. Presumably, Wedgwood's action made this unnecessary.

Raw materials for pottery decoration were mainly metallic oxides, as vegetable colours would never stand up to the heat to which the wares were exposed in firing processes. Potters relied on merchants supplying them with colour materials. An examination of the account books of Minton from 1797 onwards reveals large sums spent on colour raw materials. All these colour materials had to undergo two processes. First they had to go through a process of grinding, and later they had to be thoroughly mixed to provide a 'dip' for the biscuit ware, or for use by artists engaged in hand decoration of the wares.

Thus, after a struggle, the raw materials supply, thanks to Wedgwood's initiative, was solved to the potters' satisfaction. But solving this problem created others. Earlier the mixing, pounding and grinding of raw materials could be done by hand, for the scale of production described in Chapter 1. But now bigger and stronger means than hand tools were called for.

Here again Wedgwood was to play an important part in solving the problem.

CHAPTER 4

The Steam-Engine

Hand mills, hand blunging or treading were good enough to pound, grind and mix the potter's raw materials in the late seventeenth and early eighteenth centuries. In John Dwight's specification, mentioned by Llewellyn Jewitt[1] 'mingling and treading' were replaced by grinding with the help of the horse gin mill. One of Josiah Wedgwood's ancestors, Thomas Wedgwood, rated this means important enough to will it to his wife: 'I give and assign unto my wife during her natural life, my horse mill, with the buildings wherein it now stands.'

But eventually, treading the clays and other raw materials could not cope with the quantity used, nor produce the right quality of prepared raw materials. Even hand-milling of materials presented serious handicaps, apart from its tiresomeness and costliness. In one letter to Bentley, Wedgwood writes: 'I have made a thorough investigation of our black body since your representation of the seals being bad and can find no difference in materials or management except in grinding; and in that I know it is very deficient, and will be so long as we grind the materials in hand-mills.'

It was an easy step to adapt local corn and grist mills to perform the task of grinding flints or china stone for use in a pottery. Besides, the water-mill could grind incessantly, as long as there was a flow of water over the wheel. It also had a much larger capacity for output than horse-gins or several hand-operated mills. But even water-mills had drawbacks – their distance from the pot-banks and their failure through insufficient or irregular water flow. Some potters experimented with windmills to drive their grinding and mixing mills.[2] But even windmills were sporadic in their operation. In fact, I have discovered records of only two windmills, and these were owned by the Wedgwoods, but I examined records of over a dozen water-driven mills operating in and around the Potteries.

John Turner, the Lane End potter and friendly neighbour of Wedgwood, introduced a Newcomen fire-engine to pump water over the water-wheel installed on his potworks. He was the pioneer of the Newcomen engine in the

[1] *Ceramic Art of Great Britain, 1878*   [2] See Chapter 2

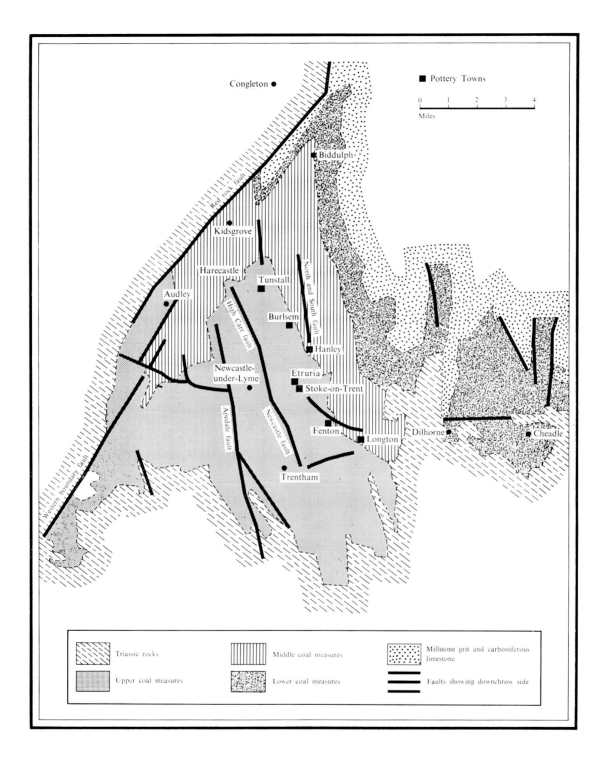

Congleton

Biddulph

Kidsgrove

Harecastle

Audley

Tunstall

Burslem

Hanley

Newcastle-under-Lyme

Etruria

Stoke-on-Trent

Fenton

Longton

Dilhorne

Cheadle

Trentham

Red rock fault

High Carr fault

North and South fault

Apedale fault

Newcastle fault

Western boundary fault

1 The coalfields of North Staffordshire

2 An atmospheric engine, *c.* 1712

3 Newcomen's Cornish fire engine and water-wheel

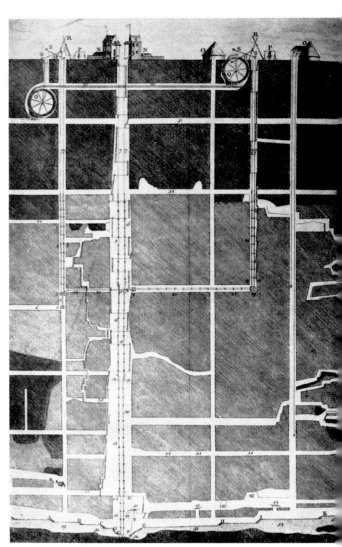

List of all engines of the Sun & Planet Type, supplied to the Various Manufactories, in the County of *Stafford.*

		Earliest date of drawings		Cylinder diar & Stroke				Number & Letters in Order Book	Owner of Engine.	Remarks.
239	1	April 1778	2	15×4·0					John Wilkinson.	Drawings marked "Double Bettering Engine" Chain on Beam Engines coupled to one shaft.
239	32	July 1782	1	42×6·0					John Wilkinson.	Old Furnace Forge Engine, Bradley, Chain on Beam. S & P. Wheels 48 & 24 dia since applied to work Reciprocating Rolls.
239		1787	1	dii.					John Wilkinson.	Bradley
239	3	April 1784	1	48×6·0					John Wilkinson.	Bradley Chain on Beam. In same house as next below.
239		April 1784	1	42×6·0					John Wilkinson.	Bradley Chain on Beam. In same house as next above.
239		1790	1	14×					John Wilkinson.	Bradley Boring & Turning.
239		1791	1	14×					John Wilkinson.	Bradley Colliery Winding Engine.
239		1790	1	48×					John Wilkinson.	Bradley Rolling & Slitting Engine.
									J. W. 9 Miscellaneous drawings	
97	1	April 1782	1						Josiah Wedgwood.	
97	9	June 1784	1	12×4·0					Josiah Wedgwood.	Single Link on Piston Rod. 5·0 Stroke S & P end.
97		Jan. 1793	1						Josiah Wedgwood.	
218	24	Sep. 1800	1	D 28×6·0	30			WB 3	Wedgwood & Byerley	
54	37	Feb. 1788	1	16×4·0					His Grace the Duke of Devonshire	Colliery Winding Engine Drawing of Winding Gear & Calculations good Drawing of Boiler Setting
48	36	Feb. 1790	1	D 16×4·0	8				Sir Nigel Bowyer Greeley Bart.	Parchment dated Sept. 1790 Winding Engine, apedale Colliery 26,000 lb 10 feet high Payment £40

4 An entry in Watt's engine book, concerning Wedgwood's first engine

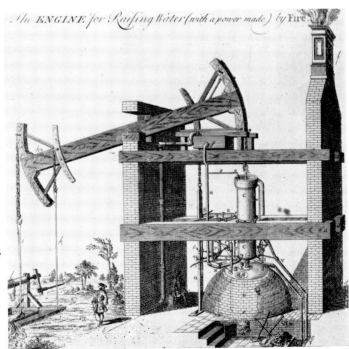

The ENGINE for Raising Water (with a power made) by Fire.

5 Newcomen's fire engine, 1717

Steam Engine —— for the power of ten horses,
to perform the following operations.

1. To grind flint in a pan   feet diameter.

2. To grind Enamel colours, in a number of small pans, in the chamber above the flint pan. The upright shaft A, which comes into the middle of this room, in order to work these small pans, must have a drum wheel upon it, B – from which is to go a strap C for every pan, which is likewise to have a drum head D – The pans, which stand some height on a plank bench, are to have bottoms made of glass, and a glass runner H in two parts In order to carry this runner round, the spindle or shaft for each pan must be divided into two parts, each part to have two prongs at bottom, which are to go into two holes left for this purpose in the upper part of the glass runners. The runners are made in two parts because, when one piece is made to turn round on its center, it does not wear away so fast there as at the circumference, So that the center remaining higher prevents the circumference from bearing upon the matter to be ground, & from doing the execution which it would do with an equal bearing.

3. To work a Stamper for pounding our broken Sagars into a powder that will pass through a coarse hair sieve – The floor of this stamper must consist of a large granite or boulder stone with a flat surface – It must be nearly square – three sides of plank – the fourth to take off when it is to be emptied – This may be made in the manner of the Stamping machines for stamping tin or other hard ores.

4. To temper clay – An upright shaft A is turned by a strap or straps on a large drum B under the floor C. The timbers D from the shaft support a circular flooring of planks E, on which the clay is to be laid. Over this, two wood rollers F F are hung, & weighted with iron or lead weights, which force the rollers down within a given distance of the Surface of the planks E. These rollers are notched halfway round in a longitudinal direction, the other half in a transverse one, and they are so placed in this respect, that the transverse notched part of one shall come over the surface of the clay which has been indented by the longitudinal notches of the other. As this pressure will have a tendency to force the clay to the edges of the circular plain, a number of bows H, H, strung with wire, are so situated as to cut off this clay in thin slices as it is protruded beyond the edges of the plain. Between the plain & the shaft is a kind of hopper I, I, into which one part of this clay will fall, and is to be taken up with a pitchfork & laid again on the plain. The clay which is cut from the outer edge will fall upon the floor, which must be kept clean to receive it, – and the clay must be returned like the other, to the plain above, till sufficiently tempered.

---

6 Wedgwood's original memorandum for a steam-engine specification

Potteries. We know through Simeon Shaw[1] that Turner installed a fire-engine 'erected in the open ground before his manufactory – open to the inspection of all the Potters of the time'. Although I have never been able to trace a description of Turner's engine, one can infer from Shaw's paragraph (where he refers also to Turner's visit in 1775 to Cornwall with Wedgwood) that the engine was a Newcomen fire-engine. Turner started as a potter at Stoke, with R. Bankes as his partner on the site. Later Josiah Spode opened his own potworks, purchasing the property from Turner on his deciding to open his own pottery at Lane Delph (today called Fenton Low, near Longton). It is difficult to fix the date when Turner installed his fire-engine. If after his visit to Cornwall, where he saw fire-engines in operation, pumping water over water-wheels to raise water from tin mines, then it was some time after 1775. To judge from a document in Wedgwood's handwriting I discovered pinned to James Watt's file of Wedgwood correspondence, in the Boulton-Watt archives in the City of Birmingham library, the Turner fire-engine must have been installed at Lane Delph before 1782.

Josiah Spode, after leaving Thomas Whieldon's Pottery, where at one time both Josiah Wedgwood and Spode had been apprentices, became a manager of Turner's Pottery at Stoke. Then, when Turner decided to open a new Pottery at Lane Delph, Josiah Spode purchased Turner's Stoke pottery. The above note of Wedgwood mentions a fire-engine at Spode's pottery raising water over his water-wheel mill.

Wedgwood knew of the existence and performance of Newcomen's fire-engines in the Cornish tin mines from his 1775 tour of Cornwall with Turner, which he must have discussed with his friend James Watt and his Birmingham partner at Soho, Matthew Boulton. Wedgwood also knew of Turner's fire-engine at Lane Delph and Spode's engine at Stoke, as can be seen from a note to James Watt.

Naturally, as an experimenter, Wedgwood was keenly interested in James Watt's invention of the steam-engine. Before deciding to install a Watt steam-engine at Etruria he invited Watt to visit the Potteries and tour the potworks, where Newcomen's engines had been installed, so as to get details of their performance in pumping water over the water-wheels. The wary Wedgwood writes at the tail of his note to Watt, anticipating possible opposition to Watt's spying round the fire-engines and mill pans of rival potters: 'Get the facts first and deliver the letter [of introduction!] after.' Watt's visit must have proved successful and entirely satisfactory to Wedgwood, for he gave an order for his first steam-engine from Boulton and Watt.

[1] *History of the Staffordshire Potteries*, 1829

Wedgwood had seen the value of water-driven mills for grinding flints and china stone during his partnership with Thomas Whieldon, before he set up on his own at Ivy House potworks and later at the Brickhouse Works in Burslem. Here Wedgwood had his flints and other raw materials ground and mixed at the Jenkins Flint Windmill, (see Chapter 2). He had great faith in this windmill, for if ever it broke down any time, it could be repaired by James Brindley, who had settled in the Potteries, erecting windmills and water-wheels for mills of local potters and landlords, such as the Earl of Gower.

As early as 3 March 1768, Wedgwood wrote to Bentley to say that he was invited to visit Dr. Erasmus Darwin at Lichfield, where Darwin had constructed a model of a new type of windmill:

(1) having no cogs or wheels or moving parts only;
(2) sails and upright shafts causing no friction;
(3) goes with all the winds night and day;
(4) has a large room under it, for the convenience of the works.

Wedgwood also describes a second visit to Lichfield to assist at a consultation about 'the windmill of Dr. Darwin's invention, which has been perfecting under the hands of Mr. Edgeworth and Mr. Watt.' In the meantime, at Etruria, Wedgwood wrote to Bentley on 3 April 1773 that 'I am going to erect a wind-mill in the middle of the front of my workshops (instead of a cupola) to grind the materials.' This was probably an ordinary windmill, with side sails like the Jenkins Flint Windmill, and not like the Darwin horizontal sails type, which Miss Meteyard states Wedgwood erected in 1779. In addition to these two windmills at Etruria, Wedgwood had a smaller mill driven by a water-wheel, deriving its driving-power from water supplied from a lodge or reservoir of water in the pottery grounds.

Even while Wedgwood was experimenting with Dr. Darwin's horizontal-sailed windmill he had a note from him as early as 15 March 1769 saying: 'I should long ago have wrote you, but waited to learn in what forwardness Mr. Watt's fire-engine was in. He has taken a partner, and I can make no conjecture how soon you may be accommodated with a power, so much more convenient than that of wind. I am of opinion it will be a powerful and con-venient windmill, but would recommend steam to you, if you can wait awhile, as it will on many accounts be preferable I believe for all purposes.'

Though Wedgwood had erected a windmill of Dr. Darwin's invention in 1779, he ultimately decided, as experimenter and progressive potter, to order a steam-engine from Boulton and Watt in April 1782, as shown by an entry on pages 56–57 in Boulton and Watt's 'Catalogue of Old Engines' in the Birmingham City Library archives. The drawing in Portfolio 97 shows a sketch of the two large flint mills, with two huge circular mill-stones, cog wheels and shaft. This was merely a preliminary sketch or drawing probably made in 1782, when the order was given, for it took a year or so to produce the complete engine and assemble it ready for erection in Etruria. So the actual date of its erection at the pottery was delayed till 1784. The engine was one of Boulton and Watt's Sun and Planet type, and destined to drive the clay mill, flint mill and smaller colour-grinding pans. The accompanying sketch in the Portfolio gives a plan of the mill house and engine room. A note marked H in the left-hand corner reads: 'the upright shafts of the three big mills pass through the next floor and has the same sort of machinery fixed to it there'.

Wedgwood's business at Etruria continued to thrive and expand. The greater demand for his wares required greater horse-power to grind and mill his clays, flints and colours. The first reference to the second steam engine for Etruria is contained in a letter from Wedgwood's son Josiah to Boulton on 15 June 1792, apologizing for his inability to give the details that Boulton had asked him to provide, on his return to the pottery after a visit to Soho. Wedgwood Senior writes to Boulton on 25 August 1792 giving the necessary details: 'As near as I can guess the engine should be from 12 to 15 horses. But on thinking upon the subject, I find I want a question answered "supposing the force of 30 horses to be wanted, how much greater expense or what other disadvantages would attend the dividing of it into 2 steam engines instead of one? That would be more convenient for us. In that case, I would have one of the engines to go direct by the force of the steam, and on the other I would throw the water upon a wheel.'

Boulton replied to this letter on 11 November 1792. 'I do not find myself possessed of any calculation for 15 h.p., but I can speak accurately as to the cost of engines of 16 h.p. and 32 h.p., which cost very little more than 15 or 30 h.p.' He then proceeded to set out the comparative costs of the two engines and the cost of their erection, in the following table:

	16 H.P. £	32 H.P. £
All the metal materials	459	846
Iron boiler	80	175
Wood work	97	162
Erection	60	77
	696	1260
Suppose Engine House	150	200
Total	846	1460

Continuing his letter Boulton writes: 'Each h.p. will take from 9 to 11 lbs. of coal per hour. To 2 engines you must have 2 men to work them, and the repairs which, but trifling, will be twice as much in two as in one.' Boulton also tried to shatter Wedgwood's faith in water-wheels, even when adapted to have water lifted over them, by bluntly stating: 'I cannot recommend the application of engines to raise water to apply to a water wheel, because there will be by that circumstance and application of your power, a loss of nearly 50% of it. Moreover, the expense of pumps and keeping them in order is much greater than by the other mode of working.'

Wedgwood appears to have studied the above details and decided to order an even less powerful engine than 16 h.p., as this letter from his son makes clear. The letter is reproduced in its entirety, though when I discovered the document the upper half (a) was found among the private papers of Matthew Boulton in the Assay Office at Birmingham, and the lower half (b) among the James Watt MSS in the Boulton and Watt Collection, Birmingham Public Library.

Etruria Dec. 24/1792.

Dear Sir,

(a) My father is just gone from home for a day or two, but desired me to tell you that the mode you proposed paying the money is perfectly agreeable to him, say £3,000 in a bill payable on 20th January, £1,000 payable the 20th February and £1,000 payable on 20th March.

(b) My father was mistaken or calculated wrong, respecting the power of the engine. He thought Mr. Spode's engine had been calculated equal to 3 horses only, and when he said 6 horses he meant an engine of double the power of Spodes, which it seems must be 10 horses. He therefore wishes it to be so.

I beg my respects to Mr. M. Boulton and am Dear Sir,

Your obedient servant

Thos. Wedgwood.

In the Boulton and Watt portfolio relating to this 1793 steam-engine, I discovered a transcription of Josiah Wedgwood's notes to Watt about the performance he expected of the 10 h.p. steam-engine. It was expected to perform 4 operations:

(1) To grind flint in a pan.

(2) To grind enamel colours in a number of small pans in the chamber above the flint pan.

(3) To work a stamper for pounding broken saggers into a powder that will pass through a coarse hair sieve.

(4) To temper clay.

In his notes Wedgwood elaborates the details of each process.

In a book which Wedgwood called a 'Commonplace Book' on pages 41–42, I discovered further notes which Alexander Chisholm, his private secretary, had extracted from Wedgwood's memorandum books for the years 1785–1788: 'Engine Mill 32 inch pump. 130 lbs. of coal per hour – gross on the most favourable supposition, cost about £1,000, including the engine house. Mr. Sherratt or Mr. Watt?' This question-mark about Sherratt or Watt probably means that Wedgwood would query Sherratt, a local ironfounder and engine and boiler repairer, or Watt himself regarding the probable cost. Wedgwood's notes continue: 'Main shaft Engine Mill goes round 40–42 times in a minute. Mr. Watt says they have had for their premium 5 guineas per horses per annum, reckoning a pair of corn mill stones at 6 horses. Can say no more till Mr. Boulton returns from Cornwall, only that they shall in the prices they fix be guided by their own and their employers' interest.'

In my search for any further data regarding this 1793 steam-engine, I was fortunate enough to find an undated letter, placed in the space September 1790, addressed to Mr. Wedgwood from Matthew Boulton in his letter book from 1780 to 1794. The letter was to be delivered by hand by Mr. Ewart, Mr. Boulton's millwright, who was in the Potteries area erecting a steam engine at Sir Nigel Gresley's colliery at Newcastle-under-Lyme. It read: 'Suppose your canal to furnish a stream of water sufficient to work a mill for 6 months in the year. I say it will burn as many coals to raise and return the water to your said mill for the remaining power for 12 months, provided the power of the engine was applied direct to the turning of the mill, without the intermediate application of the water. I therefore recommend that the water will stand on its own legs and do all it can, and that a rotative engine stands upon its own legs.'

The above letter confirmed that Wedgwood was equipped at Etruria with a water-wheel, drawing canal water to supply power, and that, as a man who had faith in existing wind- and water-power mechanisms, he was really hesitating to rely solely on steam power. Boulton, as the purveyor of steam-power engines, naturally advocated reliance on steam power direct. Boulton proved to be right, for after Josiah Wedgwood's day, Josiah, his son, abandoned wind- and water-driven power and relied on steam-power engines entirely.

I was extremely fortunate to have had access to a complete file of correspondence between Josiah Wedgwood II and Boulton and Watt in Soho. It gives details of the erection and the subsequent performance of the steam-engine at the pottery factory. In a letter sent by J. Watt Junior to Josiah Wedgwood II on 9 November 1795, the following details are given about the work performed by a

24 H.P. Engine, turning 3 pairs of 4 ft. 4 ins. stones and burning 3½ cwts. of coal per hour. The metal machinery for such an engine including our demands of every kind and an iron boiler will amount to £1,125. The wooden framing will cost about £130, and the expense of erection about £70. Total

£1,325. The first sum is the only one we contract for, as the wooden framing may probably be had cheaper upon the spot, and the expense of erection may be more or less according to the exertions of the persons employed to co-operate with the engineers furnished by us.

After receiving the engine drawings in September 1800, Josiah Wedgwood II was perplexed as to what horse-power engine to order. He wrote a letter to Boulton on 22 January 1801, describing a steam engine owned by Keeling, a neighbouring potter – a 24 h.p. engine erected by Sherratt of Manchester. Boulton was invited to send someone from Soho 'so that they could examine the new engine to find out whether the 24 h.p. is too little a horse-power for the work it had to perform'.

The result of this visit is shown in the next letter sent by Boulton to Wedgwood, who had written to say he had decided to order a 30 h.p. steam-engine:

We are favoured with your obliging order for a 30 H.P. engine . . . we can scarcely flatter ourselves with being able to complete it in less than 9 or 10 months . . . the price of the whole of the article delivered will be £1,095 and payable in 3 months. [The letter concluded:] We have some difficulty in directing your choice between a wooden beam and one of cast iron. The former has answered extremely well in the engines we have hitherto executed, and we probably should not have deviated from that construction, but for the scarcity of timber of the proper size, grain and age . . . cast iron beams are indeed superior to wooden ones in one respect – that of not warping.

In a letter on 24 November 1801, Josiah Wedgwood decided on using an iron beam, though it cost £50 more. On 9 July 1802, Boulton and Watt sent an account for all the materials supplied for this engine. The promptness with which Wedgwood paid on 3 October by a bill of £1,200, contrasted with the delay in payments made by some other potters, and especially by some of the colliery owners supplied with steam-engines. In 1803, there was some trouble with the steam-engine and the Account Books of Boulton and Watt show that on 16 May Wedgwood paid £51 for repairs. Later still, on 27 December 1810, correspondence shows 'Collar of the flywheel broken . . . our engine stands still until the new pedestal is fixed'. The despatch with which the repairs were carried out is revealed by the following entry by Boulton: 'Wedgwood had broken their flyshaft plummer block and are to have another sent immediately, completely fitted with brasses. Mr. Storey had directions to cast the block and it will be sent down to Soho 'and no time must be lost in fitting it complete'. Obviously, a cash customer and a family friend of the Boulton and Watt families must not be let down.

Later correspondence still, on 20 August 1817, discloses an expansion of production requiring greater engine power, for Wedgwood inquired about adapting his 30 h.p. engine to one of 36 h.p. by a change of cylinder size.

However, a note from Soho on 4 October 1817, states it would be unsafe to install more than 4 h.p. to the present engine which Wedgwood himself admits 'is constantly loaded to the full extent of its powers'. Further correspondence at various dates later in 1817 and 1818 shows that Wedgwood reported to Boulton and Watt alterations to boilers, including the addition of a third boiler and the erection of taller chimneys to cope with the demand for extra power.

The steam-engine in other factories

Where Wedgwood led, other potters followed. The second Josiah Spode, whose father, as already indicated, had a fire-engine at his Stoke works, installed a 6 h.p. steam-engine from Boulton and Watt. Spode's account books in 1802 show that he paid £30. 2s. 7d. for a steam-engine to pump water for an overshot-wheel, either to replace or supplement the fire-engine his father had installed.

There is documentary evidence that Josiah Spode II installed a new Watt 36 h.p. steam-engine in 1810.

Closely associated with both Spodes was a Thomas Minton, the copper engraver, who later left Spode to set up as a potter himself (see Chapter 2).

A study of Thomas Minton's account books show that he relied on the use of water-power to grind his pottery materials, but in 1819 a steam-engine was installed by a Christopher Kirk of Etruria. Shaw in his *History of the Staffordshire Potteries* refers to this engine. Shaw also mentions a steam-engine in use at Thomas Wolfe's pottery. Robert Hamilton married Wolfe's daughter, and succeeded his father-in-law as potter. Boulton and Watt records show that he had a Watt steam-engine installed, probably to replace or supplement his father-in-law's 'pirate' steam-engine, as Watt termed them. Shaw who, wrongly credits Robert Hamilton with being the first to erect a steam-engine, says that Enoch Wood installed one as well. William Adams, a friend of Wedgwood and Spode, installed a Boulton and Watt engine at one of his collieries. Shaw states that Adams installed a steam-engine at his pottery adjacent to the colliery. According to the 1833 Report of the Factory Inspectors, E. Keeling was a potter whose business was conducted on a larger scale than Etruria under Josiah Wedgwood II. He installed a 'pirate' steam-engine by Bateman and Sherratt. A Boulton and Watt entry for July 1796, under the heading 'Manchester Pirates' reads: 'Messrs. Bateman and Sherratt to pay £103. 3. 3. in one lump sum.' A later entry among the Boulton and Watt MSS shows a reference to Sherratt, who had a branch engine works in the Potteries, where their ironworks at Shelton were advertised for sale in the *Staffordshire Advertiser* on 23 August 1833.

Solving the problem of handling ever greater quantities of raw materials, then, had brought the steam-engine into pottery manufacture and established it there by the 1790s. The next step was to apply steam power to other processes.

7 Steam engine installed by Wedgwood in
1800, dismantled in 1912

...ah Spode Stoke Stafford^re Novr 17th 1802

	BRASS, &c. Cont?							
2	Brass Washers for Piston Rod X Bar							
2	Ditto ditto for Bell Crank X Bar							
2	Brass Washers for Air Pump X Bar							
4	Brass for Bell Crank Gudgeon							
4	Ditto for double Crank							
20	Ditto for Perpendicular and Horizontal Rods							
4	Ditto for Shaft Plummer Blocks							
4	Ditto for Governor							
	Feeding Valve 1/2 Inches							
	Reverse Valve							
2	Gage Cocks							
	Feet Feed Pipe, 1/2, 8 Feet Gage and Flanches							
	Copper Pipe in Stuffing Box for Feeding Apparatus							
	Brass and Iron Wire for Feeding Apparatus							
	Barometer, Pipes, Cocks, Scales and Socket							
	Steam Gage							
4	Boxes of Cement							
8	Ditto and Packing Materials							
	Cement used in making joints at the Foundery							
	Fitting the Engine complete							

Abstract

Cast Iron						
Wrought Iron						
Roller						
Brass						
Stores						
Boxes						
Part of Expence of Patterns						
Carriage &c of Boiler						
Ditto						
Commiss^n on S.F. Acct						

8 Watt's account for Spode's 1802 steam engine

9 Matthew Boulton

10 James Watt

11 A note from Wedgwood to James Watt

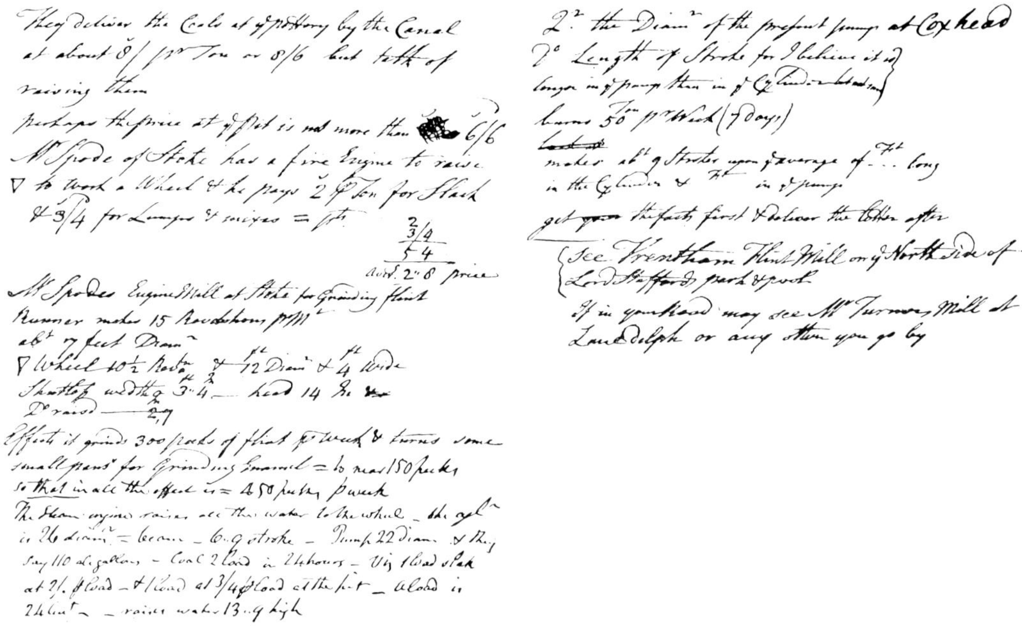

They deliver the Coals at y^e Pottery by the Canal
at about 8/ p^r Ton or 8/6 but talk of
raising them
perhaps the price at y^e Pit is not more than 6/6
Mr Spode of Stoke has a fire Engine to raise
▽ to work a Wheel & he pays 2/ p^r Ton for Slack
& 3/4 for Lumps & mixes = p^t.

2
3/4
5 4
Aver. 2"8 price

Mr Spodes Engine Mill at Stoke for Grinding flint
Runner makes 15 Revolutions p^r M^t
ab^t 7 feet Diam^r
▽ Wheel 10½ Revo^ns & 12 ft Diam^r & 4 ft Wide
Shuttles width 3"4 — head 14 In.
D^o raised — 2,7
Effects it grinds 300 pecks of flint p^r Week & turns some
small pans for Grinding Enamel = to near 150 pecks
so that in all the effect is = 450 pecks p^r week
The Steam engine raises all the water to the wheel — the cyl^r
is 26 diam^r = beam — 6..9 stroke — Pump 22 diam. & they
say 110 ale gallons — Coal 2 load in 24 hours — Viz 1 load slack
at 2/. p^r load — & 1 load at 3/4 p^r load at the pit — a load is
24 Cw^t — raises water 13..9 high

2^r the Diam^r of the present pump at Coxhead
D^o Length of Stroke for I believe it is
longer in ye pump than in ye Cylinder
burns 50 Ton p^r Week (7 days)
makes ab^t 9 Strokes upon ye average of ... Ft long
in the Cylinder & Ft in ye pump
get the facts first & deliver the letter after
{See Trentham Flint Mill on ye North side of
{Lord Stafford's park & pool
If in your Road may see Mr Turners Mill at
Lane Delph or any other you go by

CHAPTER 5

Application of Steam Power
to Pottery Processes

The success of steam-power engines in their application to the preliminary processes of preparing the raw materials, was an inducement to the employers to apply power-driven machines to other processes which hitherto had been merely hand operations, to the work of throwers, turners, moulders and even artists.

1. PROCESSES INVOLVING THE USE OF THROWERS' AND TURNERS' WHEELS

In 1730 and earlier, the potter threw the clay on to a horizontal wheel operated by a hand-driven wheel and rope attachment, or by a kick of the foot on a revolving wheel. The kick-wheel had the advantage of being self-operated by the thrower, whose hands were free to manipulate the plastic clay on the revolving wheel. The hand-driven wheel with a rope attachment would necessitate the labour of a boy or girl as an assistant. Even when these devices were replaced by artificial power later, throughout the eighteenth and nineteenth centuries and even today in some potteries these hand-driven and kick-impelled throwers' wheels may be seen side by side with steam-operated throwers' wheels. In Wedgwood's pottery, there was a throwers' table operated by a woman, who turned a large hand-wheel with a rope which drove the revolving table (see plate 18).

Arthur Young, in his *Six Months Tour through the North of England*, published in 1769, writes: 'A boy turns a perpendicular wheel, which by means of thongs turns a small horizontal one, just before the thrower with such velocity that it twirls round the lump of clay he lays on it, into any form he directs with his fingers.' Young, an observant traveller, would have noticed the hand-operated thrower's wheel, with the occasional flick from one of the thrower's free hands, had this been the method of operation in 1769. Alternatively, had the thrower operated his wheel by an occasional foot-kick, Young would have described it. So we must assume that at that date as a general rule the throwers' wheel was driven by a rope or thong attached to a perpendicular wheel hand-rotated by a boy or a girl.

Power applied to the turner's wheel

When the ware leaves the thrower's wheel, when it is dry or received from the green room, a vase or teapot, for example, can be turned, polished, fluted or finished in the turner's hand by being applied to the wheel of his revolving lathe. The turner's lathe had been used in Staffordshire much earlier than 1730, for Wedgwood in a letter to Bentley on 19 July 1777 gives full credit to David Elers for his use of the lathe on his fine teapots. Whieldon in his memorandum book, 1749–1760, wrote the following entry: 'June 2nd. 1749. Hired a boy of Ann Blowers for treading lathe: Per wk. 2/-d. Paid Ernest 6d.' A list compiled by Wedgwood's secretary in 1790 contains the following entry: '3 Turners and 5 boys turn the lathe (2/6d., 3/-d., 3/3d., 4/-d.)' in the ornamental ware section. A similar entry gives details in the useful ware section: '7 Turners of flat ware and 7 boys to turn the lathe'. And again: '*Turners* of holloware [cups, jugs etc.] 4 at piecework, 2 apprentices and 1 at 10/6d. 7 boys turn the lathe at 3/6d., 4/-d., 3/6d., 4/d., 2/6d., 2/6d., 4/-d.' Then follow details of throwers: '*Useful ware Throwers* 9 at 3/6d., 18/-d., 17/-d., 2/6d., 5/-d., 4/6d., 2/-d., 4/-d., 2/9d. *Ornamental ware Throwers* 3 at 17/-d., 3/-d., 3/3d.'

As there is no entry here for boys to turn the throwers' wheel, it may be assumed that the throwers' wheel was not turned by boys specially engaged for that purpose, as in the case of the turners' lathe. It may be that the lower-paid thrower's learner – earning rates from 2s. to 5s. in the useful ware and from 3s. to 3s. 3d. in the ornamental ware section, took turns at the thrower's wheel for the master thrower. On the other hand, it is possible that by 1790 Wedgwood had applied the artificial power of the water-wheel or one of his steam-engines to drive the throwers' wheels in the pottery.

In the House of Commons Report by the Committee of 'Inquiry into Children employed in Manufactories' (1816) we have clear evidence given by master potters of the existence of steam-engines to drive throwers' and turners' wheels. On page 69, Josiah Wedgwood II, in reply to the question, 'Your manufactory does not employ much force?' answers, 'I employ a steam-engine for grinding the materials and some of the lathes are turned by that steam-engine.' From this reply, we may conclude that since 1790, when Wedgwood's list refers to 'boys turning lathes', some of the lathes at Etruria had been mechanized between 1790 and 1816.

The purpose of an inquiry of 1834, through the circulation of a questionnaire of 50 items to pottery maufacturers and others, was to find out the effects of power-driven machinery on the employment of children. Its object was not to ascertain how much power-driven machinery was used in a pottery factory, but to what extent children were used in the working of power-driven machinery. In many cases the answers to the questions were not given, as in the case of Enoch Wood of Burslem and John Wedgwood of Tunstall. In others we get replies: 'No machinery used.' 'Machinery fenced off from children', or 'They are well fenced off.' Enoch Wood replies, 'The machinery being used does not affect the employment of children in any way.' Charles Mason replies, 'Not fenced off, because none but miller goes near it.' In reply to question 4, Copeland and Garrett (successors to Spode) state, 'Steam engine for grinding materials, also for turning and throwing wheels'. This 1834 report confirms the paragraph written by William Evans, the Editor of *The Potters' Examiner and Workman's Advocate* in his preface to the issue on 9 December 1834: 'In some manufactories, where steam-engine power is available cones inverted are placed on parallel shafts, and a belt is adapted to them, which is always adjusted because of their similar but opposed dimensions. One of these shafts has a pulley at the lower end, from which passes a belt to the thrower's wheel and the other is connected by proper gear with the moving power. The needed velocity for the thrower is obtained by the movable belt being higher or lower on the driving cone from a directing lever.'

This suggests that the practice of using steam power to drive throwers' wheels was well established and had been in operation well before 1834.

2. POWER APPLIED TO PRESSING AND CASTING WARE

The application of steam power, and its resulting mechanization of throwers' and turners' wheels, obviously suggested to progressive potters the extension of such steam power-driven engines to the processes of pressing flat ware and hollow-ware. The hollow-pressers' wheel is only a modification of the throwers' wheel in its operation. I have discovered no document giving any evidence of objection to the application of steam power to hollow-ware pressing machines. This may have been because (a) when steam power operated the pressing machine, the presser had no deductions from his earnings to pay the boy or girl engaged to turn their wheels of the press; (b) by the application of steam power to the press the presser earned more on piecework. So there was no outcry against mechanization of operations for pressing hollow-ware between 1800 and 1832.

From 1832 onwards, there was active resistance by workers in certain potteries to the introduction of special types of power-operated machines, called 'jiggers' and 'jollies'. They are in fact power-operated mechanical throwing and pressing machines to produce hollow and flat ware. Reference to these machines is found in William Evans' *The Art and History of the Potting Business*. He says on page vii, 'The machine for the manufacture of flatware is even now in the course of perfecting by George Wall of Manchester.' This machine was introduced into the pottery of Charles James Mason at Fenton, but it was abandoned after a few weeks. Evans stated, 'It was constructed so as to be made to work either by steam or hand-power. In its rude form, it was capable of producing by the power of one man and a boy, as much ware as is now produced by six adult operatives.'

There is no record of the permanent use of the 'jigger' or 'jolly' type of machines during the period of our study up to 1850. This may perhaps be explained by the leadership of William Evans, a militant trade-union leader who was a bitter opponent of mechanization processes which led to the displacement of operatives – as the jigger and jolly threatened. A vigorous campaign leading to strikes in the Potteries was undertaken by William Evans in his trade union journal *The Potters' Examiner*. But even he admits in his *Art and History of the Potting Business* on page viii, that 'In addition to Wall's machine, there is another now in use in some of the manufactories in the North of England. . . . It is principally used in the manufacture of cups and bowls and, I believe, although of a ruder construction than that of Wall's invention, is nevertheless of a more successful character.'

In B. Woodcroft's list of patents affecting machinery 1726–1850, there is a record of Ridgway and Wall's patent for a 'jigger' and 'jolly'. How soon after 1850 these power-driven machines were actually employed in North Staffordshire, it is hard to say. The master potters were agitating for the use of such machines in the North Staffordshire Potteries, according to W. H. Warburton in his *History of the Staffordshire Pottery Union*. He writes: 'In 1850 they [the North Staffordshire master potters] complained that not only were the North of England potters using machinery [i.e. 'jiggers' and 'jollies'], but that this machinery was also being used on the Continent, and in both cases without interference from the workpeople.' Josiah C. Wedgwood in his *History of Staffordshire Potteries* fixes the date of the introduction of 'jiggers' and 'jollies' as late as 1870. He appears to have based his conclusion on F. Harris' statement, and Harold Owen's view, based in turn mainly on the strong trade-union opposition in the Potteries. J. L. and B. Hammond in their *Rise of the Modern Industry* rightly state that 'certain machinery [i.e. flat and hollow pressers] was delayed'. But further, they make the astounding statement, 'Perhaps the most surprising fact about the development of the Potteries was that mechanical power played no part in it.' This statement can be flatly contradicted from the facts and evidence adduced in this and the earlier chapter.

Mechanization of tile making

One very important section of the pottery industry is that of tile making. Today, it is one of the most flourishing sections of the North Staffordshire Potteries. Some of the most noted firms, Minton, Spode-Copeland and even Wedgwood have manufactured tiles, side by side with their earthenware and china products. Today Wedgwood and Spode-Copelands have given up making tiles, and left it to specialist firms, such as the Campbell Tile Co. and the Henry Richard Tile Co.

As early as 1830, Samuel Wright of Shelton obtained a patent for an invention for making tiles. It reads: 'The patterns of the tiles are impressed by moulding them in moulds of Plaster of Paris in metal frames. The articles are reduced to the same thickness by a cutting instrument worked upon a machine, which hecks the articles at a true level'. Wright sold his patent to Minton, who produced such large quantities of tiles, that his partner Boyle thought Minton had become 'tile mad', according to Jewitt.[1] In 1840 Richard Prosser patented an invention 'for making buttons, tesserae, floor tiles and glazed tiles by pressure, by preference using screw presses of different powers for articles containing up to and including 50 sq.in. of surface in each piece. Articles of larger surface requiring greater pressure being made by hydraulic press, the pumps of which are worked by steam.' Jewitt gives further details of Minton using Prosser's patent:

In August 1840, Minton commenced making buttons and tesserae with six presses. On December 1841, 25 presses were at work. On September 5th. 1842, 62 presses were at work, and in March 1844, 90 presses were at work, employing 90 women and 180 girls. During the first 6 months of 1844, the firm received orders for 27,123 great gross and sold 22,519 great gross. In 1845, 33,928 great gross were made, and in 1846, 50,493 great gross. *Mr. Minton was lavish in his expenditure in adopting every mechanical improvement – hydraulic presses, Napier's steam hammer etc. that promised success.*

In 1852 a firm of ironfounders, William Boulton Ltd., was established in Stoke to manufacture the tile presses and steam-engines to operate them. In an

---

[1] *Ceramic Art of Great Britain*

interview with Mr. Frank Boulton, the son of the founder who was still carrying on his father's business, I was told that his father came from Madeley, and as far as he could trace, was not related to Matthew Boulton, James Watt's steam-engine partner at Soho. Further evidence of William Boulton's interest in tile-pressing machines is given by Furnival in his book on *Leadless Decorative Tiles*. Boulton took out, in 1863, a joint patent with a Joseph Worthington of Burslem to make figured encaustic tiles, by a new method called the 'dust-clay method'. This is substantially the method of tile production in all up-to-date clay and tile works even today.

During my meeting with Mr. Frank Boulton at his Stoke works, I was shown a copy of the patent granted in 1867 to his father William 'for the transmission of motive power to potters' wheels, lathes etc., by means of rope drives'. The existence of this patent before 1870 itself is evidence that there was in existence a mass of machinery and mechanical apparatus used in the pottery industry, prior to 1867, to justify William Boulton's enterprise in establishing a factory to supply the motive power for pottery machines and engines. Mr. Frank Boulton shares my view that those who date the introduction of pottery machinery around 1870, are greatly in error. His father's machinery-making firm would never have thrived and expanded, since its establishment in 1852, if there had not been in existence a demand for pottery machines and steam engines to generate motive power earlier than 1870.

Trade-union opposition to the use of the 'jigger' and 'jolly' machines for pressing flat-ware and hollow-ware from solid or ball clay, probably assisted the introduction not only of clay-dust pressing described above, and also drove the potters to adopt alternative means of mechanical production of wares. Shaw in his *History of the Staffordshire Potteries* states that even in the eighteenth century some ornamental wares – toys and trinkets for example – had been made by casting them in moulds. Dies were used for stamping out china buttons, and Wedgwood had seal-makers stamping out seals, used extensively to seal letters and agreements with sealing wax. Some of the moulds for casting were in the early stages made or carved from wood. These were later superseded by plaster-of-Paris moulds.

During the eighteenth century there was a great extension of casting by the use of slip-clay in the fluid state. This slip-clay was poured into the plaster-of-Paris mould, which when left in the warm drying-room absorbed the moisture from the slip, leaving the cast or moulded article to be extracted. Though this casting with slip-clay was a series of hand operations, the mechanical character of this production of wares by slip-casting in moulds is really an operation using a simple form of machine or mechanism – the moulds for casting.

Babbage, in his *On the Economy of Machinery and Manufactures*, writes on this question of copying by the use of moulds in the making of pottery, or the use of copper-plate engravings, or the use in textiles of the calico-printing roller. He argues cogently that all these devices are not simple tools, they are really simple machines. When moulds are made of metal, as many were, then they were pieces of machinery. In particular, moulds for making the complicated fitments of sanitary ware would be classified by Babbage as pieces of machinery and not simple tools. The mechanical reproduction of certain types of pottery ware by simple slip-casting in moulds led to a large increase of women and girls doing this lighter type of work and reducing the number of male pressers, who later operated the jiggers, jollies and heavy tile pressers.

3. MACHINERY INTRODUCED TO DECORATE POTTERY WARES

Decorative forms may result from throwing, turning, pressing or casting the plastic raw materials used by potters. But the type of decoration that easily lent itself to be applied mechanically to the pottery wares was transfer printing. Wares were sent from potworks in Staffordshire to Liverpool to be transfer-printed from about 1756 onwards, as record Meteyard, Jewitt and Smile in their volumes on Josiah Wedgwood, and W. Turner in his book *Transfer Printing*.

It is not till 1775 that we get a record of transfer printing being introduced at a factory in North Staffordshire. Turner gives the credit for the first on-glaze transfer printing to W. Adams at his Tunstall pottery. Simeon Shaw credits John Turner of Lane End with the introduction of the first under-glaze transfer printing in 1783. In *Spode and His Successors* Hayden challenges this claim by stating that Josiah Spode I introduced it into his pottery factory in 1781.

Transfer printing, at first from copper plates, and later from steel engravings, finally led to the introduction of printing presses. Some of these were hand-operated and others, later, steam power-operated. The engraved plates with the desired decoration were smeared over with printers' oils of various colours and the engraving was transferred mechanically on to the biscuit ware for under-glaze printing or – on the glazed ware – for on-glaze printing, a process performed either by what was termed 'bat-printing' or the application of transfer-printed paper. This decoration by transfer printing cheapened the process of decoration, which hitherto had been long tedious hand work by artists. Now the decoration of wares could be undertaken on a mass-production scale, by the application of a piece of printed tissue paper placed on wares by transferrers –

mostly by young girls and women. Later, the use of transfer printing of a mere outline design was another step to cheapen and speed up the painting of colours on pottery wares.

The mechanical decoration of pottery wares with the installation of transfer-printing presses was in full swing from 1790 onwards. The rapid extension of mechanical decoration by the use of transfer printing from copper engravings is confirmed by the increasing number of patents for transfer printing on pottery recorded by B. Woodcroft in his *List of Patents*; and by evidence from ledgers recording expenditure by potters on transfer printing paper and on copper-plate. I examined several ledgers and account books of Minton, covering the years 1817 to 1835. There is an account totalling £593. 6s. 9d. for transfer paper from Robert Bradbury & Co. of Stoke, an account also from Smith and Rhead, Newcastle-under-Lyme, and one in 1822 from Mr. Holden, Burslem. There are accounts also in 1817 showing purchases of tissue paper for printing from Messrs. Chance and Chance of Birmingham, and from Reece and Wall, another Birmingham paper firm. Minton purchased tissue paper from Fourdrinier Hunt of London, who owned Colthrop Mills near Newbury. This last entry is most interesting, for this London firm removed their paper mill from Hertfordshire and established a paper mill in Hanley in 1827, to meet the growing demand for transfer printing paper by potters.

Hand-made ceramic transfer paper had been made at Cheddleton in 1797. But Fourdrinier's London paper mill, first established to export his 1804 Patent Paper Machine, and his Hanley factory, opened in 1827, soon put William Adams' paper mill out of business. Then Fourdrinier rented the paper mill from Adams in Cheddleton, where he built a new paper factory. Fourdrinier's former Ivy House Paper Mill at Hanley was purchased by a Thomas Brittain, who later followed Fourdrinier, and erected a new paper mill there. The Fourdrinier interests in the Cheddleton Paper Mills were purchased later by a Mr. Goldstraw. In 1888, he sold the concern to a Mr. Steele. He took as his partner Mr. Fred Haigh, one of the ancestors of the present owner. Today, the paper mill employs 400 hands, and supplies transfer tissue paper, not only to the North Staffordshire pottery factories, but to potteries throughout various parts of the world.

One or two writers on the pottery industry have attempted to break down the traditional view that the impact of machinery on it dates only from 1870 or later. The first of these is W. Burton, who published in 1922 his well-informed book, *Josiah Wedgwood and His Pottery*. He was on the staff at Etruria, and as a ceramic chemist he was conversant with the pottery as a working concern. On page 20, writing of Josiah Wedgwood, Burton states: 'A constant preoccupation of his mind from the time [in 1759] of his settlement in Burslem, as a manufacturer, was the imperative necessity that his workmen should be trained in more precise methods than such as served elsewhere, as well as in the use of improved machinery, i.e. that to the industry should be applied scientific and mechanical improvements'. The practical manager-ceramic-chemist proceeds to elaborate: 'He realised that the aid of machinery could be usefully applied in two directions, *first* in replacing the exhausting and deleterious labour involved in pounding and grinding the hard materials and rocks used as prime constituents of the bodies and glazes of the pottery, as well as the more perfect levigation of the various colouring oxides and their compounds; and *second* by effecting mechanical improvements, which increased the precision of the potters' throwing wheels and turning lathes, used in shaping and finishing the pottery before it was fired.' Proceeding with the subject of mechanization, Burton states: 'This change which had been slow and gradual, throughout the seventeenth century . . . was somewhat quickened, when improved tools and machinery were invented on the spot or were adapted from those used in other manufacturing industries.' This is corroborated by a letter that Wedgwood wrote Bentley on 22 February 1768: 'We have an ingenious and indefatigable smith, who has, ever since engine lathes were first introduced here, been constantly employed in that business.'

I was fortunate in securing access to Minton's Account Books from 1797–1850. If space permitted, I could produce ample evidence from Minton's pottery, adjacent to Spode's factory, to contradict the traditional view of 'not

MINTON'S PAYMENTS FOR MACHINERY 1824–1834

Year	Amount		
	£	s.	d.
1824	79	3	0
1825	38	1	0
1826	10	4	0
1827	31	3	6
1828	109	2	4
1829	60	15	0
1830	367	13	$7\frac{1}{2}$
1831	556	2	5
1832	26	11	1
1833	56	10	0
1834	91	19	6
Total	1427	5	$5\frac{1}{2}$

till 1840 or possibly 1870 or 1876' for the introduction of machinery in the Potteries. But one extract must suffice here. It is under the heading 'Payments for machinery' of annual disbursements. Unfortunately, the ledgers giving this financial data do not specify the type of machinery purchased or the source from which it came. There is an item in another ledger which implies that some of the expenditure was for printing presses, as there was a total of £4,307. 17s. 1½d. paid for ceramic printing tissue paper from 1823 to 1835, and an item of £788. 0s. 6d. for copper, on which engravers worked out copper plate designs to transfer them to the tissue paper.

To clinch my main argument on the very early use of machinery in the potteries of North Staffordshire, I have set out in five tables data taken from Boulton and Watt's archives showing the distribution of the sales of their steam-engines, according to counties of installation.

Watt's Steam Engines according to County dispersal 1775—1800
TABLE I DURING DECADE 1775–1800

Order	County	No. of Engines	Total H.Power
I	Cornwall	21	420
2	*Staffs.*	*12*	*181*
3	Salop	10	301
4	Notts.	2	9
5	Warwicks.	I	20
6	Derbys.	I	20

Excluding Cornwall, with its numerous steam-engine pumps, Staffordshire is easily first. Lancashire and Yorkshire are simply not on the list at all during this first decade.

TABLE II DURING DECADE 1785–1795

Order	County	No. of Engines	Total H.Power
I	Lancs.	19	267
2	*Staffs.*	*16*	*248*
3	Salop	14	120
4	Notts.	13	166
5	Yorks.	9	217
6	Cheshire	7	91
7	Warwicks.	3	23
8	Leics.	2	22
9	Derbys.	2	12

This decade sees Lancashire first with Staffordshire a close second, both in number of steam-engines and in horse-power. Yorkshire is fifth in list of steam-engines, but third in order of horse-power used.

Unfortunately, the Watt records end in 1800, and thus the statistics cover only half the last decade.

TABLE III STEAM-ENGINES FROM 1795 TO 1800

Order	County	No. of Engines	Total H.Power
1	Lancs.	35	619
2	Yorks.	6	100
3	Cheshire	4	68
4	Staffs.	3	74
5	Leics.	1	8
6	Notts.	1	30
7	Salop	1	20
8	Warwicks.	1	20

Note how the three textile counties shoot up, leaving Staffordshire fourth in number of engines, but third in horse-power.

Combining Tables I and II shows how over a longer period the race for motive power develops, according to Watt's careful records of the sale and use of his steam-engines.

TABLE IV COMBINING RECORDS OF TABLES I AND II, 1775–1795

Order	County	No. of Engines	Total H.Power
1	*Staffs.*	*28*	*429*
2	Salop	24	421
3	Cornwall	21	420
4	*Lancs.*	*19*	*269*
5	Notts.	15	175
6	*Yorks.*	*9*	*217*
7	Cheshire	6	91
8	Warwicks.	4	43
9	Derbys.	3	32
10	Leics.	2	22

Note over this span of 20 years, Staffordshire is easily first, with Lancashire fourth and Yorkshire fifth in use of horse-power. This particular Table IV brings out more clearly than any other evidence that as far as either the number of steam-engines or horse-power used, Staffordshire, predominantly a pottery county, used more steam-driven machinery than either of the textile counties of Lancashire or Yorkshire.

TABLE V, STEAM ENGINES FROM 1775 TO 1800

Order	County	No. of Engines	Total H.Power
1	Lancs.	54	886
2	*Staffs.*	*31*	*503*
3	Salop	25	441

TABLE V—*contd.*

Order	County	No. of Engines	Total H.Power
4	Cornwall	21	420
5	Notts.	16	205
6	Yorks.	15	317
7	Cheshire	11	159
8	Warwicks.	5	63
9	Derbys.	3	32
10	Leics.	3	30

This last quarter of the eighteenth century Staffordshire is a runner-up to Lancashire in the number of steam-engines and horse-power.

BRIEF SUMMARY OF CONCLUSIONS

(1) *From 1730 to 1775*

The pottery industry in Staffordshire as early as 1730 used power-driven machinery – water-driven wheels, horse-gin mills or windmills for grinding flints and stones, and tempering clays and similar arduous and laborious tasks. About 1775 Newcomen's fire-engine came into the field to supplement the above power apparatus, but not to supplant it.

(2) *From 1775 to 1782*

All the four methods of supplying motive power were in operation during this period. James Watt had been perfecting his steam-engine, and the first to be installed in a factory was installed at Etruria by Wedgwood. At first it was used to pump water over water-wheels to conserve canal water. Later, as Watt perfected his steam-engine, it became a direct source of power, driving mills and turning throwers' wheels and turners' lathes direct.

(3) *From 1782 to 1800*

The improved Watt steam-engine proved successful, and in addition to pumping water over water-wheels to operate the heavy stamping and grinding of flints and clays, it was later used as motive power to drive wheels operating throwing wheels, lathes and decorating printing presses.

(4) *From 1800 to 1830*

A great increase in the number of steam-engines installed in the Potteries – both Watt steam-engines and those Watt termed 'pirate' engines – and an increase in their horse-power.

(5) From 1830 to 1850

A great extension of the use of steam power in potteries inside the Potteries area, as well as in 'out-potteries', a term used by the Pottery Trade Union for potters outside Staffordshire.

This briefly summarises my case against the traditional view that the Industrial Revolution, which altered industry in Lancashire, particularly the textile industry, did not affect the Potteries at all till the 40's or even the 70's of the nineteenth century.

Further, the application of steam power and machinery was not confined to the Pottery industry alone in Staffordshire. It crept steadily into ancillary industries like the coal industry, colour industry, metal industries and even Staffordshire transport.

CHAPTER 6

The Potters' Search for Fuel

The steady increase in the use of steam-engines to supply power for the increasing mechanization of pottery processes first of all drove the potters to search for appropriate supplies of coal to fire the steam-raising boilers. The increase in the use of steam-powered machinery, from the early grinding and pounding of clay, flints and stones, led to an increase in the bulk of raw materials later passing through the mills to the hands of the craftsmen – throwers, turners, pressers, moulders, casters, and later to the artists and designers. Then the potters found it needed large quantities of fuel to fire the kilns of pottery ware. The question facing them was, 'what is the most suitable fuel?'

Miss Meteyard[1] suggests no date for the use of coal. But from the following extract, one may infer that she would fix a point of time between the fifteenth century and 1715. 'Carts and waggons were unknown, and they were rare in 1715. Yet the traffic was considerable, and it must have grown as the woodland receded and billets and charcoal for firing the ovens had to be brought from increasing distances. The absorption of the neighbouring woods undoubtedly led to an early use of coal, more especially as it cropped out from the surface.'

There is on record, as early as 25 June 1635, a patent No. 83, on page 21 of *The Abridgements of the specifications relating to bricks, tiles and pottery* (pub. 1862). It reads: 'Franke Thornese – An invention for the saving of fewell labour, iron and tyme heretofore unnecessarily spent and consumed . . . with the saving of more than a full third of the fuel consumed in Kylnes for making bricks, tyles, earthen potts . . . and done by altering the shape and contracting the ayre of the furnaces.' Ashton and Sykes in their book on *The Coal Industry of the Eighteenth Century*[2] state, 'By the early seventeenth century coal had come to take the place of charcoal in brewing, distilling and in the making of bricks, tiles and pottery.' J. V. Nef in his more recent researches into the *Pre-Industrial development of the British Coal Industry* confirms this view.

[1] Eliza Meteyard, *Life of Josiah Wedgwood*
[2] T. S. Ashton and J. Sykes, *The Coal Industry of the Eighteenth Century*

Wedgwood in a letter to Bentley on 7 July 1768, writes, 'I have read your queries and answers, which are very clear, but *charcoal* is not to be had here on any moderate terms, indeed you hint as if *coals* will do.' Here Wedgwood is referring to the problem of firing enamel kilns. Wood was the fuel used in the firing of porcelain in Cookworthy's, and later Champion's pottery works in Bristol.[1] Shaw has an interesting paragraph in his *History of the Staffordshire Potteries*. 'William Littler of Brownhills about 1765 was manager of a porcelain manufactory in Skelton for Baddeley and Fletcher . . . they fired with wood, because the body would not bear coals.' As late as 7 September 1796, Josiah Wedgwood II was concerned about the use of wood in his enamel kilns. His objection to the use of wood was 'that the flames will burst forth from the top of the chimney to any height'. James Watt tries to help him with the suggestion of building a cupola above the chimney of the muffle kiln, as it was called. Then Watt adds, 'I think also you should try the burning of coals in your present kilns.' Wedgwood carried out Watt's suggestion. The following extracts are from Wedgwood's account books (1801–1806) pages 34, 107, 155 and 212 in Ledger A.:

CHARCOAL, COKE AND COAL USED IN POTTERY KILNS (ENAMEL)
IN LONDON

Year	Charcoal	Coke	Coal	Total £.
1801–2	—	£109	£12	121
1802–3	£59	£75	£12	146
1803–4	£60	£113	£29	202
1805–6	£56	£124	£15	195

The progressive increase in the use of coal to fire kilns is brought out more clearly in a further series of accounts for the same period for two sections of the pottery. Wedgwood always referred to his ornamental side of the pottery as the 'O' works, and the 'Useful' side as the 'U' works.

COAL USED IN THE STEAM ENGINE BOILERS AND KILNS AT
ETRURIA

Year	Tons	"O" Works £	Tons	"U" Works £	Total tonnage	Total Value £
1801–2	852	367	5038	2085	5890	2452
1802–3	555	248	5064	2271	5619	2519
1803–4	465	281	?	2794	?	3075
1804–5	228	240	6283	3146	6511	3386
1805–6	382	163	6825	2866	7207	3929

From the above tables, it can be seen that coal used exceeded the rival fuels, charcoal and coke.

[1] Hugh Owen, *Two Centuries of Ceramic Art in Bristol* (1873)

The first table quoted below, taken from Thomas Minton's account book for 1796–1803, shows a steady increase in two heavy items – 'wages and coal', which are combined in this first table showing weekly expenditure.

Year	Week	Wages and Coal	£	s.	d.
1796	May 21	,, ,, ,,	12	19	5½
1803	Jan. 8	,, ,, ,,	206	13	10

After the above date a new system of book-keeping was adopted by Minton, separating items of cost on wages, coal and clay, as the following table shows.

MINTON'S EXPENDITURE ON WAGES, COAL AND CLAY 1823–1835

Payments expressed in £ (shillings and pence ignored)

Year	Wages	Coal	Cornish Clay	Dorset Clay	Total Clay
1823	9,469	2,860	1,083	656	1,739
1824	9,477	2,740	723	486	1,209
1825	12,421	2,964	1,248	463	1,711
1826	12,518	2,836	788	415	1,203
1827	13,772	3,084	1,046	451	1,497
1828	15,981	3,323	1,205	454	1,659
1829	17,326	3,275	1,717	306	2,023
1830	17,668	3,153	841	342	1,183
1831	18,104	3,235	1,169	382	1,551
1832	19,823	3,136	861	318	1,179
1833	20,485	3,244	758	443	1,201
1834	22,684	3,871	748	524	1,272
1835	23,226	3,932	746	418	1,164
Totals	213,954	41,653	12,933	5,658	18,591

These amounts from 1823 to 1835 are a compact statement extracted from 75 items analyzing pottery costs for the period. They reveal that next to labour costs, coal costs are the heaviest single item, even more than clay costs. Coal costs are about one fifth of labour costs, and over twice the cost of clay.

Herein lies the economic significance of coal, as a decisive element in the localization of the pottery industry in North Staffordshire. It was cheaper to bring clays and other raw materials to the North Staffordshire coalfield, than to transport the required bulky and costly coal to Cornwall, Devon and Dorset.

From the period 1730 to 1850, there survive a number of original documents available in the archives of individual potters who kept coal accounts. Wedgwood's earliest accounts, dated April 1763, show that he paid R. Mollatt £10 on account for coal. A letter dated 9 September 1763, shows Mollatt asking for

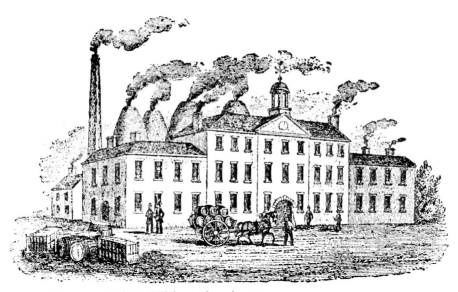

12 Greengates, built by William Adams in 1770

13 A porcelain factory in Worcester, 1752: figure 9 indicates the coal-yard, thus showing that coal was being used by this date

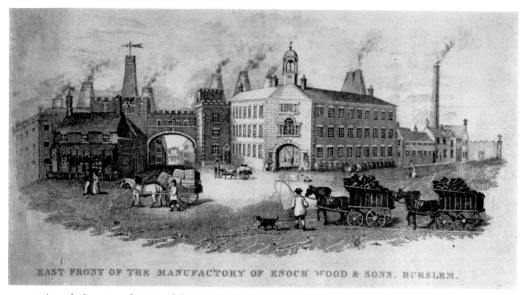

EAST FRONT OF THE MANUFACTORY OF ENOCH WOOD & SONS, BURSLEM.

14 A typical pottery factory of the early nineteenth century

15 The pithead colliery of Wm. Adams & Sons, situated on a potbank

'3 or 4 gineys if you possibly can', and a further letter, dated 2 October 1764, states, 'Mister Whedgood, I desire you will be so good has to send me 3 or 4 ginneys'. In the same bundle of accounts, we find details showing Mollatt overcharging as recorded below:

> Overcharge a/c of R. Mollatt shows
> 10 loads @ 4d.   3s. 6d.
> 17 „ @ 2½d.   3s. 6½d.
> Overcharge on 2 horses to Lane Delf.   8d.
> 1 load to Burslem mill   1s. od.

These 'loads' at 4d. and 2½d. were obviously packhorse pannier loads.

The coal accounts show that Wedgwood was supplied by other packhorse teamsters – a W. Coles supplying 'Great Row' coal on 10 December 1763, and a Richard Taylor, on 5 September 1764 supplied to 'Mr. Say Weehood 30 Drips of coal at 6½ for load come to sum of £1. 0. 7'.

Here is a typical account, showing that Wedgwood had some of his coal supplies delivered by canal to Etruria.

JOSIAH WEDGWOOD TO SPARROW & CO.

1788.	£.	s.	d.
April 30. To 18 tons coal del^d at Etruria @ 6/6	5.	17.	0.
Later dates „ „ „ „	5.	17.	0.
regularly. etc.		etc.	
Total	£115.	12.	0.

In connection with the Trent & Mersey Canal, which passed the Etruria works, on its way northwards towards the Mersey, Wedgwood as a canal proprietor and treasurer put forward an interesting scheme for cutting into rich coal seams by piercing the Whitfield Hill. There was a precedent for coal extraction from canal tunnels in the case of the Duke of Bridgewater's Canal at Worsley, where he extracted coal and brought it to the surface by canal barges. Wedgwood's coal plan by means of the proposed canal tunnel came to nothing, as explained in his 'Common Place Book', and noted by Smiles in his *Lives of the Engineers*.

The following extract is from accounts for road delivery from 26 March to 24 June 1789.

RSP F

JOSIAH WEDGWOOD DR. TO R. BILLINGTON FOR COALS

Name of coal seam and sometimes coalowner.	Tons	Cwts.
Engine coals	116	19
Grister „	265	13
Burnwood „	47	19
Heath's Cannel Row Coal	12	17
„ Spencroft	45	11
Whitfield Coal.	73	3½
Baddeley's Spencroft.	19	4½
Heath's Peacock Coals.	34	10½
Bagguley Cannel Row Coal.	4	15½
Gallimore's Spencroft Coal.	1	10½
Winghay Coals.	5	16
Cockshead „	1	11½
Adams Great Row Coal.	1	9½

Total £235. 7. 10d.

Josiah Spode I did much the same as Wedgwood and purchased his supplies of coal from various persons, as shown in his accounts from 1775 to 1795. He had coals delivered by horse panniers at first, but later used carts on roads, and barges on canals for delivery. Josiah Wedgwood II was content to follow his father's policy in purchasing coals from various sources. This extract from his Ledger A (1800–1807) shows a great increase in the use of coals, and coal costs, as compared with those revealed in earlier accounts.

COALS AT USEFUL WORKS

1800–1801	Tons	Cwts.
Gutter	2604	6
Burnwood.	176	15½
Camp.	871	4½
Rohurst.	63	13
Cockshead.	1112	19
Whitfield.	126	16½
Newcastle.	4	8
Total	4960	2

Value £1,940. 7. 8.

Up to this time no potters are found involved directly in coal mining ventures. But soon, in the first decade of the nineteenth century, Josiah Spode II became directly interested in coal mines to supply fuel to his steam-engines and kilns. Later, other potters followed his example, among them William Adams.

In 1802 Josiah Spode II took out a lease for 21 years of coal mines in Lane Delph. One of the other lessees was Thomas Fenton, who married Spode's sister Anne in 1808. The lease is a most interesting document, but for lack of space the following extracts must suffice:

'To this end the said Josiah Spode shall have permission to stack, set up, sell, dispose of and carry away the said coals cannels slack, marle and clay. And also to set up, erect and build any Fire or Steam Engine or Engines, or any other Engine or Engines Buildings Machinery and works in and upon the said lands.'

The lease allowed him to use these steam-engines 'for the purpose of drawing the water from the mines or any other use or purpose' . . . 'or the said Josiah Spode shall be at liberty to use and employ them for the purpose of grinding or preparing colours, flints, glazes and other materials for the use of his or their earthenware or china manufacture.'

The Fenton Park Colliery Co., in the days before Josiah Spode II decided to become associated with it, seems to have had financial difficulties. They were behind in their payment of the engine premium, as the following account, sent with a letter from Boulton & Watt pressing for payment, shows:

FENTON PARK COLLIERY CO. DR. TO BOULTON & WATT

1799. Nov. 30. To premium of Engine from Aug. 11.		
to 30th Nov. 1799. 111 days @ £30.	£9.	2. 5d.
1800. June 27. Cylinder top piston rod.	£137.	8. 8d.
Total	£146.	11. 1d.

This amount must have been paid, for by the time Josiah Spode II had taken things in hand the Watt records (in a letter dated 11 October 1803) disclose the delivery of a new engine to the value of £1,476. 8s. On 21 November 1803, there is a letter from Spode acknowledging a bill for £1,000, which at maturity will be placed to the credit of the Colliery. The balance on the engines seems to have been unpaid, for on 4 July 1814, Watt sends a stiff letter:

Josiah Spode & Partners, Soho.
Gentlemen,

Annexed, we hand you a statement of our account, which according to our agreement with you should have been liquidated a 12 months ago. We beg to solicit that no more time may be lost, and that we may be favoured with your remittance at an early date.

Boulton & Watt.

On 13 November 1804 came a much stronger letter ending with the words:

such a continued disregard to our claims might be thought to warrant other measures on our part than the renewal of our solicitations . . . . . .

Boulton & Watt.

This had the desired effect for on 26 November 1804, Spode forwarded a bill to the amount of £500 to the credit of the Fenton Park Co.

While the Fenton Park Colliery was struggling to pay for its engines, there was a rival colliery – Cockshead – in which William Adams and Benjamin Godwin, potters, were interested as partners. They apparently felt the particular premium charged by Watt for the first steam-engine installed at the colliery was heavy, as they refer to this in a letter to Watt, ordering a second engine through John Sparrow, the Secretary of Cockshead Colliery.

Watt in his reply on 17 February 1792 asks several questions relative to the colliery.

(1) Its depth.

(2) Diameter of pump and length of stroke to clear pit water.

(3) 'Do you want the same engine to draw water and your coal like the one we have erected at Newcastle for Sir Nigel Gresley?'

The answers given by Mr. Sparrow were satisfactorily answered, for in 1794 the following account was sent by Boulton & Watt:

ACCOUNT OF JOHN SPARROW ESQ., NO. 6. DR. TO BOULTON & WATT.

		£.	s.	d.
1794.				
April 3. To a/c transmitted.		334.	2.	2.
Aug. 4. To 1 day of J. Law at engine.			5.	0.
„ 4. To premium on full Rotative Engine.		135.	0.	0.
Oct. 1. To ½ year's premium first engine.		60.	0.	0.
		529.	7.	2.
Deduct remittance 1 Sept. 1794. £100.				
„ 4 Dec. £199.		299.	0.	0.
Balance		230.	7.	2.

In the letter accompanying this account Watt replies to Mr. Sparrow's complaints about the performance of the pit engine:

We are extremely sorry to hear that any stoppages have taken place from the failure of one or other of our engines. We have always understood that they performed their work perfectly. . . . Accidents in the pumps or pitwork ought not to be attributed to the engines, and you will please recollect, that the principal parts of the wrought iron work were made at Cockshead by your own workmen. . . . You will please observe that in a powerful machine consisting of so many parts, it is scarcely in the power of man to make them so, but that some trifling part at times will fail or break.

Presumably Sparrow had complained about engine troubles in the hope that Watt would reduce the annual premiums. But Watt, the stern Scottish business man, was unmoved:

We were sorry to find that you look upon the colliery as a hopeless project. Perhaps you have had only money to disburse, and we have no doubt your expenses have been considerable, but we hope you will be amply repaid. At all events you know it is a rule in trade, not to share the losses without a share of the profits. . . . . Although it is painful to us to say 'No' to anything you ask, we must act uniformly and consistently and not establish a precedent which would be extremely ruinous to us.

Further correspondence between Sparrow and Watt show that Watt agreed to commuting the annual premiums for the engines for a final lump sum of £650 on 12 June 1795. Then, on 2 December 1795, Watt installed a further new steam-engine at Cockshead Colliery.

Difficult as were the financial transactions between Watt and the potters interested in coal-mine engines, they were more satisfactory than Watt's dealings with Sir Nigel Gresley, a personal friend of Wedgwood and James Brindley. Watt installed a steam-engine for Sir Nigel at his Apedale Colliery at a cost of £325. 7s. 6d., which Sir Nigel never paid.

CHAPTER 7

The Transport Revolution: Roads

The early decades of this period could rightly be described as an age of no roads, or at best of bad roads. All that existed in the Potteries were beaten tracks or winding narrow lanes (for example, the old name often used for Longton today is 'Lane End'). A study of the earliest North Staffordshire maps – Kid's 1607, Speed's 1611, and later modifications by Janssom and Bleeu in 1646 – show no roads. Ogilby's strip-map of 1675 shows roads from London to Chester and Carlisle, the latter by-passing the Potteries. When roads are first marked on maps, we find traces of the traditional Roman roads put in some. A map of 1750 shows lanes and some parish roads, many of which must have existed earlier, for there are records in the Tunstall Court Rolls of the seventeenth century showing penalties being imposed for neglecting to keep roads and lanes in repair.

As late as 1768, Arthur Young in his *Tour through the North of England* wrote: 'A more dreadful road cannot be imagined, and wherever the country is the least sandy, the pavement is discontinued and the ruts and holes most execrable. I was forced to hire two men at one place to support my chaise from overthrowing in turning, but for a sort of cart of goods overthrown and almost buried. Let me persuade all travellers to avoid this terrible country.' If this was Young's assessment of the main road from Knutsford to Newcastle, we may leave to the imagination the actual state of the narrow lanes in the Potteries, where Llewellyn Jewitt says 'packhorses laboured along lanes where clay pits had been dug out and left unfilled'. Eliza Meteyard states 'that vehicular traffic of carts and pot waggons taking wares to Bridgenorth and Bewdley on the Severn and to Wellington Ferry on the Trent for shipment on boats on the navigable rivers there, did not make these roads any better'. The return loads from these places bringing flints and clays were a heavy burden, for which these roads and lanes were totally unfitted. In spite of the good supply of rivers and streams in the Potteries, not one is navigable. There were numerous fords crossing these, and when the rivers were flooded, road traffic was not only difficult, but extremely dangerous, and crates of earthenware were often submerged, according to Meteyard. It is therefore not surprising to find potters, particularly, pressing for road improvements.

The first road to be turnpiked near the Potteries was on the eight computed miles from Tittensor to Talk o' the Hill, on the post road from London. This Act was passed in 1714, and renewed in 1734. In a later Turnpike Act of 1759, we find the potters of that period as Trustees erecting turnpikes on the old road from Newcastle-under-Lyme through Stoke, Lane Delph and Draycott on to Uttoxeter and Derby. Among the names of the trustees were famous potters – Whieldon, Turner, Shelley, Ralph Wood, Thomas Wedgwood (Senior), Bourne and William Adams. All these potters were users of the road, taking their wares to Uttoxeter Market and beyond to Derbyshire, as well as for bringing return loads of flints and clay.

Two features of this Act are interesting for their favourable terms to potters. First, no toll gate was to be erected nearer to Newcastle than the Mere – which meant that within the Potteries a stretch of turnpike road from there, through to beyond Longton, was toll-free. Secondly, special exemption from toll was given to all who carried coals from Crakemarsh to Uttoxeter – another concession to potters, as consumers of coal for their kilns. Another road joining these was turnpiked in 1761. Here the provision was made that 'No tolls for carriages or cattle over Hug Bridge into Staffordshire unloaden or loaden with lime or coal'.

The pre-Wedgwood potters paid attention first to turnpiking roads taking out their fragile wares to Uttoxeter, and more distant markets in the North and South-East of England via Hull. Wedgwood, when he first interested himself personally in the improvements of roads in the Potteries, concentrated on improving roads from Chester, port for clay from Devon and Cornwall, roads on which he used to send wares to be decorated in Liverpool and then brought back to the Potteries after decoration.

A petition supporting 'high-road' improvements was presented on 16 February 1763. It is recorded in full in the House of Commons Journal:

A petition of the several towns and villages, and of several merchants and traders residing in Newcastle-under-Lyme was presented. . . setting forth, that the road from the Red Bull to Lawton, Cheshire to and thro Killegrew (Kidsgrove) Goldenhill, Tunstall, Burslem, Cobridge, Hanley and Skelton to Cliff Bank near Stoke-upon-Trent, is in a ruinous condition and in many places ponderous, narrow and incommodious, and at each end falls into a great Turnpike road, leading to Winsford ferries, and at the other end into a Turnpike leading to Uttoxeter, and so on to Willington Ferry, where the navigation to Gainsborough and Hull commences, whereby the materials for the manufacture of earthenware are chiefly brought and conveyed, and the manufactured goods are chiefly carried to markets, whereby great profits and advantage arise, in case the said communication between the said Turnpikes was made easy and passable for carriages. That some of the petitioners have already subscribed the sum of £1,200 for and towards the repairs, and only wait for the power of erecting Turnpikes to reimburse them and to complete the said roads.

According to the House of Commons Journal, an amending petition was presented a few days later, on 19 February 1763, altering the route slightly. Opposition to the Petition came from the Mayor and Corporation of Newcastle-under-Lyne, as it would divert Liverpool–London traffic into Burslem, Hanley and Stoke, and deprive Newcastle of trade, and besides 'it would only lead through small villages, so that the same seems only calculated to serve the interests of a few private persons'. The matter was referred to a special Committee, an amended route which satisfied objectors was accepted, and the Act was passed on 31 March 1763.

Under this Act, over 300 trustees were appointed. Amongst them, naturally, in a district like the Potteries, were several potters. In the list of trustees we find the following names of leading pottery manufacturers – 9 Wedgwoods, 5 Warburtons, 4 Whieldons, the Wood Brothers, Hares, Adams, Cartwrights, Daniels, Heaths and Cartlidges. Among the others, of course, were the leading aristocratic landowners and coal-owners. But the outstanding promoter of this Turnpike Act and others later added, was Josiah Wedgwood.

In his commonplace book he recorded his speech delivered at a meeting of the Gentlemen of Newcastle at the Town Hall in 1763. 'It is apprehended that the interests of Newcastle rightly understood will not be injured, but rather promoted by the intended Turnpike, since it is not intended to be continued further than Burslem. On Mondays (Market days) no horse shall pay more than ½d nor carriage more than half toll at Tunstall gate. These concessions have been made out of regard to the interests of Newcastle to continue the friendly intercourse between the two neighbourhoods.' Wedgwood cleverly weighed the few half pence in tolls from 'salt and malt horses, and a few hackney carriages' against 'the welfare of a manufactory, which putteth bread into the mouths and findeth employment for many thousands of poor people, and which hath raw materials and manufactured goods of upwards of 6,000 tons yearly passing.' If this did not convince Newcastle, Wedgwood plainly told them that if they objected 'then a few of the Pottery owners would privately subscribe to repair this road, without an Act of Parliament and then travellers will have a stronger inducement to come our way if the tolls were equal. . . . Your conduct in opposing would be unneighbourly and ungenerous, and whether you carry your point or not, it cannot be to your advantage.'

Having met the Newcastle-under-Lyne opponents face to face, Wedgwood pulled all possible strings to get the Turnpike Act through Parliament, as shown by his plea to Lord Gower in a letter also recorded in his commonplace book.

May it please your Lordship.

We, the Freeholders, Tradesmen and Principal inhabitants of Burslem and the parts adjacent, humbly pray your Lordship's favour and patronage in petitioning Parliament to obtain an Act to widen and repair 4 miles of a road from Red Bull, Lawton to Burslem. . . the manufacturers of earthenware in these parts are greatly obstructed, as they are obliged to pay exorbitant prices for carriage on this road, both to and from Liverpool, for clay, flints etc., and of the goods when manufactured, besides for salt, coals etc. . . . . The hamlets cannot keep the road in repair and the manufacturers have to do it and labour is so dear. It adds to the cost of production and he feared they would undersold be in the markets to the great prejudice, if not entire ruin, to the manufactory.

Wedgwood also took advantage of the efforts of the Trustees of the Uttoxeter Turnpike Act of 1758 to insert an amendment to the original Act, by including in it the portion of road from Cliff Bank to Snape's Marsh in Shelton, a portion of the route strongly objected to by Newcastle. Having beaten the Newcastle opponents over this new Act, he set about completing his victory by getting another Act passed continuing the road from Shelton to Cobridge and on to Burslem. He had to be busy canvassing for support for his petition, for opposition from Newcastle against this extension could only be overcome by raising a substantial subscription list. In a letter, dated 1 February 1765, Wedgwood wrote to his brother John:

We have another Turnpike broke out here betwixt Leek and Newcastle. They have mounted me upon my hobbyhorse again and a prancing rogue he is at present. I am just returned from Leek, and I am much satisfied with our reception there. Tomorrow, I wait on Sir Nigel [Gresley] and on Monday at your friend Isaac Whieldon's. We pray to have the Burslem-Uttoxeter Turnpikes joined and the road made Turnpike from Buxton and Bakewell to Leek and from Leek to Buxton. £2,000 is waiting for the road. Uncles Thos, and John have – I am quite serious – I know you will not believe me, – subscribed £500. I have done the like, intending 2 or £300 of it for you.

This particular Act was passed in 1765, and included several pottery manufacturers as Trustees. Specially reduced tolls were allowed potters:

All waggons and carts going for and returning loaden with coals for the particular use and consumption of the potteries in Burslem, Cobridge, Shelton and Hanley Green, and the Potworks, shall pay at the Cobridge Toll-gate:

	s.	*d.*
Waggon 8d usual Toll	1.	0d.
Cart 4d „ „		6d.

Horse and cattle loaden upon their backs with coal exempt.

After 1765, the pottery owners, led by Josiah Wedgwood, continually pressed for extensions to existing Turnpike Acts, or for new ones to build up a compact and comprehensive network of turnpike roads through and around the Potteries and its Six Towns. There were nine such Acts passed in 1766. The next campaign led by Wedgwood was to press for various Acts linking these local roads with the main London highways. This he achieved by extension of the 1714 London Tittensor-Talke road, by additions to previous Acts of 1756, 1777 and 1783. After Wedgwood's day the Act was further extended in 1804 and 1833 to cope with increased road traffic.

The Turnpike Road Book 1791–1893 is among the Hanley Museum MSS. This record is interesting, because the Turnpike Road Act in 1791 shows canal promoters as Trustees, as well as the usual landowners, pottery owners, colliery proprietors, clerks in Holy Orders, bankers, lawyers, doctors and others — possessed of land or receivers of rents of yearly value of £50, or heirs-apparent of a person possessed of lands etc., to the clear value of £200 yearly. This showed that only propertied persons could be Turnpike Trustees. In the 1779 Act, there were 130 Trustees, and of these 22 were landowners and 22 pottery owners. The Wedgwoods were represented by Josiah Wedgwood I, Josiah Wedgwood II, John Wedgwood and Thomas Wedgwood. The Spode pottery interests were represented by Josiah Spode I and II, George Steedman, Spode's partner in the flint mill. Thomas Fenton was the Clerk to the Board of Trustees, and he was Spode's son-in-law's father. Other potting families were the Adams, Brindley, Caldwell, Hollins, Warburton and Whieldons. Last, but not least, were the potters who were interested with Spode and Partners in the Fenton Park Colliery.

The first recorded Committee Meeting of Trustees on 13 July 1791 shows six potters out of 11, among them Josiah Wedgwood, Thos. Whieldon, Harrison, Josiah Spode and his partner, flint merchant Steedman, and Ephraim Booth. Josiah Spode Senior was the most regular attender at the Trustee Meetings, because his factory was the largest pottery in the 1½ miles of the turnpike road, from its junction with the Black Lion Inn.

The Trustees on the Committee often went to sites to value land required for the turnpike road. Then they decided to whom the contract for road widening and construction should be given, and considered estimates or tenders for the job. When these were unsatisfactory, they often undertook to do the contract themselves:

'At this meeting [held 10 August 1791] Messrs. Sherratt, Orme and Hammersley, offered proposals for making the new road at certain prices per rood, which not being agreed to by the Trustees present – Messrs. Lovatt,

Steedman, Booth, Smith and Spode are hereby empowered and desired immediately to take under the direction, forming and making that part of the new road.'

Steedman and Booth, like Spode, were pottery owners. The minute book records purchases of land from potters to make the new roads, e.g. 'To E. Booth for 6026 yards of land at Stoke at £70 per acre and to the Trustees of Ann Warburton the sum of £52. 10s. for land at the rate of £70 per acre.' Potters sold 'shords' from their potbank heaps, of broken and spoilt wares, e.g. 'To Jas. Warner for carriage of shords and gravel £5.3.6d.' The coal masters of Fenton Park Colliery, in which Spode was interested, sold posts and rails for the Turnpike for £38.0.2d, and 'bricks for the use of the road £3.1.6d.'

One entry in the minute book shows potters and their relatives contributing capital to defray the costs of turnpike roads: 'Ordered that the Clerk prepare a short statement of the Securities to the several persons following, who have subscribed sums for defraying expenses for making the new road, with interest at 5%'. Then follows, in a separate column, a total of £1,700 in capital subscribed – £300 from Josiah Wedgwood and then seven sums of £200 each from Whieldon, Lovatt, Steedman, Harrison, Spode, Wolfe and Booth, all potters excepting Lovatt, a son-in-law of Booth.

By 19 December 1793 the Trustees were short of money to complete the turnpike repairs. 'Ordered that the moneylenders in this road be acquainted that there is a considerable debt due from the Trustees, which is not in their power to pay without having money on the credit of the road.' This financial SOS brought in extra capital, as shown by the minute for 21 January 1794: 'Mr. Steedman and Mr. Spode offered at this meeting to advance £150 each, and ordered two several securities be prepared against the next meeting.'

This particular stretch seems to have been a safe investment, judging from bids for farming out of tolls collected. On 7 September 1791, item recorded 'Knappers Gate tolls £558'. Because there was no bidder for Dimsdale Gate Tolls, it was 'Ordered that W. Whittaker be collector at a salary of 10/- a week'. On 5 October 1791, 'Ordered that the tolls from the Dimsdale Gate be let to W. Whittaker, the present collector for one year at a rent of £295'. The record of progressively increasing bids for toll gate receipts probably reflects the increasing traffic along the routes. The bid for Dimsdale Gate of £295 was raised to £296 in 1795, £340 in 1797, while the bid for Knappers Gate was £558 in 1791, increased to £565 in 1792, £625 in 1795, £700 in 1799 and £731 in 1800. The balance sheet for this Toll gate shows a progressive profit. The Balance in hand in 1795 of £135. 6s. 0d. rose to £356 in 1797.

The main items of income were the collected tolls imposed as below:

For every horse, mare, gelding, drawing coach, chariot, Landau, Berlin, Phaeton, Curricle, Hearse, Calash, chaise or suchlike carriages, except Post Chaise drawn only by 2 horses, mares or gelding, the sum of 3d. For every Post-chaise drawn by 2 horses etc. . . . 8d. For every horse or other beast drawing any waggon, wain, cart or other such like carriage, having the soles of the fellies of the wheels of the breadth or gauge of six inches or upwards, the sum of 3d. For every horse etc. – soles of fellies less than six inches, the sum of 4½d.

For every horse etc., laden or unladen and not drawing. . the sum of 1d. For every drove of calves, swine, sheep, lambs, 5d. per score. [There were the usual exemptions from tolls. . . . : horses etc., drawing carts with manure, lime, or horses for funerals, military, post, mail coaches etc.]

A careful perusal of the minute book of the Potters' Chamber of Commerce[1] reveals that they were very much alive to the need for a national improvement of roads, especially with reference to the national post system. Their chairman, Wedgwood, could always be relied on to bring to the notice of his fellow potters issues of national importance. This he did on a question of vital importance to an expanding pottery industry, with its markets spreading to all points in the country and even crossing the national boundaries, to the European and American continents. This pottery market relied on the quick despatch and punctuality in the sending and receiving of letters containing orders for their wares. At a meeting held at Swan Inn, Hanley, on 17 June 1786, the potters recorded: 'The irregularity and delay attending the cross-posts, since the establishment of the mail coaches, having been stated by the chairman, a resolution was carried to memorialize the Post Master General.' They passed the following resolution: 'Ordered that a memorial be prepared and presented to the P.M. General setting forth the inconveniences occasioned thereby to the manufactory, and praying that such relief may be provided against this evil in future.'

The minute book for 6 November 1786 records that Wedgwood had been in correspondence with two Commercial Societies in Wolverhampton and Edinburgh as well as with the General Chamber of Commerce.

The reply from T. Gibbons, Secretary of the Wolverhampton Commercial Society states that he had received a reply from Mr. Palmer, that as a result of their memorial to the P.M. General 'an immediate alteration shall take place in their western letters, through Salop instead of Birmingham . . . and that shortly there will be a Mail Coach every day to and from the North and West'. The potters wisely took the cue from Mr. Gibbons and Wedgwood offered to meet Mr. Palmer, when next in London.

Wedgwood alerted his fellow potters to the danger of the Government's

[1] See Chapter 14

proposed tax on transport. He wrote a letter to Sir John Wrottersley in 1782, noted in his commonplace book. Fearing a revival of the Government's suggestion to lay a tax upon the carriage of goods, he thought Sir John would like his views on the subject. Wedgwood ends his letter:

The tax would fall heaviest upon those in which we find the greatest difficulty to preserve our footing in foreign markets. The Potters in Staffordshire are a trifling object when compared with our works in iron and other metals, but in proportion to their extent and value, they suffer so much perhaps as any of them, for the whole of our raw materials is carried some 100 miles, so that carriage alone constitutes in some of them $\frac{3}{4}$ or in others $\frac{5}{8}$ of the value. In the carriage of the cheaper kinds of goods to market, it amounts often to more than the original price of the goods.

It is easy to understand why potters owners packed Turnpike Trust committees, when transport played such a big part in the disposal of their production, and carriage was such a big item in the cost of production.

CHAPTER 8

Canals

It was to be expected that the potters of Staffordshire would be swift to draw conclusions from the success of the country's first canal opened a little way to the north, in Lancashire.

There were certainly enough connections to ensure that the message was passed on.

James Brindley, appointed Canal Engineer by the Duke of Bridgewater for the first navigation scheme connecting Worsley Hall with Manchester (later extended via Runcorn in Cheshire to the port of Liverpool) was well-known to the potters before he started on the Bridgewater project in 1759. He lived in Leek, where he established a reputation as a millwright, and before he turned his attention to canals he had been employed in the potteries to erect and repair windmills and water-wheels (see Chapter 2).

But there were other connections. Earl Gower, who probably wanted to emulate his brother-in-law, the Duke of Bridgewater, engaged Brindley in 1758 to survey land between Longbridge in Staffordshire and King's Mills in Derbyshire (where Brindley was born). But as Samuel Smiles in his life of the famous engineer says: 'Brindley was hard at work on the Duke's canal and the Staffordshire promoters were disposed to wait the issue of the experiment.'

While waiting, they presumably discussed. Wedgwood often met Earl Gower at the Turnpike Road meetings described in the last chapter, and would know of Brindley's canal survey for Staffordshire.

By 1765, Wedgwood was busy soliciting support for a canal scheme for the Potteries. Brindley's memorandum book records that 'On 23 December 1765, Wedgwood of Burslem sent for me and we dined with Lord Grey. Mr. Wedgwood came to seliset Lord Grey in faver of the Staffordshire canal, and on Fryday set out to wait on Mr. Egerton to seliset him'.

Other people were 'seliseting' support for canal schemes in Staffordshire, including T. Gilbert M.P., brother of the agent of the Duke of Bridgwater. He put out a printed circular whose contents, not to speak of the very act of publishing it, annoyed Wedgwood, who referred to it in a letter to Bentley on 2 January 1765: 'His printing and circulating such a paper without once consulting the persons who had hitherto lent their heads, hands and purses too in planning and forwarding out scheme of Navigation was as indelicate as the insinuations were gross and ill-founded.'

But Wedgwood's party had their way, as this letter later reveals.

It tells of a Wolseley Bridge meeting of canal supporters. 'There were rival canal schemes before the meeting, but Brindley's scheme ultimately won.' It was the one strongly supported by the Duke of Bridgewater, Earl Gower, Bentley and Wedgwood. Jewitt in his account of this historic meeting states: 'Wedgwood took so prominent a part in the discussion, that the Chairman, Earl Gower, asked him, what was he prepared to embark in it? Wedgwood replied that he would at once subscribe a £1,000 towards the preliminary expense and take, I know not how many shares besides.'

Wedgwood lost no time in persuading his partner Bentley to write a pamphlet to describe the proposed Staffordshire Canal and urge support for it. Wedgwood wound up his letter of 2 January 1765: 'You want a good plan for raising the money. That I hope, is now fixed, and I am in no fear of the subscription being filled, and as to a general letter on the advantage of the Inland Navigation, I have no time to think or write. . . . I Scarcely know, without a good deal of recollection, whether I am a Landed Gentleman, an Engineer or a Potter, for I am indeed all three.' So Bentley agreed to draft the suggested letter in the form of a convincing pamphlet, which Dr. Darwin and Wedgwood corrected and finally improved. Dr. Erasmus Darwin was interested in the Staffordshire canal scheme, because it would benefit his Midlands manufacturing friends Matthew Boulton, James Watt and others, who later became very enthusiastic canal promoters for their own advantage in the development of the Staffordshire Canal, which became known as the Trent and Mersey Canal.

Wedgwood, from the early date 2 January 1765 until 3 June 1766, when the General Assembly of Commissioners and Proprietors of the Navigation from the Trent to the Mersey met, was engaged in writing letters to his relatives and friends, to interest them in the canal project. He also dined with prominent and aristocratic friends, such as Earl Gower, the Duke of Bridgewater and Sir W. Bagot, or with his Birmingham circle of friends Darwin, Garbett, Boulton and Watt, and attended deputations to wait on Corporations, boroughs, towns and Chambers of Commerce, to enlist their support and subscriptions towards the canal scheme. Where Wedgwood himself could not go, he sent well-versed canal missionaries, armed with a copy of one of the Bentley pamphlets on the Inland Navigation. It is not surprising that Wedgwood ended one of his letters to Bentley: 'I wish this bustle [over the canal] was over, and I was quietly settled a Potter only again.'

At the first meeting of the General Assembly of Commissioners and Proprietors of the Canal on 3 June 1766, Wedgwood was the obvious choice as treasurer of the project. He had been most active, along with Thomas Whieldon, in securing a large subscription list from local landlords and pottery manufacturers. The potters outnumbered all others in the subscription list raised to defray the cost of obtaining the Act of Parliament, which received the Royal Assent on 14 May 1766. Wedgwood, writing to his brother John, jocularly remarked that he was appointed treasurer 'at a salary of £0,000 per annum, and had to find a security for £10,000'.

Wedgwood's campaign and propaganda for the Trent and Mersey Canal ensured a certain and successful passage of the Bill through Parliament. The House of Commons Journal 1766 records that the petition for the Bill, when presented, was signed by 'Gentlemen, Landowners, Tradesmen, Manufacturers and others of the Counties of Lancaster, Chester, Stafford, Warwick, Derby, Leicester, Nottingham, Lincoln and York, as well as the town of Kingston-upon-Hull'. Wedgwood knew the value of enlisting the support and patronage of the landed gentry, as he told Bentley: 'To secure the patronage of Lord Gower was the only measure that could give us any of that importance with the land-owners and Country Gentlemen which was necessary, for carrying the great design into Parliament this Session.' At the Committee of the House of Commons, Wedgwood himself, supported strongly by Bentley, was well equipped to put forward arguments on behalf of industry and commerce, while Brindley completed the trio, to answer any technical engineering questions raised. Wedgwood discloses, in one of his manuscripts, that it cost £925. 0s. 1d. to secure the Act.

The Act itself, a ponderous document of 106 pages, and 103 clauses, names two Governing Bodies: the Company of Proprietors of the Navigation from the Trent to the Mersey; and the Commissioners of the Navigation. The Proprietors consisted of 101 persons headed by Earl Gower and the Duke of Bridgewater, and including 10 pottery owners or their relatives representing them — J. Whieldon, John Brindley, G. Challoner, John Wedgwood of Smallwood, John Wedgwood of Burslem, H. Palmer, John Mare, E. Leigh, J. Falconer, W. Willett (brother-in-law of Wedgwood), and T. Storer, a partner of Bentley and Wedgwood in London. There was also a list of 12 women members as proprietors. Other significant names among the 101 were Matthew Boulton

16 The churchyard house and works at Burslem

17 A kick-wheel

18 A hand-turned wheel

and Samuel Garbett, both of Birmingham, and staunch friends of Wedgwood, whom he roped in to secure an extension of the Canal from the Black Country end.

Each proprietor might contribute a minimum of a £200 share or 20 such shares. Thus the 101 Proprietors might raise the capital sum of £130,000 by 650 shares of £200. If this were not sufficient then £70,000 capital might be raised from outside subscribers, who could become Proprietors, if they purchased shares to the value of £200. The proprietors met on 3 June 1766 at the Roe Buck in Newcastle-under-Lyme, also the headquarters of the Turnpike Road Trustees, referred to in the previous chapter.

There were 816 Commissioners named in the Act. Their function was 'to settle, determine and adjust all questions, matters and differences, which may arise between the Proprietors and any persons interested in any lands or waters, that shall be affected by the powers hereby granted and to settle recompense'. Seven of the Commissioners could form a quorum and settle issues after examining witnesses. Failing a settlement, a jury could be empanelled. Among these 816 Commissioners were 22 pottery manufacturers and their relatives. Sir Rowland Hill of Penny Postage fame was also a Commissioner. The name of one well-known pottery owner is missing from this formidable list, however, — that of Josiah Spode, who figured so prominently on the Board of Turnpike Trustees.

Important though both the Assembly of Proprietors and the Commissioners were, the real management of the affairs of the Canal was in the hands of the Executive Committee: James Brindley, Surveyor-General; Hugh Henshall, Clerk to the Canal Works; J. Sparrow, Clerk to the Proprietors; Josiah Wedgwood, Hon. Treasurer; T. Nailor, R. Parrott and T. Bateman, Clerks to the Commissioners of Cheshire, Staffs. and Derbys. respectively.

In the appointment of Wedgwood as Treasurer, the pottery industry secured the man-in-charge of the purse strings. In appointing Henshall as Clerk of the Works, they secured not only the services of the brother-in-law of Brindley, but also a member closely linked with the pottery of Spode, who was related to the Henshalls by marriage. On the executive committee (excluding the above officers) were 10 representing pottery manufacturers, eight representatives of Landowners, two representing Birmingham manufacturers — two close friends of Wedgwood, Boulton and Garbett — and one canal expert, R. Whitworth. So we can see that in actual practice, the pottery owners could always secure a majority on the executive committee.

The Canal Executive Committee at their very first meeting showed their

RSP G

deep appreciation of the signal services rendered by Wedgwood and his partner Bentley – the two most ardent public relations officers, who carried out the successful publicity and behind-the-scenes correspondence, negotiations and lobby pressure to secure the successful passing of the Canal Act. They voted Josiah Wedgwood 150 guineas, and £90 to Bentley, besides what Wedgwood calls 'the balance in your hands for extensive services'.

Bentley's standing as a Liverpool merchant, even before he linked up with Wedgwood as a partner in Etruria, was such that the City of Liverpool and the corporate body of merchants subscribed to the funds to secure the passage of the Act in Parliament. In return, Wedgwood arranged with Bentley to send any goods from Etruria via Liverpool on the Canal, rather than via Hull. Then again, Wedgwood showed his appreciation of the co-operation of Liverpool City and its merchants by taking them into his confidence about the proposals made by Chester City and its merchants to construct a canal to connect with the Trent and Mersey. He invited a Mr. Tarleton to attend a meeting of the Canal Committee to put Liverpool's point of view on the proposed Chester–Mersey Canal.

James Brindley had planned to complete the canal construction, begun in 1766, by 1773. But there were engineering difficulties in the construction of the Harecastle Tunnel, and Brindley's illness that led to his death in 1772, and the canal was not completed till 1777 under the supervision of his brother-in-law, Hugh Henshall. He was promoted from being Clerk of the Works to Brindley's successor, with the title of Surveyor-General or Canal Engineer. Writing to Bentley on 2 March 1767, barely a year after cutting the first sod for the Canal, Wedgwood wrote: 'I think Mr. Brindley *The Great* – the fortunate money-getting Brindley, an object of pity, and a real sufferer for the Public Good. He may get a few thousands but what does he give in exchange? – His health and I fear, his life too!' How right Wedgwood was – Brindley died five years before the Trent and Mersey Canal was completed.

Wedgwood got on very well with the aristocratic landowning proprietors of the Canal Assembly. In one of his letters to Bentley, he states: 'We were honoured at our General Assembly of the Navigation with the company of the Duke of Bridgewater and Lord Gower, who approved much of our proceedings. Lord Gower told us pleasantly, he thought we should be styled '*The Amicable Society of Navigators*'. At this meeting, the Duke invited Wedgwood to view the Bridgewater Canal and its terminus at Runcorn, with its famous locks constructed by Brindley. Describing this visit Wedgwood later wrote Bentley: 'I do not wonder that the Duke is so enamoured of his handiworks. He very courteously invited me to dine with him, which I readily accepted, and after dinner, he condescended to show me all his canal works, so we had a long tête-à-tête upon navigation and other matters. His Grace has promised to come to see me at Etruria, a place he has never seen yet.'

Later, on 11 September 1774, Wedgwood journeyed along with his fellow committee members of the Canal to see the Duke's canal to its Runcorn terminus. They travelled via the Harecastle Tunnel to Sandbach, Middlewich and on to Preston-on-the-Hill. From there, they travelled in the Duke's boats to Worsley Hall and Manchester via Warrington. Wedgwood was no armchair treasurer. He was up and down the canal route, almost as much as Brindley, until it was completed. Probably, he was too active a proprietor to suit certain others. His first real conflict with some of the canal proprietors occurred during the construction of the canal through Wedgwood's estate at Etruria. Wedgwood wrote Bentley about the incident:

Mr. Henshall and I have spent yesterday and today at Etruria, setting out the Canal through the district, and on Monday next, I shall begin to make it. The canal will run in a straight line through the district, at least so it is set out. I could not prevail upon the inflexible vandal to give me one line of grace. He must go the nearest and best way or Mr. Brindley will go mad.

A second letter on this subject to Bentley continues:

I shall not go to London, as soon as I expected, though it is a very disagreeable business which will keep me so long at home. Some of my good neighbours have taken it into their heads to think that I shall have too pleasant and valuable a situation by the side of the Canal, as it is planned and executed through my estate. This has raised a little envy in their breasts, and as they are Proprietors, they have represented to the Committee that the Canal ought to be made along the meadows, as that is the shortest and most natural course. This cloud had been gathering for some time and no pains are spared by the party who have blown it up to make it alight as heavy upon me as possible.

Wedgwood continues:

But notwithstanding all this bustle, I am in no fear for the event, I know my cause is good and feel myself a match for them all. I am preparing a little ammunition for the battle, and I know you will come in time to assist me, to give it full force. Mr. Brindley's brother is at the head of this affair, but that circumstance does not alarm me at all, as I know *Brindley the Great* to be an honest man.

Wedgwood triumphed and the canal through Etruria remained as planned, thanks to Brindley's support and friends of Wedgwood among the Proprietors.

Later in 1773, a 'junta of our Proprietors', as Wedgwood described them, in a letter to Bentley, made a more serious imputation against Wedgwood, over a transaction that he, as Treasurer, carried out on behalf of the Navigation Committee. He was authorized to bid up to £1,000 more than the highest bid made for a plot of land opposite Etruria Pottery by the Burton Company. Wedgwood reported to Bentley that this 'junta' had accused him of receiving money for nothing. 'They represented the transaction as a fraud upon the Company by myself, the Deputy Treasurer and many of our Proprietors'. Wedgwood felt this accusation very seriously, and took the whole matter to the committee, over which Lord Gower presided, and there the matter was settled once and for all, as reported by Wedgwood in his later letter to Bentley: 'I called upon my dear friend to rejoice with me upon another overthrow of my enemies in the line of the Navigation. The Chairman summed up the evidence by which it appeared to the entire satisfaction of all present, and the transaction was a fair one, and it was unanimously satisfied and confirmed, not to be disturbed again. Mr. Gilbert observed, that he and the Proprietors had ever placed unlimited confidence in me.' Wedgwood summed up this personal attack on him in a later letter to Bentley, as the action of 'Malevolent Persons, who envied my situation upon the Canal, and I believe, my situation in life too'. The attack, to say the least, was a most ungrateful gesture to one who had put so much of his personal energy and enthusiasm into the transport project, as well as sinking a good deal of his personal wealth to secure the success of the canal. The incident probably only urged Wedgwood to further efforts to perfect the transport facilities of the Potteries, and indeed, of the whole country, by linking the Trent and Mersey Canal with a huge network of Canals in the Midlands, with Bristol, Hull, Liverpool and London.

Though the Trent and Mersey Canal formed the main artery of what later developed as the Grand Trunk Canal, there were quite a large number of smaller canals that later acted as feeders to the Grand Trunk system. There were seven of these small stretches of canals in the Potteries, which were later incorporated in the Grand Trunk scheme:

(1) Newcastle Canal from Stoke to Newcastle (1759).
(2) Caldon Canal from Shelton to Leek and Froghall (1773).
(3) Froghall Canal from Froghall to Uttoxeter (1797).
(4) Longport-Burslem Branch of the Grand Trunk (1797).
(5) Shelton-Cobridge Branch of the Grand Trunk (1797).
(6) Stoke to Lane End Canal (1797).
(7) Newcastle Junction Canal (1798).

(1) *Newcastle–Stoke Canal.* This was one of the earliest 'cuts' in the Potteries. It was very little used, except by Spode, Minton and Wolfe, whose pottery

works were adjacent to its Stoke terminal. As a dividend earner, it was a disastrous failure.

(2) *Caldon Canal.* This canal was an extension of the Grand Trunk Canal from Shelton to Hanley, Milton, Norton, Endon and on to Leek and Froghall. It was constructed to transport lime and coal from these outlying areas to the Potteries. It was in the construction of this canal that Wedgwood suggested they should tunnel through the Colliery at Whitfield and work the coal seams. The Duke of Bridgewater did this at his Worsley Collieries by means of his Bridgewater Canal, which entered the pit and transported the coal in barges, direct from the coal-seams and headings. But Wedgwood's idea was not put into operation. At Froghall there was a rail-road connecting the Canal terminus with the Caldon Quarry and Lime Works, a distance of three miles one furlong seven chains.

(3) *The Froghall–Uttoxeter Canal* is really an extension of the Caldon–Froghall Canal. It never paid much dividend to its shareholders.

(4) *The Longport–Burslem,*

(5) *The Shelton–Cobridge and*

(6) *The Stoke–Lane End Canals* – all three were live branches of the Grand Trunk Canal system, serving a busy pottery and colliery area. This Stoke to Lane End Canal was really constructed to replace a tram-road or rail-way that had been laid in the latter decades of the eighteenth century, linking the collieries of Lane End with Stoke.

(7) *The Newcastle Junction Canal.* This canal was constructed in 1798 to join up with an earlier 'cut' of Sir Nigel Gresley's collieries, and the ironworks of Sir John Heathcote and Thomas Kinnersley, M.P. This early cut was started after the Act of 1775 to connect Apedale Collieries with Newcastle. It did not flourish and soon became disused.

Though the pottery owners did not use this canal themselves, they benefited for a time, but only by using it to secure supplies of coal from the Newcastle coalfield. The enthusiasm of the pottery owners in providing the Potteries with a network of local canals was soon transferred to linking the Grand Trunk Canal to other Inland Navigations outside Staffordshire.

So far I have dealt only with the Trent and Mersey Canal, and the later group of seven local canals, that made up what came to be known as the Grand Trunk Canal, so compactly contained in the Potteries with outlets through the Trent River Navigation to Hull on the East coast, and through the Mersey to Liverpool. But the potters were most anxious to secure quick and as direct a transport facility to London for their wares in the capital, as well as to export them to the Continent. Hence, their interest in getting an Act to consolidate the Grank Trunk Canal with seven other important canals, which when amalgamated with the Grand Trunk Canal could provide the missing links with London. These canals were:

(1) The Staffordshire and Worcester Canal (1766).
(2) The Coventry Canal (1768).
(3) The Oxford Canal (1769).
(4) The Fazeley Canal (1771).
(5) The Birmingham Canal (1783).
(6) The Birmingham and Worcester Canal (1791).
(7) The Grand Junction Canal to London (1793).

(1) *The Staffordshire–Worcester Canal*, surveyed by Brindley and originally called the Wolverhampton Canal, was later merged into a larger venture and called the Staffordshire–Worcester Canal connecting with Stourport on the Severn. It was finished five years before the completion of the Staffordshire Grand Trunk. By means of this canal the Potteries were able to reach Bristol, their third port for exports after Liverpool and Hull.

(2) *The Coventry Canal.* This was the most immediate link in the chain of canals to enable the pottery manufacturers to get their wares to London, and cut out the heavy carriage cost by road. This point is well brought out by Wedgwood in a letter to Mr. Lloyd of Coventry in 1769, only a year after its official opening:

I am obliged to you and beg leave to thank you in the name of my neighbours, for your kind attention to our interest, respecting the junction of the Oxfordshire and Coventry Canals. As common travellers and freighters to the Metropolis, we look upon your Canal, the Oxford Canal and any other which may join with that, and point towards the Metropolis, as so many extensions of the Grand Trunk, as Mr. Brindley emphatically calls 'this navigation, which runs through the heart of the Kingdom'. We therefore wish to have this great and public road made as straight, easy and commodious as may be, and in this idea, I flatter myself, we shall have your concurrence and every other public spirited encourager of Inland Navigation.

(3) *The Oxford Canal.* This was the next link after Coventry Canal, to reach the Thames. Writing Bentley from London, where Wedgwood was resting while his wooden leg[1] was being repaired, he wrote: 'I should have attended a

---

[1] Wedgwood's leg had been hurt by a fall and amputated on the advice of a Liverpool doctor to whom he was introduced by Bentley.

meeting at Marlborough House concerning the Oxford Canal. There were present Dukes of Bridgewater, Marlborough, Bedford, Lord Gower, Hartford and several others, to get a petition in favour of the Oxford Canal from our Proprietors and another from the Potters, both of which I proposed at our last Committee, but the motion was over-ruled.' This letter indicates that even amongst the proprietors of the Trent and Mersey Canal and among Wedgwood's fellow potters, there was not a majority for the extension of the canals to London, as well as Hull, Bristol and Liverpool. Perhaps the majority of the Trent and Mersey proprietors were afraid that bringing more canals to join the Trent and Mersey Canal, might affect the high dividends earned by their Potteries Canal. Wedgwood's fellow potters probably felt that as Hull, Bristol and Liverpool sufficed for their export trade, they did not need the metropolis as a market on the scale required by Wedgwood's wares. Wedgwood, as ever a pioneer, pushed ahead with his extension and consolidation of canals most enthusiastically as shown by his letter in October 1772 to Sir Roger Newdigate. 'We have got our Canal completed from the Trent to the Pottery, and shall be very anxious to have the Coventry and Oxford Canals finished so that land carriage may be totally abolished betwixt us and London.'

(4) *The Fazeby Canal,*
(5) *The Birmingham Canal* and
(6) *The Birmingham–Worcester Canal.*

These three may be described as the hub of the Midland Canals. Canals (4) and (5) were soon consolidated in 1784, a year after the opening of the Birmingham Canal No. 4. This was facilitated by the fact that the proprietors of both canals were almost identical subscribers. The leading proprietors of both these canals were Wedgwood's close friends, Messrs. Boulton and Garbett – both of whom were original proprietors of the Trent and Mersey Canal. But Matthew Boulton was to be transformed from a canal enthusiast to a violent anti-inland navigationist, to the bitter disappointment of Wedgwood, his close friend and business associate.

Birmingham was not as fortunate as the Potteries, with their almost boundless supplies of water from innumerable, unnavigable streams to feed its water-driven mills, and even to replenish the Grand Trunk Canal with water supply. Further, most of the surface-water Birmingham could collect from its meagre supply of streams seeped down into the pit-shafts of collieries and earth fissures. At this stage Matthew Boulton and Watt, at their metal works and foundries at Soho, relied entirely on water-power to drive their mills and rollers. Boulton, who had spent £20,000 at his Soho works in buildings, machinery and equipments, driven by water-power, could not afford to lose one drop from his mill-pool. So in 1771, when proposals were put into operation to drain off water that naturally fed his mill-pool, so as to feed the proposed Birmingham Canals, he reacted strongly. His feeling and action against these canals is revealed in the following extracts from letters sent to two of his closest friends, T. Gilbert, M.P., and Samuel Garbett. The letter to Gilbert read:

Let Smeaton or Brindley or all the engineers upon earth give what evidence they will before Parliament, I am convinced from last summer's experience, that if the Proprietors of the Birmingham Canal continue to take the two streams on which my mill depends, it is ruined. Think of my summer situation, my workpeople standing still. What a reward this is for my labour and hazards, to deprive me of my very existence, to gratify the whim of a single man As an M.P., as an old acquaintance, as a friend to your country, as a good man, I beg you will save from destruction your friend – Matthew Boulton.

Boulton followed this letter of 2 February with another pleading letter to his friend Garbett on 12 February 1771. 'I value the opinion of neither Smeaton or Yeoman, nor Brindley, nor Simcox in this case, nor of the whole tribe of jobbing ditchers.' He then poured his contempt for the passing of the Canal Act in Parliament as 'the deception of a wretched managed cause by a House consisting of landowners, in favour of a landowner. I dare say you will judge precisely as I do and you have too, often reflected on the Government of England not to perceive some Parliaments have exceedingly reserved conspiracies of landowners formed for the oppression of the rest of the community.'

This forthright opinion anticipates the conclusion of the pottery manufacturers, after the Reform Act, when they elected potters to replace the landowning class as their Parliamentary representatives.

Poor Matthew Boulton, had he been as skilful a diplomat and collaborator with members of the aristocracy and landowners as his friend Wedgwood, who knew how to cajole and coax them to support his canal schemes, he could have prevented the diversion of the streams feeding his Soho mill-pool. Because of this unpleasantness over the Birmingham Canal in 1771, Boulton withdrew his interest in the Trent and Mersey Canal, much to Wedgwood's personal chagrin.

The Grand Junction Canal to London was the last link to complete the Grand Trunk junction of the Potteries with the capital. The Oxford Canal, though linking the Potteries via the Coventry Canal to the Thames, was inadequate for taking traffic from the North and from the Midlands to London. Hence the proposals to have a better navigation, such as the Grand Junction Canal, by a new route from the Oxford–Coventry Canal at Braunston and through Uxbridge, Leighton Buzzard on to London. As W. T. Jackmann states in his *Transportation in Modern England*, this last canal in the chain of canals was 'the most successful in resisting the paralyzing influence of the railroads'.

The construction of the Trent and Mersey Canal was undoubtedly a great financial undertaking, begun and completed as we have seen with the full exercise of Brindley's ingenuity, and Wedgwood's drive and determination. There was a real spirit of adventure and enterprise about the scheme to provide the Potteries with a canal that eventually became the core or 'Grand Trunk' of the consolidated canal system of England. The proprietors were fully rewarded for their enterprise and speculative investment of £130,000 in nominal Capital.

There are two tests of the financial success of the Canal: the dividend paid annually on capital, and the prices of Canal shares when sold in the open market.

(1) DIVIDEND YIELD OF THE GRAND TRUNK CANAL

Year	*Dividend %*
1766–1777	5 each year
1813	50
1821	75
1824	75 plus bonus
1825	75
1829	37½
1838	130
1846	30

(2) TABLE OF SHARE PRICES OF GRAND TRUNK CANAL

Year	£ *Prices quoted*
1766	200 at par
1792	200 to 700
1821	1,750
1824	4,600
1834	2,560
1836	2,400

The table below shows the Grand Trunk Canal as the most successful of all canals in England and Wales, both in share price quotations and dividend paid on capital.

(3)   TABLE OF CANAL QUOTATIONS FOR 1824 FROM WETTENHALL'S
COMMERCIAL LIST

Canals	£ Shares	£ Price	Dividend %
Grand Trunk	100	2,300	75 plus bonus
Mersey and Irwell	—	1,000	35
Standwater	150	450	$31\frac{1}{2}$
Neath	100	400	15
Leicester	140	390	14
Barnsley	160	340	12
Warwick & Birmingham	100	320	11
Ashton and Oldham	$97\frac{9}{10}$	310	5
Grand Junction	100	296	10
Glamorganshire	$172\frac{2}{3}$	280	£13. 12s. 8d.
Melton Mowbray	100	255	11
Monmouthshire	100	245	10

CHAPTER 9

Railways

In the third and final stage of the transport revolution in the Potteries, between 1730 and 1850, the potters, who had put their money into Turnpike roads, then canals, now turned their attention to railways. The canal era was to be eclipsed by the railway era.

Yet there was no clear-cut division between the stages. One grew out of the other and the changeover was full of oppositions and confusions. Before the locomotive reached the potteries, rail, or tram roads as they were called locally, with horses to draw goods or passengers, already existed. Indeed by 1750 there was scarcely any important colliery that did not have its own railway for private use. All that was required was agreement with the landowners concerned with the route of the rail or tram-road. The railway or railroad which was eventually to supersede the canal was then seen as an adjunct or offshoot to it.

We find the Trent and Mersey Proprietors seeking an extension of their powers in an Act of 1776, granting permission to construct a rail-way from the Canal to the Froghall quarries, a distance of $3\frac{1}{2}$ miles. Then, in later amendments of the Canal Act, in 1783 and 1785, the line was still referred to as a 'rail-way' (with hyphen). It worked by gravitation with four inclined planes of various lengths and inclinations. It ultimately reached a height of 400 feet above the canal, after passing through the tunnel. Later, the Canal Company erected an iron rail-road to connect with their canal at Stone. In 1802, the proprietors of the canal applied for an Act to allow them to construct three railways extending their traffic from the canal.

Simeon Shaw states: 'From the market-place of Hanley, the Company of the Proprietors of the Navigation from the Trent to the Mersey have a Rail-Road on which, by waggons, they bring up all packages into the town and return with crates and casks of porcelain and pottery. This Rail-Way terminates in Vale Pleasant near Etruria. . . . From Stoke to Lane-End the navigation have a Rail Road on which the waggons regularly convey materials to Fenton, Lane Delph and Lane End.' John Ward, another contemporary, says: 'A Rail-Road for horse draft extends from Longton through the Fentons for the conveyance of the merchandise of these places.[1] Parliament itself came to regard these 'dram-roads' as accessories to canals in an Act of 1799, under which the Trent and Mersey proprietors applied in 1802 for an Act, enabling them to construct the three rail-roads mentioned earlier. Robert Fulton, in his *Treatise on the Improvements of Canal Navigation* of 1796, states: 'Rail-roads have been considered as a medium between lock-canals and cartage in consequence of the expense of extending the Canal to the particular works. Rail-Ways of 1 mile or thereabouts will be frequently necessary where it is difficult to find water.' But already there were signs that the railway was not to remain an extension of the canal system. Thomas Telford in 1800 wrote: 'Experience has convinced us that in countries where the surface is rugged or where it is difficult to obtain water for lockage, in those cases iron rail-ways are in general preferable to a Canal navigation.'[2] Thomas Gray, another contemporary rail-road enthusiast, goes further: 'The time was fast approaching when rail-ways must, from their manifest superiority in every respect, supersede the necessity of both Canals and Turnpike roads.' It is not surprising that the Duke of Bridgwater, in reply to Lord Kenyon's query about his canals and their prospects said, 'We may do well if we can keep clear of those damn tram-roads.'

Great impetus to this stage of the transport revolution was given by the successful application of locomotive power to the railway that Liverpool traders decided to construct from Liverpool to Manchester in 1824. They failed to secure an Act in 1825, but succeeded in 1826 in buying off the Duke of Bridgewater's canal opposition with a gift of 1,000 shares in the Railway Company and the privilege of nominating three of the Railway directors – to the Marquis of Stafford, the new family name of the Lord Gower of Wedgwood's day, who later inherited the Bridgewater estate.

The first railway in Britain, the Liverpool and Manchester, was constructed, opened and operated then, in an area where goods from the Potteries and goods to the pottery manufactories were constantly flowing in transit. So it was natural that the pottery manufacturers in particular would watch its development with deep interest.

Some of the leading proprietors of the Trent and Mersey Canal, like the Marquis of Stafford, having inherited the Bridgewater estate, naturally kept a watchful eye on the progress of the Liverpool and Manchester railway pro-

[1] John Ward, *History of Stoke on Trent*
[2] *A General View of Shropshire*

moters, for fear traffic on the Duke of Bridgewater's Canal from Worsley to Runcorn and Liverpool, should be affected.

At first, the Trustees of the Bridgewater Canal rallied all canal proprietors in England and Wales to oppose not only the Bill for the Manchester and Liverpool Railway, but all railways. This is disclosed in the following letter issued in 1824 by Charles Lawrence, their Chairman:

Sir,

    The Leeds and Liverpool, the Birmingham, the Grand Trunk and other Canal Companies having issued circulars calling upon every Canal and River Navigation Company in the Kingdom to oppose '*in limine*' and by a united effort the establishment wherever contemplated, I have most earnestly to solicit your active exertions on behalf of the Liverpool and Manchester Railroad Co. to counteract the avowed purpose of the Canal Proprietors.

Baines in his *History of the Commerce of Liverpool* writes: 'seldom has any scheme gone before Parliament that excited so much interest. The Canal Proprietors, with an instinctive sense of danger, justly appreciated what they affected to despise and with one accord, and one heart and mind, resolved to crush the rival project.' Baines gives a detailed account of the proceedings before the Committees of the House of Commons, where no fewer than 150 petitions were submitted in opposition to the Bill, which was lost on 1 June 1825. Pratt, in his *History of Inland Transport and Communications in England*, says: 'The combined Canal and landed interests scored the first victory against the Bill. Lords Derby and Sefton were the diehards in the House of Lords against it, with the Marquis of Stafford and his friends.' A second attempt was made in 1826 with a new Bill. Yet with this second attempt Baines writes, 'There appeared but little chance of overcoming the opposition of the combined water carriers', while in his *Guide to Liverpool* Osborne states, 'The most powerful opposition had been found to arise from the Marquis of Stafford, who was the party pecuniarily interested in the Duke of Bridgewater's Canal.'

Baines then discloses how opposition to the 1826 Bill was overcome by detaching from the opposition 'the trustees of the Duke of Bridgewater – an affair of the greatest delicacy'. Baines states that a secret committee from the railway promoters approached Mr. Lock, the agent of the Marquis of Stafford. Baines continues the story that led to the complete somersault of the Marquis of Stafford, in changing his attitude to the Bill. 'Mr. Lock, with the penetration and zeal for the interests of those beneficially interested in the Trust under his management, received the proposition with the frankness and candour which had suggested it. A course so obviously consistent with the interest of his employers, was promptly adopted. He consented, on the part of the Trust, to the terms proposed, to accept a fifth share in the Railway undertaking.' Pratt refers to this transaction in one significant sentence: 'The opposition of the Bridgewater Trustees having been overcome by a judicious presentation to them of a thousand shares in the Railway. . . .'

The winning over of the chief landowner in the Potteries, with large collieries, ironworks, his interest as one of the leading proprietors of the Trunk Canal and of the turnpike road trusts, must sooner or later influence the pottery manufacturers in throwing in their lot with the promoters of railways. One must remember that there were yet considerable doubts in the minds of hard-headed and practical potters as to the success or failure of the railways as a satisfactory mode of transport. This is reflected in a letter to Josiah Wedgwood II from James Watt Junior, dated 30 December 1829. It was obviously written by James Watt after Josiah Wedgwood had sought his reaction to the Rocket triumph of George Stephenson at Rainhill on the Manchester–Liverpool Railway on 9 October 1829.

To Josiah Wedgwood.   Soho, 30 Dec. 1829.
    I send a parcel per coach, with Mr. Walker and Rastrick Report to the Directors of the Liverpool and Manchester Railway on the comparative merits of Locomotive and Fixed Engines. You will observe that it was made before the Prize Contest Exhibition and I know not how far they may consider their conclusions affected by the result of these trials. To me the results have appeared to lead to exaggerated conclusions made no doubt with a view to keeping up or increasing the price of shares in that jobbing speculation. Nor can anything be yet predicted of the wear and tear of the rail-ways and engines, the firmness and the efficiency of the former and the safety and economy of the latter and the regularity of performance.
    My creed remains as it has been for these 30 years past, that where the heavy tonnage is downhill the railways have a decided advantage over Canals, but where the ground is level, the advantage is with Canals, where slow motion – 2 to 3 miles per hour, are sufficient but for greater speeds railways should be preferred. Where the heavy carriage is uphill or the line consists of considerable ups and downs, railways must have stationary as well as locomotive engines, and I conceive that here also the advantage of economy in slow motion will be with Canals. With regard to such goods as from the majority of heavy freights, it is of little importance whether conveyance is at the rate of 3 or 10 miles an hour.

Even the cautious James Watt Junior, ends his letter with a tilt at the up and coming younger generation –

'but the double quick times seem to suit the notions of the rising generation better than those of their seniors.'
                                                              My dear Sir, James Watt.

If the contents of this letter from the son of the inventor of the Steam Engine represents the doubts of some of his contemporaries, among them probably Josiah Wedgwood II, it is not to be wondered that the pottery manufacturers and many of the senior members of the Canal Proprietors suspended judgment and action over railways in the Potteries.

The railways that progressively, from 1830 on, spread outwards from Manchester only encircled the area of the Potteries without penetrating it and thus challenging the transport monopoly enjoyed hitherto by the Grand Trunk Canal. This may have been by design, so as not to injure the navigation in which the Marquis of Stafford was so deeply interested. There were three such, built in the 1820s and 30s.

First, The Grand Junction Railway which obtained its Act in 1833, flanking the Potteries to the South from Birmingham, on to Warrington. This company was a consolidation of two companies that had failed to secure Acts of Parliament between 1824 and 1826, to construct a line from Liverpool and another from Birmingham to make rail connections between the two cities. The Birmingham Co. made a further effort to get their Act in 1830, but this failed. The Grand Junction Railway was primarily a passenger service.

The Grand Junction Railway in 1838 was linked to London by an Act ultimately obtained after great opposition from landed and other vested interest. This extension benefitted Liverpool and Manchester, but did not benefit the Potteries, as the pottery manufacturers still found the Grand Trunk Canal more useful to send their goods to and from the Potteries to Liverpool, Bristol, Hull and London. The Manchester and Stafford Railway entering just above North Staffordshire at Congleton, and the South Union Railway from Manchester via Macclesfield, were two schemes that never got beyond the project stage – the latter having been surveyed by George Stephenson. They would both plan to hem in the Potteries from the North from Manchester, while the first railway, the Grand Junction, would hem the Potteries to the south from Liverpool and Warrington on to Birmingham.

There were sound economic reasons for delay in projecting any distinct railway for the North Staffordshire Potteries. The potters were obviously satisfied with the transport services afforded by their own Grand Trunk Canal. As practical business men, they probably wanted other folk to burn their fingers with promoting experimental railways before they would invest any money in them. Then again from 1834 to 1837, the potters had enough to cope with on their own doorstep with the strikes, without risking their capital on railways which were, at that time, highly speculative ventures. Besides, as onlookers this early railway development must have seemed to them piecemeal, a mass of unrelated, unconnected strips of railways with no system of consolidated rail transport, like the consolidation of canals.

The railway companies themselves realized the chaos and inefficiency of this patchwork of unrelated stretches of railways. Local amalgamations of neighbouring railways were effected, despite opposition from landed and navigation vested interests. There were also technical difficulties, connected with the railway gauge, the rolling stock types of carriages, variations of fares, freight rates and problems of running services according to a timetable. When voluntary agreement could not be arrived at between railway companies, Parliament had to step in and settle the matter by legislation after wordy warfare between experts and engineers.

The decisive step for constructing a railway to serve the Potteries was taken during the period of railway mania, 1844–1846. According to Tuck's *Guide*[1] 1,118 schemes for railways to be constructed were prepared by various railway companies. Of these, seven Companies were registered to construct projected railways to pass through the Potteries. They are listed here in order of their registration:

No.

(1) 151 Central Staffordshire.
(2) 411 Grt. Grimsby, Sheffield, The Potteries and Grand Junction.
(3) 791 N. Staffs or Churnet, Potteries and Trent Junction.
(4) 975 S. Union or Manchester, Potteries and London.
(5) 991 Staffordshire and Shropshire Union.
(6) 992 Staffordshire Potteries.
(7) 993 Staffordshire Potteries and Liverpool, Manchester direct.

Railway companies (5) and (6) failed to secure an Act in Parliament. Of the remaining five Companies, only one survived to proceed with the construction of a railway through and in the Potteries. That company was registered No. 791, the third on the above list. The others failed to secure Acts of Parliament in 1845, but the company registered No. 791 was authorized by three separate Acts in 1846 – (9 & 10 Vic., C. 84, 85 and 86) to construct what later became known as the North Staffordshire Railway. These three Acts enabled the company to construct the main pottery line from Stafford through Stoke-on-Trent towards Macclesfield in Cheshire. At North Rode it formed a branch line along the Churnet River Valley, through Leek to Uttoxeter. Then another branch line from Harecastle on to Sandbach linked up with the London North Western Railway. In its general outline the Railway might just as well have been called The Grand Trunk and Cauldon Canal Railway. These two Canals decided the location and siting of the railway. In the accompanying sketch map, one can detect the lay-out of the railway and the canals. But there is more than geographical affinity between the two forms of transport (Fig. 44).

[1] H. Tuck: *Railway Shareholders' Annual Guide* (1845)

19 Aerial view of the Etruria Pottery

20 A potter at his wheel

21 Dipping and glazing ware

22 A pottery artist decorating ware

23 The original flint-crushing mill at Etruria

24 A bottle-type oven or kiln

25 A turner placing a 'runner bead'

It is very difficult to decide whether the New North Staffordshire Railway Company absorbed the older established Trent and Mersey Navigation Company, or the Trent and Mersey Navigation Company created the New North Staffordshire Railway Company. J. H. Clapham in his *Economic History of Birtain* states: 'The Trent and Mersey [Grand Trunk] Canal was more fortunate, it really made a railway. It had seen its superb dividends so cut into by the competition of the Grand Junction Railway and the Midland Railway, and its shares worth £1,200 in the days of 75% dividends, had fallen to £450. But it retained vitality enough to turn itself by a series of Acts in 1846, into the North Staffs. Railway Co.'

Bradshaw's *Railway Manual* gives the following information: 'The North Staffordshire Railway incorporated by three separate Acts in 1846. . . . The Trent and Mersey Canal was purchased in 1846 (except the Newcastle-under-Lyme Branch) by the North Staffs. Railway Co., for £1,170,000 5% Preference Stock.'

Scrivenor in his *Railways of the United Kingdom*, published in 1849, records that 'This North Staffordshire Railway Co. was incorporated by an Act of Parliament, passed 26 June 1846. Under three Acts this Company has been authorized to raise Capital to the extent of £2,900,000 and to borrow £965,000 and to amalgamate with the Trent and Mersey Co. The Trent and Mersey Navigation has under the Act of 1846 been incorporated with the N.S. Railway Co., from 15 January, 1847 and the Capital of £1,170,000 divided into 58,500 shares of £20 each, have been merged into the Capital of the North Staffordshire Railway Company.'

The official history of the North Staffordshire Railway Co., published by the London, Midland and Scottish Railway Co., in 1925, states 'The North Staffordshire Railway Company were the owners of the Trent and Mersey Canal'.

Clapham records that 'the Chairman of the Trent and Mersey Canal at the time of its metamorphosis, was Ricardo' (i.e. J. L. Ricardo, the M.P. for Stoke from 1841 to 1862). Several of the original proprietors of the Trent and Mersey were made directors of the new railway company, including descendants of the original treasurer of the navigation, Josiah Wedgwood.

Josiah C. Wedgwood in his *Staffordshire Pottery and its History* appears to lay the blame on Parliament for this merger of the Canal Company with the new Railway Company. He states 'with the help of Alderman W. T. Copeland's partner, Thomas Garrett, Lord Ingestre, Richard Cobden and some London financiers, the North Staffordshire Railway was formed. Bills were passed

RSP H

through Parliament in 1846. . . . They were foxed by Parliament to buy out the Canal Company's monopoly at a very high figure of £1,170,000'.

This account of the transaction by J. C. Wedgwood underestimates the influence exerted by J. L. Ricardo. He was the Chairman of the Canal Company, besides being the son of Jacob Ricardo, the famous railway contractor and a director of the Westminster Bank. He was also a personal friend of Richard Cobden M.P. Wedgwood, in his book, does not mention the name of J. L. Ricardo or make any reference to the prominent part he played in the formation of the North Staffordshire Railway. He gives the credit to W. T. Copeland of Spode's Pottery, who was Ricardo's fellow M.P. in the Potteries.

We know from Hayden's book, *Spode and his Successors*, that Alderman Copeland was specially interested in this North Staffordshire Railway, not only as a pottery manufacturer and a Stoke M.P., but 'as an original Director of the old London and Birmingham Company, that was absorbed by the London North Western Railway in 1846, the year that the North Staffordshire Railway was authorized.

A contemporary account of the official opening of the North Staffordshire Railway in the *Illustrated London News* of 3 October 1846 gives Ricardo and Copeland equal honours:

On Wednesday week, the commencement of the works of this important Railway was celebrated by great rejoicings at Stoke-upon-Trent, the day being kept as a general holiday. The spot chosen was Shelton New Road, where a piece of ground was fenced off for the ceremony of turning the first turf. Mr J. L. Ricardo officiated with the spade and Ald. Copeland with the wheelbarrow. Just as Mr Ricardo was putting the turf into the barrow, the crowd broke the ring and Mr. Ricardo lost his hat in the confusion, but after mounting his horse, rode off the ground with the spade over his shoulder. . . . The affair of the day was conducted with much ceremony. There was a public breakfast at the new Town Hall at Stoke, in the evening a ball at which the Duke of Sutherland's quadrille band attended, and the outdoor merrymaking concluded with a brilliant display of fireworks.

Thus the potters made the transition from being promoters of canals to promoters of railways.

In the span of little more than a century, then, the supply of raw materials, technical processes, use of power and transport, in the Potteries, were revolutionised. Hand in hand with these enormous changes, went changes in the way the vastly increased production of the potteries was distributed and sold. These changes will be examined in the next three chapters.

CHAPTER 10

The Commercial Revolution

In the period 1730–1850, the whole mechanism of distribution of wares changed in its character; new methods of salesmanship and new centres for the display of goods replaced the earlier periodical trips to fairs and local markets by huckster or hawking pedlar. Though this commercial revolution, like the transport revolution, happened outside the walls of the pottery factory, nevertheless, it was as real as the industrial revolution that affected the productive process inside the factory.

Today, we are so accustomed to associating cups and saucers of earthenware, china or porcelain with tea, that we are apt to forget that our earliest ancestors in this island neither knew tea as a beverage, nor used tea cups and saucers to grace their table. Today, however, in antique shops, we can see pewter pots, jugs and other vessels, as well as wooden bowls and platters. These for centuries did service on the table, where today we have replaced them with tea cups and saucers, and complete tea services.

Had the oriental habit of hot drinks – the tea beverage – not been introduced into the western countries in the late seventeenth and eighteenth centuries, it is doubtful whether pottery ware would have been so much in demand today throughout European countries, and later in America.

It is almost impossible to drink hot tea from a pewter pot – contact between the heated metal and the lips is too painful. Nor is a hot tea drink from a wooden bowl very appetizing. The horn 'tot' was equally unsuitable. But even before the growing popularity of hot tea, coffee and cocoa reduced and finally eliminated the use of pewter, wood and horn vessels for everyday drinking, there is evidence that pot mugs were ousting pewter, because they were cheaper. The scarcity of tin and lead made pewter pots difficult to obtain. As C. Welch points out in his *History of the Worshipful Company of Pewterers of the City of London*, the competition was causing concern:

'That for encouraging the consumption of tin, and advancing the price thereof, no wine, beer, ale, brandy, rum or other spirits be sold by retail in any tavern

103

or any public house, but in sealed measures made of pewter. . . . The Company of Pewterers for this purpose is to draw and bring in the same in a Bill'. On 23 September 1702 the Court of Pewterers was informed of 'the great increase of mugs made of earth and a mark impressed thereon in imitation of sealed pewter measures to sell liquid commodities in'.

D. Macpherson in his *Annals of Commerce* gives details of the great increases in the consumption of tea in England. Then, side by side with the tremendous increase in the quantity of tea drunk, there was a striking drop in price per lb. from 1728, when it was £1. 12s. 6d. per lb., to 1833 when it ranged from 2s. 6d. to 4s. 6d. per lb. according to quality.

TEA CONSUMPTION IN BRITAIN IN THE

EIGHTEENTH CENTURY

Date	lbs.
1728	1,493,626
67	3,762,800
68	6,862,075
69	6,965,899
70	7,149,245
80	5,152,399
1833	31,829,620

R. O. Mennell, in his book *Tea, an Historical Sketch*, quotes the following copy of an East India Co. Catalogue of sale in January 1785:

The Court of Directors of the United Co. of Merchants in England, trading to the East Indies declare, they will put up for sale on Tues. March 1st.

China Ware more or less	1050 lots	
Tea large chests	3021 @	1s5d per lb.
Tea small ,,	415 @	,, ,, ,,

Not only did tea come in during the eighteenth century, but also the table ware to use with it.

The potters of North Staffordshire became so expert in imitating the original Chinese tea and table ware, that they were able to oust it from the market in a short time. The aristocracy had long developed a craze for china, which Defoe in his *Tour of the Whole Island of Great Britain* attributes to Queen Mary, who was influenced by the Dutch merchants, the first to deal in Chinese merchandise.

It was not only the change in drinking habits of the people of England that led to the increased demand for earthenware for table use. Their food habits changed also. The increase in cooked-meat consumption, and the habit of a hot meal as an item in the national diet, led to a demand for dinner ware, as well as tea services. The higher the standard of living of the population and the better the cooked meals they obtained, the more the demand for earthenware pottery to deck the table increased. But this rise in demand for earthenware, whether crockery or the better type delph or delft ware, (or the china and porcelain produced in Chelsea, or later at Bristol and Worcester) was not the whole story of this eighteenth-century demand for pottery. There was the 'useful' side of demand, represented by the farmers' need for butter-pots, and the market for ale mugs, jugs and pots to the country inn and the town and city public houses – wherever the writ of the Pewterers Guild did not run. This common earthenware mug, jug and pot-ware trade had its distribution by means of fairs, markets and itinerant pot-peddlars or hawkers.

The early butter-pot type of earthenware, produced from the peasant pot-works of the early decades of the eighteenth century, had a very limited local market. As J. C. Wedgwood puts it in his *History of Staffordshire Pottery*, 'The ware was produced and sold to the travelling packman, and at great cost – distributed on horseback.'

But, even at this stage, Staffordshire pottery products were trickling through into a limited national market. Dwight's tea-pots are mentioned in the 1694 litigation against Josiah Wedgwood's ancestors. After 1730, we find in Thomas Whieldon's memorandum book the following entries: 'Aug 11. To make for Mr. Green at Hevingham, Eylsham, Norfolk – 4 Tortoiseshell Tea pots, 4 coffee Pots, 4 shop bowls, 4 ewers, 4 ginger boxes, 4 mustard pots, 8 salts, 12 dishes, 5 doz pails, 2 doz piggins, 6 dozen large plates.' On p. 81, Whieldon records, 'For Miss Ferney order directed to Capt Blake in Surrey St., in the Strand'. Whieldon also despatched his goods for sale at fairs and markets held in Staffordshire. W. Pitt's *View of Agriculture* lists 24 towns in Staffordshire holding periodical fairs and markets. It is interesting to note that Whieldon includes in his list of products both ornamental as well as useful wares.

This development of ornamental production has an important bearing on the marketing of North Staffordshire pottery wares. Customers were prepared to pay more for 'ornamental' ware than they would for plain 'useful' ware. Hence, we find more ornamental ware being made for sale, outside the local useful-ware market. Wedgwood was one of the first potters to exploit the demand for ornamental ware. Here he was only expanding a part of production that Whieldon and some of his contemporaries carried out in their potworks. Whieldon entered in his memo book on p. 77, 'To Mr. Broad 32 desert handles' – probably his characteristic imitation agate handles.

A good deal of the demand for ornamental pottery came from the Birmingham and Sheffield metal-ware and cutlery manufacturers. They ordered knife handles, pottery buttons for inserting into buckles, sleevelinks, tiepins and brooches. These Birmingham merchants bought the ornamental pottery ware wholesale, and after mounting, sold them retail to shops. Eliza Meteyard says that 'Much of Whieldon's trade in articles of this kind being with the Birmingham hardwaremen, who buying snuff boxes by the gross, sold them after mounting to the retail dealers'.

These hardware manufacturers of Birmingham and district had long been exporting their goods to the Continent. Matthew Boulton himself, in addition to his hardware manufactory at Soho, had a merchant's business jointly with his partner Fothergill, trading as 'Boulton & Fothergill'.

Wedgwood did a good deal of his early trade through a firm of Liverpool merchants – Thomas Bentley[1] and James Boardman. The first letter from Wedgwood referring to this business connection was sent to Bentley by Wedgwood on 26 June 1766:

My Worthy Friend,

I am extremely happy in the thoughts of having our connections increased in any way. . . . And as you are a Pot Merchant, you may rest assured, that in everything I can make or purchase, you shall be enabled to serve your friends to the utmost of their wishes. So take in orders for anything this country produces, and in what way you think fit, but whole crates will certainly be attended with the least trouble.

With respect to commission or profit upon the goods you sell I shall very readily conform to any plan you may have determined upon, or if you have not settled that matter, I would make a proposal. A very simple one, which is that whatever goods I purchase to send you, we divide the profit laid upon them equally between us, which is to pay you for the trouble of selling, and me for that of buying in the goods. For the goods of my own manufacture, I allow you 10 per cent commission.

I must know whether the goods you order at any time are for wholesale or retail customers, as the prices must be made accordingly. For this reason, I should know if the waggon of crate now ordered is for export, a shop or a private family. If for the former, the profits must be more moderate, and a discount of 5 per cent allowed for ready money. But we never allow any discount to the latter as that is properly selling them retail.

To this letter, dealing mostly with home trade, Wedgwood adds a significant paragraph, hinting at export trade to the West Indies, 'On Thursday next you may expect another cargo of cream colour, and perhaps a little green and gold for hot climates.' Later, on 14 July 1766, Wedgwood wrote: 'If you should not sell the green and gold at home, they are very suitable for the West Indies. I have sold many sets to private families in Manchester. The cream colour articles in No. 21 crate are charged just as I sell them to all my retail customers. If any of your purchasers should think them dear, do what you please

[1] Later Wedgwood's partner

in these out of the way articles, only you'll make a memo of the abatement, then I may credit you for the amount.' This 'home-trade' business of Wedgwood through Bentley & Boardman as agents or merchants seems to have thrived, for a letter dated 29 June 1767, shows an order to Messrs. Pringle and Adams for £58. 2s. 2½d.

Although Wedgwood did a good deal of export business with foreign merchants on the Continent, and with retailers through his brother John, it is to be noted that he had earlier transacted his London exporting through merchants, as he did his American exports from Liverpool through Bentley and Boardman. His foreign orders were progressively increasing as early as 1765, when he wrote his brother John: 'If you can spare Tom Byerley, I shall be glad. Our London and some foreign orders just come to hand are very large and I am confined to writing more than is anyway convenient to my interest.' Later in 1767 Wedgwood wrote to Bentley: 'I have an order, part of which neither my correspondent [probably an export merchant], nor myself can understand. Shall be glad, if you can get it translated for me. The present order amounts to £400 or upwards, and I would credit them with double that sum.' After his brother's death in 1767, Wedgwood did a good deal of exporting from London through Hodgson, a merchant in Coleman Street.

In 1765, Wedgwood wrote to Sir William Meredith, M.P. for Liverpool: 'The bulk of our particular manufacture is exported to foreign markets, for our home consumption is very trifling in comparison with what is sent abroad and the principal parts of these markets are the Continent of Europe and North America. . . . To the Continent, we send an amazing quantity of white stone ware, and some of the finer kinds, but for the islands of North America, we cannot make anything too rich and costly.'

There is evidence of the export of pottery from North Staffordshire, in the letter books of 'Fothergill and Boulton' in the Assay Office books and manuscripts for 1772. The information refers to Josiah Wedgwood and another pottery firm – of Ann Warburton. As manufacturers they used the services of Fothergill and Boulton to handle their exports to the continent of Europe up to 1774, when the partnership of Fothergill and Boulton as merchants was dissolved.

But there is more to be learnt from these archives. As merchants Fothergill and Boulton had arrangements for exporting from Hull or London. At the former port, they had as their agent a Mr. Isaac Broadly at the quay, to despatch goods to Russia and elsewhere. Repeated instructions are given to Wedgwood and Ann Warburton about the vital importance of packing goods carefully –

'They are to go a long way by land, and our friend particularly requests you will be very careful in packing them'. Fothergill and Boulton laid emphasis on punctual delivery at the port 'as they are intended for a port of the Eastern Country, when no opportunity of shipping will offer after that time.' They insisted: 'We are desirous of having the goods forwarded during the present shipping season, we therefore beg you will do everything in your power, even if your servants work nights, as well as all the day to execute and deliver the goods'. The bulk of the orders from Wedgwood were for his lemon or yellow colour wares (what Wedgwood called his Queen's ware or cream-colour). The quality required was sometimes 'firsts' and sometimes 'seconds'. Where Wedgwood cannot make up the complete order himself, he is instructed to procure them from some other potter (as he did for some orders from Bentley and Boardman, as we have stated earlier). Repeated pressure is brought on both Wedgwood and Ann Warburton to quote the lowest possible prices, as one footnote states: 'P.S. We are told the prices of earthenware are considerably reduced, and trust that you will enable us to serve our friends [i.e. customers] upon the most advantageous terms.' There is evidence that Fothergill and Boulton had to complain and even reprimand Ann Warburton for despatching supplies of un-ordered goods. She was told to forward only seven crates of ware to Isaac Broadly at Hull. She actually consigned nine crates, but crates numbered seven and eight were missing. As Fothergill and Boulton's letter puts it: 'there has been some grand fault upon the Trent and Mersey Canal. It is very wrong to forward orders in so straggling a manner, and still worse, to omit invoice or any advice thereof.'

In a later letter, dated 4 August 1773, more serious complaints were made against Ann Warburton: 'In answer to what you write re 56 crates of earthenware, that have been lying in the hands of Broadly, if you have any means of disposing of them in England, we would rather advise that method than sending them to a foreign market on your account, as we have found by experience, that many of the foreigners are sharpers, when they have goods sent them without orders.' However, they would try to sell the 56 crates in St. Petersburg for Ann Warburton 'to be sold on your own account and risk. There will be an insurance fee of 1 or 1½ guineas per crate, because of the late season of shipping'. They advised sale in Russia, rather than in any other country. Mrs. Warburton agreed to their proposals, and she valued the 56 crates at £300 for insurance purposes. In a letter dated 19 May 1774 she received a statement of the net sales and a draft for £150. Below, is a copy of the actual account, recording the transaction and the breakdown of the deductions in roubles:

	Roubles	Roubles
Produce of sales 56 crates		2850
Deduct for breakage and pilferage	276.96	
Duty to insurers	671.50	
Accidents	20.14	
Freight and duty in the Sound	87.71	
Warehouse room in St. Petersburg	84	
Brokerage	14.94	
Commission for selling	89.64	1244.89
	Balance due	1605.11

Note that the commission charged by Fothergill and Boulton was only one tenth of the deduction for breakage, pilferage and insurance. This 'unordered' or 'forward' selling of crates of earthenware does not appear to have been very profitable.

The correspondence reveals a good many countersales for Fothergill and Boulton, as button makers or seal and cameo mounters to Wedgwood and Ann Warburton. Wedgwood wrote Bentley on 22 November 1773: 'Mr. Fothergill mentioned our selling some of their articles in our [show] rooms. I thought, we could with propriety show anything, in which our manufacture has a place. They will do the same for us.' Ann Warburton sent a parcel of seals to be framed in gilt metal at 10s. a dozen. Then another entry shows she was debited with £12.14s.3d. for buttons, and an order for 12 pairs of sword swivels. There are orders from Wedgwood for white metal cameo mounts and mounted snuff boxes, showing a discount of 15 per cent. allowed. But the bulk of trading shows a balance of £861.14s.11d. due to Wedgwood from Fothergill and Boulton. Another service rendered by this merchant house was to recommend or give unfavourable accounts of certain clients abroad, who tried to place orders direct with potters. They replied to Ann Warburton on 30 November 1773. 'Respecting Henry Van Doreen of Breda, we know but little of him, but he hath always paid regularly for them and from what we could ever learn of him is an honest and industrious young man.'

While the potters used a middleman merchant-house in the early phases of export trade, the bigger pottery manufacturers such as Wedgwood, Spode, Minton and Adams began to set up a sales department of their own to handle both home and export trade direct with customers. Wedgwood made a successful Liverpool merchant his partner, Spode a successful London merchant, William Copeland (his agent in London in 1782), while his son Josiah Spode II made him a full partner in 1824, as Wedgwood had done years earlier in 1766 with Thomas Bentley. Thomas Minton made William Pownall, another successful Liverpool merchant, his partner in 1803.

I have already referred to Wedgwood's exports to the West Indies through Bentley and Boardman, his Liverpool merchants. This trade was extended to the mainland itself, and by 1769 it was of great importance. It was a natural development for English potters generally, and North Staffordshire pottery manufacturers in particular, to capture the North American trade. They were the nearest extensive and concentrated pottery centre to Liverpool, the North American entrepôt. They were nearer than the scattered pottery centres in Worcestershire, Shropshire, Yorkshire or the Chelsea and other London factories. Bristol potters could be ignored for, after the defeat of Champion by Wedgwood,[1] Bristol rapidly declined as a pottery producing area.

Wedgwood blazed the trail in America with his wares, but other potters reaped the harvest in the nineteenth century. Because of Josiah Wedgwood II's retirement to live in Dorset, and probably his entry into politics, the lead given by his father in American exports was not followed up as vigorously as hitherto despite the efforts of Byerley, Wedgwood's partner. Perhaps one reason for the temporary decline of Wedgwood sales in America during the early decades of the nineteenth century was the fact that the plain and less decorative wares of Etruria did not appeal as much to the Americans as the pottery with American scenes and events depicted on the printed transfer-decorated wares of the other potters. The aristocracy and wealthy patrons of Wedgwood's basalt and jasper vases, urns, cameos and medallions, which had such a large sale in Europe, had not yet appeared on the scene in the covered waggon era of the U.S.A. As America grew richer during the nineteenth and twentieth centuries, so did the demand for Wedgwood products revive and soar. After 1906, a direct descendant of Josiah Wedgwood, Kennard L. Wedgwood and his family, organized a sales department in the U.S.A. and established a company known as 'Josiah Wedgwood and Sons Inc. of U.S.A. and Canada'. In the 1967 financial report of the company it was recorded that for 1966, exports were 70 per cent. of the business of the firm, an increase of 19 per cent.

In its attempt to penetrate the European markets Staffordshire pottery had to meet the full force of native competition from some well-established and often state-subsidized manufactories. Later, exporters from Staffordshire also had high tariff-walls to surmount. The Staffordshire potters were at a further disadvantage of being in the heart of England, while many of their competitors were near the East coast in Yorkshire, and in particular in London. This was the great driving force behind the collective efforts of Wedgwood, Whieldon and the other pottery manufacturers in North Staffordshire to improve roads, canal

[1] See Chapter 3

and rail transport. It also explains the collective efforts of the potters, not only in their various local committees, but in particular their support of Wedgwood in his fight to establish a permanent General Chamber of Commerce for Britain.[1] This desire to be able to compete with others for the European trade to a large extent explains the resistance of the potters to the threatened interference by the Government in conditions of work, hours of employment and the restriction on child labour – all of which, they claimed, would add to the cost of labour and production. This, they declared would seriously hamper them in competing with foreigners in the export of goods to Europe. This drive to reduce costs probably underlies the bitter resistance of the potters to trade-union organization amongst the workpeople during this period.

The North Staffordshire Potters succeeded earliest in exports to Europe in those markets where they encountered least resistance and competition – the ports of the Baltic – as Miss Meteyard points out in her book *A Group of Englishmen*. In France, because of royal patronage of the Sèvres porcelain factory, the manufacture of wares had reached a high standard. For design and decoration, they were some of the finest products of the ceramic world, second only to those of China. But France's domestic utility wares were very poor, and of common pot of the worst quality. In this type of market Wedgwood's cream-colour-ware and domestic table product would sell well, if British pottery were granted an entry. This explains Wedgwood's keenness to win in the struggle for a commercial treaty with France. It is not surprising that he secured 60 signatories from his fellow potters to a memorial to the Customs commissioners. It was presented personally by Wedgwood and two of his neighbouring potters, Warburton and Neale.

In 1776, Wedgwood arranged for his partner Bentley to spend seven weeks in Paris and its environs, where he had personal friends. Miss Meteyard writes that Bentley asked 'his friend M. Sayde, if he would like to undertake a commission for the sale of Wedgwood's ornamental goods'. On Bentley's return, Wedgwood appointed a M. Perregaux as his Paris agent, and Miss Meteyard states 'through a merchant called M. Honoré a large number of choice articles infiltrated into the possession of French nobility'. As early as 1784, when the French commercial treaty seemed likely to become a fact, Wedgwood exchanged letters with a Versailles shopkeeper, M. Chappins, offering to accept his wares, either to sell on commission or for export. Wedgwood, however, waited for the commercial treaty to be ratified before he arranged to sell his goods in Paris, whither he sent Tom Byerley, his nephew, and his young son John Wedgwood. These representatives of the firm concluded an agreement with two merchants,

[1] See Chapter 15

one of whom was M. Sykes & Co. in the Place du Palais Royal, to import Wedgwood's goods for sale. A letter from Sykes' manager, dated 14 February 1788, shows the force of Wedgwood's assault on the French market: 'Your manufactory goods form a brilliant and capital part of our commerce. The flower pots pleased beyond description. They did not remain one hour with us, after they were unpacked. There is not an hour in the day passes without people sending to know if more have arrived. I should be particularly pleased to have some plain Queen's ware. They could be enchanting and sell without limit as to quantity. I believe your depot of cameos will become an object more considerable than I imagined. The merchants have begun to find us out.'

Unfortunately, the favourable clauses of the 1786 commercial treaty were not allowed to operate for long. As Miss Meteyard put it, 'The breaking out of the French Revolution annulled at once the Treaty'. This was due to the passing of the 'Prohibition of Pottery Law'. The reason given for this Law is eloquent testimony to Wedgwood and his fellow Staffordshire potters, for the French Government stated, 'We have to fear the English, who excel in the manufacture of pottery'.

In Germany, or as Wedgwood's correspondence calls it 'The States of Prussia', pottery manufacture in imitation of Dutch Delft ware had become fairly advanced. The German pottery industry was encouraged by the various German princes, much in the way French kings had patronized the Sèvres porcelain factory. If Wedgwood and the other Staffordshire potters wished to penetrate the German market, they could do so only on the excellence of their ware and its comparative cheapness in price.

As early as 1770, Wedgwood had direct inquiries at his London showroom from a Hanover merchant. Bentley did so well in his foreign trade from the London Showroom that Wedgwood wrote to him on 11 May 1771, 'I have received a pretty good order from Mr. Krause of Brunswick.' Then later, on 26 October 1771, Wedgwood had to restrain Bentley's enthusiasm for sales abroad. 'I think we should not sell all to Italy to the merchant de Schoning, and neglect the other Princes in Germany and elsewhere, who are waiting with so much patience for their turn to be served with our fine things.' A year later, Bentley received the following grateful letter from Wedgwood: 'I rejoice in the continuation of such agreeable dispatches from the Princes of Germany. May they hold out to the end, till we have a good account of all our remaining adventures. I shall be glad to hear from you every time you hear from your Princes and the Great Men of the Earth.'

Before he died Wedgwood had the pleasure of displaying his famous copy of the Barberini Vase in jasper to admiring members of the Royal family and Princes in Germany. His son Josiah and Tom Byerley visited all the chief cities in Germany to show off the Vase and also to settle intricate business matters with various correspondents, and opening new agencies for the sale of jaspers and cameos. They heard lavish praise bestowed on Wedgwood wares, and they paid a visit to the Royal Porcelain works at Meissen.

Correspondence with Josiah Wedgwood II in 1800 from a Herr Schilling tells of the serious effect of the Franco–German War on sales of ware at the Frankfort Fair, because the French prohibited the delivery of English pottery on the left bank of the Rhine. Later on, Schilling repeated his magnificent order for Wedgwood ornamental wares – vases, figures, tritons and cameos.

Holland, through trade with the Orient, was able to imitate Chinese pottery (at least in decoration, if not in material), in its later famous Delft ware. This Delft ware was introduced to England and an English version was developed at Lambeth, Bristol and Liverpool. But the wares of Whieldon and Wedgwood ousted the Delft. The fame of Wedgwood's pottery reached Amsterdam in the 1760s. D. Macpherson writes in his *Annals of Commerce* (1805): 'Staffordshire earthenware had lately come into request in Holland. The increase of this trade in Holland from 1760 was surprisingly great.' At first, Wedgwood employed as his agent a Du Burk, who opened a warehouse in Amsterdam. He sold large quantities of Wedgwood ware, and paid his accounts promptly. Later, though, he defaulted, ended up in prison and Wedgwood sent out his own representative to recoup his lost trade, before he secured the services of a new agent, Veldhuysen. Under him, Meteyard reports, 'The business sprang into new life, like a phoenix from its ashes. The sales became remarkable, depots were opened in other parts of Holland, and Veldhuysen had the pleasure and advantage of dispersing Wedgwood's beautiful productions over a wide extent of the country and adding substantially to his fame'.

It was while Veldhuysen was Wedgwood's agent that his son and Byerley made their historic trip in Wedgwood's own chaise, minus his coat of arms or cypher, from Etruria. They took with them the famous Barberini vase and a magnificent collection of cameos mounted in necklaces, bracelets and eardrops. At the Hague, young Wedgwood and Byerley were fêted and entertained by Lord Auckland, Wedgwood's personal friend, who as Mr. Eden had negotiated the French Commercial Treaty. Lord Auckland made a special display of all Wedgwood's wares in his house, where 'all the first people that are at the Hague were there. The Prince and Princess with their daughter, who is to be married to the Duke of Brunswick. . . . They said everything, that was to be expected.'

So writes young Wedgwood to his father on 26 July 1790. Continuing his letter young Josiah added, 'We did business with the Princess, who desired a pair of bracelets, which came to 14 guineas. We displayed wares in Amsterdam at Weldhuysen's – a very capital magasin of earthenware and furniture, where all the nobility and first people resort.' Other North Staffordshire potters – Warburtons, Daniels, the Turners and Adams – were also doing a considerable trade with Holland.

In spite of the patronage from royalty and the Italian nobility that maiolica and other pottery had received in Italy, Wedgwood and Bentley, through one of the latter's friends, a Mr. de Schoning, made successful inroads into Italian export trade. Wedgwood's account books record orders from Naples in 1774, Leghorn in 1775, in Trieste, Venice and Rome in 1781, Genoa and Palermo in 1784, Bologna in 1786, Turin in 1787 and Milan in 1789. Portugal was supplied with Wedgwood pottery in 1784, despite the prohibition of foreign wares. According to Meteyard, 'In 1785 the prohibition of exports of pottery to Portugal was lifted and more Wedgwood wares were sold.'

Wedgwood's entry into the Russian market dates from 1768. He wrote Boulton on 19 March 1768: 'I have waited on Lord Cathcart, the Russian Ambassador, to bring about the plan we settled of introducing our manufacture at the Court of Russia. The Ambassador and his Lady came into my measures with the utmost readiness, and I am to get done a plate by way of a specimen with the Russian arms and an edging round the plate.' This ambassadorial introduction worked the oracle for Wedgwood ware. Miss Meteyard confirms: 'Lord Cathcart's Embassy had literally opened the Russian Capital to whatever goods Wedgwood might choose to send there.' When Mr. Baxter, the British Consul at St. Petersburg, returned to this country later he brought back orders from Russian nobility for four large Wedgwood services. Wedgwood had already supplied Lord Cathcart with a full table service for display to Russian nobles.

The most famous order that Wedgwood ever received from Russia, or from any other foreign country, was that obtained through the British Consul, Mr. Baxter, for the Empress Catherine. It was referred to as 'The Russian Service'. It consisted of more than 2,000 pieces, and on the scale Wedgwood wanted to execute it, would take no less than two or three years. Originally, Wedgwood estimated it would cost £1,000 or £1,500 to produce, but later the estimate reached £2,400. The price paid for the service by the Empress, who was very pleased with it, is said to have been £3,000. The whole story, with coloured illustrations of nearly 1,000 of the scenes depicted on the service pieces, may be read in a magnificent volume entitled *The Wedgwood Russian Service*, by

G. Williamson. This great admirer and collector of Wedgwoodiana was led to believe, after the Bolshevik Revolution in 1917, that the revolutionists in St. Petersburg had destroyed the Empress Catherine Wedgwood service when they captured the Palace.

The author and his wife disbelieved this rumour, and in 1935 we paid a special visit to the U.S.S.R. at the invitation of Josiah Wedgwood and Sons to probe the mystery of the alleged disappearance of the Service. To our delight, we discovered the whole Service hidden in cases in the cellars of 'The Hermitage', Leningrad, which were brought out specially for our inspection and admiration.

Some of the difficulties attendant on Wedgwood's delivery of his wares to Russia are recounted in a letter from Lady Cathcart to Wedgwood on 28 January 1770. She reports that the ship taking the goods into port had been wrecked, and that pirates from nearby islands had pilfered a lot of the ware; the rest of the cases had been badly damaged. However, in spite of such accidents at sea, Miss Meteyard records: 'The Russian Service for Empress Catherine served as a splendid advertisement to the whole continent of Europe, and spread Wedgwood and Bentley's fame to the most distant Courts. In 1774, large consignments were made to Reval and Moscow. The vast tide of commerce grows year by year till 1786, when the whole continent and something more is embraced. Capper, a Birmingham merchant having a great establishment in St. Petersburg, gave orders for cream ware and useful goods by 'thousands of dozens.'

When Spanish duty on British earthenware was 16 per cent. (in 1776), Wedgwood delivered a consignment through Fothergill and Boulton. Wedgwood wrote to a M. Riva of Lisbon on 5 November 1774 giving details of a cargo of wares to Cadiz, for sale to Mexico. 'We have been packing up 500 dozen of table plates and other wares to make them into a table service for two houses in Manchester and Liverpool. The House of Manchester is Hulme, who was here, and I had a good deal of talk with him relative to the trade to New Spain [Mexico]. As his partner Mr. Walmesley resides at Cadiz, I hope to do something considerable in the way of trade with us in time. I apprehend some articles should be made on purpose for this trade relative to their religion. They will wear crucifixes, Saints etc., for bracelets, lockets, snuffboxes etc. In one of these orders, we were told not to send more than was ordered, unless we had some Saints.' Other potters though were shipping to Spain and New Spain, for he wrote, 'Mr. Hulme had bought 1,000 dozen plates and dishes, with a great deal of coffee, chocolate and tea ware before he called upon me.'

Sweden was yet another country which had placed a prohibition on British pottery and when a friend of Wedgwood, a Mr. Liston, who had helped him to secure orders in Spain, became Envoy Extraordinary to the Court of Sweden, Wedgwood sought his co-operation to get the prohibition of pottery removed, and he also enlisted the help of the Marquis of Stafford to use his influence with the Lords of the Committee of the Council for Trade. The minute of the Potters' Committee records that on 24 August 1789 the potters fully endorsed Wedgwood's efforts by signing a petition.

A Commercial Revolution had been accomplished between 1730 and 1850 in the scale and character of trade in pottery, from its local character in the early decades of the eighteenth century to the national and international trade of the later decades of the eighteenth century and the nineteenth century. This foreign or international trade is referred to in a resolution of the potters' minute book of 22 February 1785: 'It is the opinion of this meeting that not less than five-sixths of the earthenware manufactured in Staffordshire is exported.'

Monsieur F. de Saint-Fond in his book *Travels in England*, published in 1797, wrote of Wedgwood pottery: 'Its excellent workmanship, its durability, the advantage it possesses of withstanding the action of fire, its fire glaze impenetrable by acids, the beauty, convenience and variety of its forms together with its moderate price, have created a commerce so active and so universal, that in travelling from Paris to St. Petersburg, from Amsterdam to Sweden, from Dunkirk to France, one is served at every inn from English earthenware. The same fine article adorns the tables of Spain, Portugal and Italy, and it provides the cargoes of ships to the East Indies, the West Indies and America.'

In November 1830, the Potters of North Staffordshire presented a petition to the House of Commons 'praying for the opening of the trade to China'. As early as 1792 the Liverpool merchants had protested against the monopoly of the East India Company. Wedgwood in one of his letters to Bentley wrote: 'I am going upon a large scale with our models, but I hope to bring the whole in compass for your next winter's show and astonish the "world" all at once.' If Wesley considered the world as his parish, his contemporary Prince of Potters considered the world his market.

26 A thrower at his wheel

27 Josiah Spode I

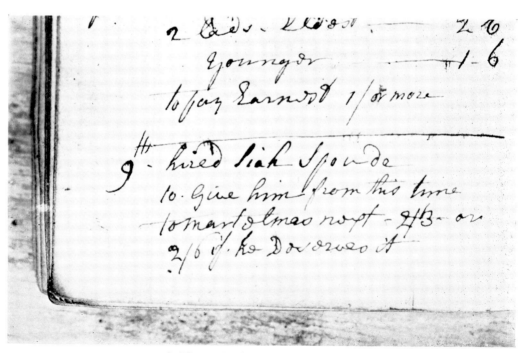

28 An entry in Thomas Whieldon's books, hiring Josiah Spode

29 Thomas Whieldon, Wedgwood's early partner

30 Thomas Bentley, Wedgwood's
first partner at Etruria

31 W. T. Copeland

CHAPTER II

Commercial Technique

Up to the middle of the eighteenth century, the peasant potter took his own wares by packhorse to the local market staff or fair. But, as the industry developed after 1730, itinerant pedlars or hawkers began to act as middlemen between potmaker and customer in country or town. Later still came the more respectable and flourishing middleman or merchant, who took consignments of crockery and pottery to be sold at shops and stores, particularly in the large towns and even in London itself.

Strangely enough, when, in 1785, the Government appealed for the abolition of pedlars and hawkers, the potters were reluctant to respond, as can be seen by a minute of a potters' committee meeting on June 14 that year: 'It was resolved that it is the opinion of this meeting that the abolition of hawkers and pedlars will, in many respects, be injurious to the general interest of the manufactory, particularly as it will tend to lessen consumption and check the sales of the manufacturers.' Even though many, if not most, of the potters had developed business connections with merchants and middlemen at home and abroad for their wares, they were still of the opinion that the humble pedlar and hawker of crockery, with a shoulder-crate strapped to his back, was a necessary part of the commercial distribution scheme of things. The pedlars and hawkers, in their opinion, were an essential link between the scattered rural customers, inaccessible in towns supplied with shops, stores, or regular markets. Again, even in 1785 transport by road was very poor in rural areas, or even in the poorer quarters of a town, and the housewife isolated in her home welcomed the visit of the pedlar or hawker, bringing crockery to her doorstep. Besides, there is sound sales-psychology about a pedlar or hawker offering his wares. He literally brings them to the notice of his would-be customers – under their very noses! It goes without saying that his wares are cheap for he is a cheap-man or chap-man. Odd bits of crockery are bought from the pedlar or hawker to replace chipped or cracked ware. If their customers could have visited a shop, it is quite possible they could not have purchased single pieces of pottery. The itinerant pedlar could make out a very good case that his wares were cheaper, precisely because he was on the road and had no high rents, rates, or other heavy overheads to meet like the retailers, market stall-holders or fair-pitch-holders. The existence of the chapman, pedlar or hawker was often a check on shopkeepers who tried to keep up prices and thus retard pottery sales. Further, from the point of view of the pottery manufacturer, the pedlars and hawkers were essential for disposing of many articles that left the pottery kiln as imperfect articles – those with a blemish, or 'seconds'.

Nevertheless, however much potters wanted to retain pedlars and hawkers to dispose of their second quality wares, they relied on merchant houses for the distribution of their more-or-less perfect wares to the home market and foreign markets. In the first instance, the potter resorted to merchants because selling pottery in bulk was a much more risky adventure than that of disposing of small quantities direct to a pedlar or hawker or even to a small retail shop. This was true even in the home trade, and was more so in foreign trade. Even in the home trade, some risks were taken because of the bankruptcy of even a respectable merchant in times of economic depression. In fact, the bankruptcy of a merchant house sometimes brought in its train the downfall of the pottery firm. John Boyle in his *Diary* 1832–1842[1] gives details of a Mr. Thelwell, a pottery merchant of Manchester who became bankrupt in 1841, and dividend of £9,600 at the rate of 8s. in the pound was declared on all his debts. Fortunately, Minton's pottery firm was able to stand this heavy loss.

Boyle records in his *Diary* for 9 November 1833, a visit he had to make to inquire about transactions of foreign merchants with Minton's: 'The business which led me to Montreal was to settle Rollasons' account with Buchanan and Co., and my observations have given me a very humble opinion of the capacity and what is more, the honour of these gentlemen. Their prevarication, their inattention and inaccuracies, accompanied wherewithal of an overbearing estimate of themselves, surpasses anything I could have believed of British Merchants. Nor is this all. The charges they make in the account are such as could not be maintained.' Boyle caustically closed his entry with the words: 'Of such as these, it would appear are merchants composed. May my conscience always protect me from imitating their conduct.'

Wedgwood in a letter to Bentley of 9 October 1776 expressed himself in equally strong terms about merchants of the unsatisfactory type – the defaulters. 'This is the best plan I can think of, supposing Du Burk (of Amsterdam)[2] to

[1] MSS. Spode Archives
[2] See Chapter 10

behave properly. If he does not, I am determined at all events to take the shortest course and have done with it, for when a man shows himself to be a determined villain, the sooner one has done him the better. . . . I have been with Mr. Sparrow [Solicitor] this morning, and he advises me to treat Du Burk as the Ministry do, with the Americans, sword in hand, is to have a writ ready, and if he will not do what is right, to secure him.' Whether dealing with honest or dishonest merchants, the tendency of the leading potters, if not of most of them, was to arrange their business in the home and foreign market so as to dispense, as far as possible, with commission-charging merchants. There were definite advantages in establishing direct dealings with customers, at home and abroad, from a sales agency, warehouse or showroom of one's own. There was not only a saving of the middleman's or merchant's commission, but also the satisfaction to the potter and his salesmen, of meeting their customers and clients at first hand, to explain the merits of their particular wares. From such a sales centre, the pottery firm could push its own ware to the exclusion of other firms' products.

Wedgwood began his direct sales agency in London, with his brother John established in Cateaton Street with only a clerk and his nephew Tom Byerley to help him. Later, the sales office was developed into a warehouse. As early as 1767, Wedgwood wrote Bentley, 'I have some thoughts of opening a warehouse, not merely a pattern room in the City.' He took great care to search for a suitable site, first finding a place in Pall Mall, then later, at the bottom end of St. Martin's Lane. Later still, in 1768, he discovered a more suitable and attractive premises, 'at the top end of St. Martin's Lane, in Great Newport Street.' It was a Corner House, 60 feet long, the streets wide which led to it, and 'carriages may come to it either from Westminster or the City, without being incommoded with drays full of timber and coals.' This was the London warehouse and headquarters of the home and export trade of Wedgwood, till the lease expired about the time of his death. Then 'a more palatial, aristocratic, but eminently dull showroom' (to use Meteyard's words) was chosen in York Street, St. James' Square. Here Wedgwood II and Byerley carried on business till 1829, when the London showroom was discontinued.

Josiah Spode also opened a London warehouse, first at Fore Street, Cripplegate, later at a more aristocratic centre in Portugal Street in Lincoln's Inn Fields. Here William Copeland, the London tea merchant, was put in charge to train young Josiah Spode in the art of salesmanship. Thomas Minton later followed suit with a warehouse in London, where his brother Arthur was in charge.

From the sixteenth century onwards, London had been the starting point of foreign ventures. Great financial concerns like the East India Company and other monopolies found it convenient to be established in the capital of the Empire. The outlying industrial areas of the North and Midlands poured their goods – cotton, woollen and hardware – into London, scene of financial transactions on a large scale. Bills on all parts of the globe could be exchanged for it was the banking centre for all trades dealing in cash or credit transactions. It was also a clearing house for information concerning the credentials of foreign merchants and business houses – in Europe, particularly, since London was the nearest port serving the Continent.

In 1793 Spode's sales from his London warehouse totalled £9,485. Minton – a beginner in 1800, had sales totalling £2,000. But Wedgwood and Byerley's sales from their new showroom totalled £18,813 in 1801. Wedgwood's account books for 1793–1795 show the sales of their chief European merchant houses.

Name	Place	Amount £
Veldhuysen.	Amsterdam.	1,853
Wagnon.	St. Petersburg.	1,793
Perisco.	Genoa.	1,091
V. Axon.	Hamburg.	840
Krause.	Brunswick.	763
Dooren.	Antwerp.	568
Boreriller.	Frankfurt.	495
G. Smith.	Hamburg.	448

The wars and political revolutions in Europe at the close of the eighteenth and in the early nineteenth century led to impoverishment and the European market for pottery dwindled.

London was a good centre for home trade, as well as an entrepôt for foreign trade. The most populous centre in Britain, it had the largest concentration of potential customers. Besides, it had the greatest concentration of wealthy, aristocratic, titled people, who could afford to purchase lavishly from the stock of table and ornamental wares for their drawing rooms and salons. The development of road, canal and railway transport brought people in large numbers to live in and around London, and its neighbouring counties. It took a long time for the transport revolution to open up large centres of home trade in the north, west and centre of Britain. When the European trade, and with it London's importance as an entrepôt, the potters looked across the Atlantic for another outlet.

During the road and canal transport revolution of the eighteenth century, the North Staffordshire pottery manufacturers had developed their export trade through Liverpool, Hull and Bristol (and of course, later, London) by using the services of merchant houses. Wedgwood had used the services of Bentley and

Boardman, and the Manchester firm of Hulme and Walmesley, while Spode employed Pownall, a Liverpool merchant, to deal with exports of pottery to America.

While most potters in North Staffordshire used Liverpool merchants, as middlemen, to export their wares across the Atlantic, there were some potters who set up their own warehouses in Liverpool, and in New York, to handle their American trade. One of the earliest Staffordshire firms to do this was William Adams and Sons who opened up large premises in Liverpool, first at 19 Erskine Street, and at Wellington Buildings, Poole Lane, using these as centres to carry on not only their own export trade, but also to act as merchants for several of the leading potteries manufacturers. In 1821, under the title of Adams Brothers, they opened a branch office and warehouse in New York. Adams and Sons exported a lot of their wares to South America, but because of the language difficulties, they employed Liverpool general merchants for this trade.

This American export trade became more important than either the home trade or European exports. With the declining of London export trade to Europe, some potters refused to transact any more business through foreign merchants, unless they did so from the London warehouse or through some accredited London merchant. Wedgwood II closed their London warehouse in 1829. They were content to use the services of general merchant houses, till they opened their own Branch House in 1906.

Based on their experience of home sales, through the warehouses that they had established in the capital, many potters decided to establish branch warehouses or agencies, to display and sell their wares at important centres like Liverpool, Bath, Buxton, Edinburgh and even in Dublin. Adams and Minton established warehouses in Liverpool, and Palmer had an agency in Bath. When showrooms opened at Bath and Buxton, Wedgwood himself visited these two centres, where people of wealth and fashion were in attendance practically all the year round, seeking health and pleasure. Writing to Bentley from Buxton, Wedgwood said, 'I met with a Hue and Cry after our seals at Buxton'. Writing later from Bath on 2 January 1772, Wedgwood tells Bentley, 'We find Mr. Palmer here, trying to establish a warehouse for his goods.' Palmer, one of his keenest rivals in the Potteries, thus not only imitated Wedgwood's products, but also imitated his method of selling his wares in Bath.

In order to sell the ever increasing products of their increasingly mechanized factories, the potters appointed persons whom they termed 'riders'. In those early days, they travelled on horseback, taking samples or patterns to show retail shops or private families. This 'rider' salesman was a kind of mounted pedlar or hawker, appointed officially to represent the potter. Wedgwood gives us a picture of such a rider in a letter to Bentley in 1778.

As Mr. Brownhill has asked to be set at liberty, perhaps he would like to travel for a year or two, and it might do very well to have our things shown in the shops. He should take patterns [or samples] of flower pots, bouquet pots, tablets, figures, ink-pots, ink-stands, seals etc. Also some pieces of useful ware. I am afraid he cannot carry them by any contrivance on horseback, though I know much may be done by means of little boxes and large rider's saddle bags. He might begin his year's business in London, that he might learn it under your eye, and it will give you time to provide a travelling machine etc.

This term 'travelling machine' was used for a horse-drawn vehicle, which today we would call a horse-drawn trade van.

Other potters followed Wedgwood's example of appointing riders. John Boyle, a rider for Thomas Minton, who made him his partner, has left us an account of his frustrations on his tour of the western counties of England, in his *Diary*. 'Most assuredly this mode of life is to me the most uncomfortable that can be imagined. Within the last week, I have passed through four towns without having obtained a single order in Gloster, Worcester, Buglawton and Taunton. I am apprehensive that I shall have to add Exeter to this list. In three places I have not been enabled to show my patterns even. 'No want of goods' is the constant remark.' Boyle was more successful in his tour in Ireland. He entered in his *Diary* for 3 April 1839: 'My journey on the whole has not been a prosperous one, but the amount of my orders £575.' On the other hand, we find Wedgwood writing to Bentley in March 1771, 'Byerley is stripped of all his Garricks and Shakespeare framed in black, and says he could sell thousands of Keppel at any price. Oh Keppel, Keppel, why will you not send me a Keppel! I am persuaded if we have our wits about us we ought to have had two or three months since we might have sold £1,000 worth of Keppel's heads.' The very success of these 'riders' like Byerley brought problems to Etruria, because some shopkeeper customers of Wedgwood complained that the riders 'hawked' his wares to their own shop customers. When Bentley wrote that Mr. Brownhill's machine had broken down, Wedgwood wrote: 'I cannot say that I am in my heart very sorry for it, being a little of Mrs. Cooper's opinion, that we should not only avoid the evil of hawking, but even the appearance of the evil.' Mrs. Cooper was one of Wedgwood's best shopkeeping retailers.

Nevertheless, it is clear from a letter to Bentley in March 1771 that Wedgwood decided to proceed with his riders: 'I have great expectations from a rider, and I think we may employ one constantly to advantage. I suppose he is to confine himself to the shops and merchants, and not attempt to take any orders from any private families, unless where he calls with an odd account, if an order should be offered, he could not decently refuse it.'

Wedgwood, as noted earlier, had close connections with Birmingham shops. He wrote Bentley: 'In this line I think we might employ a rider with safety to our reputation and advantage to our business. But, as our goods in Birmingham are already in the possession of all the jewellers' shops for mounted seals, and they will be our best customers for the stones, I think I should not interfere with them in Birmingham, nor show any of them as patterns to the shops' [through riders].

Wedgwood, and Whieldon before him, used the metal and jewellery manu-facturers as middlemen, to purchase much of their ornamental ware in bulk, to be mounted in their factories. Seeing the efforts of his riders equipped with samples and patterns so successful, Wedgwood thought he might undertake the mounting of his seals and cameos at Etruria, and save the cost of sending them to the jewellers. 'I have two reasons for wishing to send the seals abroad and for selling them set to the shops in England. One is to sell the greater quantity, as soon as may be, and the other was to have more profit upon them. I may add another motive, which should have some weight with us, that we may have a correspondence of our own, independent of the setters and wholesale jewellers too.'[1]

Wedgwood then discloses his plans: 'There is a jeweller in Uttoxeter, who employs one to two hundred hands – a Mr. Copestake, whom I intend to take the first opportunity of seeing, but should wish to have a good bracelet or two to show him. Sleeve buttons and lockets must come next in play, and we may as well sell a quantity of them ourselves as give all the profit to others.'

Josiah C. Wedgwood, in a lecture reviewing the growth of the pottery industry in North Staffordshire, was inclined to attribute the large fortunes of Wedgwood, Spode, Minton, Adams and others to this inter-pottery trading or merchandizing of one another's goods. He stated: 'When one thought of the fortunes made by some pottery manufacturers, one must not imagine that they made their fortunes solely by their own potting.' He was certain that all the big manufacturers, who employed agents or merchants in London or Liverpool, also acted as merchants for the smaller potters. The 'getaway' for one week in Etruria in 1780, according to the records, amounted to £12,000. It was quite obvious that Etruria was not capable of such an output. What must have hap-pened was that Josiah Wedgwood bought a good deal of ware from the smaller potters and sold this through his own agents, thereby acting as a wholesale

[1] Letter to Bentley 2 December 1773

merchant, as well as a manufacturer. This is a feasible explanation of the fortunes made by some of the earlier potters.

Spode-Copeland's account books show this pottery firm acting as glass
merchants, to supply customers with glass ware, as well as Spode pottery. Many
shops selling earthenware also sold glass ware, used extensively as table ware.
Indeed, one of the most successful potters – Davenport, owned one of the
biggest glass factories of his day. Even today, one of the best known pottery
trade journals, circulating amongst pottery and glassware shops and stores is
called *The Pottery Gazette and Glass Trade Review.*

However, large pottery manufacturers often had sources of income outside
their factories. Many, like Wedgwood and Adams, inherited large sums of
money and sometimes estates from their richer relatives, or through marriage
into wealthy families. This was true of both Josiah Wedgwood and Josiah
Spode II. Most, if not all, like Whieldon, Wedgwood and Adams, were
propertied persons owning land. Some like Adams, Josiah Spode I, and later his
son Josiah were local colliery owners. Most of the potters, as we have seen, were
shareholders in turnpike roads as trustees and held shares, as proprietors of the
Trent and Mersey Canal, and later many became railway shareholders, when
the canal was taken over. W. T. Copeland, in addition to owning Spode's
factory, was a large coalowner, and a director of the Grand Junction Railway.
J. Ridgeway, another successful potter, was a director of the Trent Valley
Railway.

Probably then, J. C. Wedgwood over-estimates the part played by inter-
potter-trading, as a source of the fortunes of many of the largest potters. The
truth is that these very successful and wealthy pottery manufacturers were more
than pottery capitalists. They invested their surplus capital in several financial
ventures or enterprises in coalmining, transport schemes on roads, canals and
railway, and some were interested in banking.

During this period of the Industrial Revolution, from 1730 to 1850, there
was no traditional or single method of sales adopted by the pottery manufacturers. They resorted to several methods of transacting their sales, so as to
secure the best result from the marketing of the mass production of wares. One
thing they did not do was to attempt to organize a co-operative concern to sell
their wares, similar to their ventures in organizing a co-operative Clay Company
to purchase and produce clay supplies from Cornwall, Devon and Dorset. The
nearest they approached to such a joint venture was to try to work out a common
scheme concerning prices. This I shall deal with in the next chapter.

CHAPTER 12

Price Agreements

For the small peasant master potter of the pre-1730 period, the question of what price to charge for the plain and simple pots was not hard to decide. The wages to be paid his journeymen were fixed and there was a small amount for his apprentices' upkeep and training. He could judge from these wages items what his remuneration or wage as a master potter should be. He also knew what the cost of his raw materials were. As he delivered his wares himself on horseback to local fairs or markets, he knew what transport costs to add to fix his prices. In those early days his neighbouring potters were master potters, like himself, with small pot-works, and prices of goods were known to the potters, as they travelled to the same market or fair to dispose of their products. There was little danger of one master potter undercutting or underselling his neighbour in such a close neighbourhood as Burslem — merely an enlarged village.

Later, in the decades after 1730, rapid changes took place in the number of potbanks and in the scale of pottery operations including, as we have seen, the application of power-driven machinery to replace and supplement human labour. Sub-division of labour and specialization of skilled trades resulted in the number of employees being increased from the half-dozen or so in the peasant potbank, to several hundreds, even 1,000 employees engaged in some of the largest pottery establishments, before the end of 1850. Competition became very keen between potters, and mass production on a large scale in some factories made it difficult for very small potbanks to survive.

This state of affairs led to the first recorded attempt to establish a price-fixing agreement, in 1770. Space does not permit the reproduction in full of this important agreement, but it may be referred to in Appendix XXI of a Thesis by the writer on *The Industrial Revolution in the North Staffordshire Potteries since 1730*. It was a legal document, signed on 4 February 1770 by 27 potters, who were manufacturers of dishes, tureens, stoolpans, sauce boats, twyflers — large plates, cups and saucers, butter tubs and stands. This list contains no ornamental wares, but only domestic plain wares and useful pottery. In the list of 27 potters who signed this price agreement there are many names conspicuous by their absence. Josiah Wedgwood, Thomas Whieldon, Josiah Spode, William Turner, R. & J. Baddeley, W. Adams and Palmer, to mention just a few of the large potters who produced ornamental wares, as well as the above listed useful wares, are not among the 27 signatories. Written into the agreement is the distinction in qualities of the wares. For example, this classification distinguishes the qualities or standard of wares from the best and dearest, down to the worse, and worse than worser, the cheapest.

Quality	*Price*	
	s.	*d.*
The Best or Firsts	2.	0.
Best Seconds	1.	9.
Seconds	1.	6.
Worser or Thirds	1.	0.
A degree worser		9.
None sold under		9. and not to be picked, but taken as they are put together.

There is a discount off the above prices – 5 per cent. for breakage, and 5 per cent. for cash and ready money. These were the prices to manufacturers of earthenware, but no more than $7\frac{1}{2}$ per cent. was to be allowed in addition to discounts for breakage and cash: that is, $17\frac{1}{2}$ per cent. all told. This is evidence of sales by the smaller potters to larger manufacturers, and confirms the inter-trading referred to in the last chapter.

In 1771 Wedgwood (who had refused to sign the 1770 price agreement) noticed the tendency to cut prices of some of his fellow potters, especially R. & J. Baddeley (who had also refused to sign). He wrote on 21 April to Bentley that Baddeley 'who makes the best ware perhaps of any of the potters here, has led the way and the rest must follow, unless he can be prevailed upon to raise it again, we are to see him tomorrow about a dozen of us for that purpose.'

The result was a meeting of the potters (so Wedgwood reports to Bentley on 30 May 1771) at which 'They have all promised to be very good, and to keep up their prices and we are to have a weekly meeting and to be very sociable and harmonious together.'

The question of price-cutting by other firms than his own had certainly exercised his mind for some time before he rallied his fellow potters to stand firm. He wrote Bentley in this 1771 letter:

This Russian trade comes very opportunely for the useful wares, and may prevent me lowering the prices of useful wares, though it may be expedient to lower the prices of the tableplates per dozen in London, as our people are lowering them to 2/- here. In short, the general trade seems to be going to ruin on the gallop, large stocks on hand, both in London and the country, and little demand. The potters seem sensible of their situation and are quite in a panic for their trade, and indeed with great reason for *low prices* must beget *low quality* in the manufacture, which *will beget contempt, neglect and disuse* and there is an end of trade. But, if any one warehouse distinguished from the rest will continue to keep up the quality of the manufacture or improve it, that house may perhaps keep up its price.

Though Wedgwood's view in this letter carried weight with his fellow potters for a few years, this bolstering up of prices did not last long. On 14 April 1773 Wedgwood writes to Bentley: 'Our Potters had a sort of General Assembly last week to consider a reduction of their prices, and came to a resolution *nem-con to lower them* 20%, and I find that our Society and the whole pottery abide by this resolution.' This sort of a resolution posed for Wedgwood some sales problems. He asked Bentley: 'Do you think we can stand our ground in London at 5/- for plates, when everybody round us will be selling at 2/6 and 3/-?' Wedgwood, then suggested to Bentley that they should have two prices at the warehouse, 3s. 6d. and 5s. 'When the price of our plates is asked, Mr. Jennings (the warehouse clerk) may tell them that we have good plates at 3s. 6d. but that our highest finished, and as such we hold perfect and of the finest materials, are still 5/-' or, as Wedgwood suggests in keeping with the resolution to cut prices by 20 per cent., 'shall we drop the best to 4/-', or again yielding to his desire to keep prices up 'or shall we continue as we are?'

During the eighteenth century potters were always trying to establish some reliable basis for estimating the cost price of producing various wares. Wedgwood, in his correspondence with his partner Bentley from early in 1772 till Bentley's death in 1780, and even as late as 1790 in a letter to his son Josiah, was bothered with the task of finding a satisfactory method of costing his wares. Fixing prices by rule-of-thumb methods for certain plain useful pottery, that had been traditional for a century or more on the peasant potbank, may have been comparatively easy and satisfactory. But in Etruria, where Wedgwood, with his inventive and creative mind, as an artist, and practical potter, was continually experimenting with new materials, new shapes and designs, and with his production of ornamental ware, found it a great problem both for himself and his partner Bentley to determine accurate cost prices for the prolific and varying output.

A long letter to Bentley on 23 August 1772, shows Wedgwood attempting to work out a satisfactory method of breaking down into its component parts the cost price of his wares:

I have been puzzling my brains all the last week to find out proper data and methods of calculating the expense of manufacture, sale, loss etc., to be lain upon each article of our manufacture. And a very tedious business it has been, but what is worse, I find what I have done is *wrong* somewhere, very essentially so. But, I do not know where or how to amend it. What I now send you is only to show you what steps I have taken and the grounds I have gone upon. I desire you to sit down and consider the subject, and try to put me in a better way. *It will be of the greatest use to us to establish some such scale, as I have been attempting to examine all our new articles so that we may not fix the prices too high* as to prevent the sale, and not too low as to leave no profit upon them.

In some memoranda enclosed with this letter, Wedgwood attempts to set out the component items in his cost price of a vase. He has taken the cost of the clay to the wheel, allowed for loss of weight in firing, added the cost of turning the vase and finishing. These items are mainly based on wages paid for these tasks. Then he added the estimate of firing the ware, finally based on details worked out when in partnership with Whieldon. Wedgwood is frank here, and states, 'I *guessed* this from my general knowledge as a potter.' Then he added items for rent, wear and tear by working them out as a ratio of the whole factory in proportion to labour used. From these calculations Wedgwood constructed the following table:

(a) Rent, Wear and Tear $= \frac{1}{2}$
(b) Modelling and Moulds $= \frac{1}{3}$ of whole expense.
(c) Interest on Capital $= \frac{1}{4}$
(d) Loss in breakage etc. $= \frac{1}{3}$

He then proceeded to apply this yardstick to each article. The result surprised him, he said, when he compared his calculated cost of production with the fixed price of the article when sold from the factory. He wrote:

It appears very clearly from this calculation, that we have advanced the prices by inches, out of all proportion to the real expense for instance:-

	Cost Price	Selling Price
	s. d.	£. s. d.
Article 1–9 ins.	4. 10¾d.	12. 0.
„ 9–12 ins.	5. 7½.	1. 17. 0.
„ 12–14 ins.	7. 11½.	2. 0. 0.

and so on you'll observe. The total expense of manufacturing and selling of the articles at cost price is £12.12.5¾d. while the corresponding selling prices total £46.4.6d. There is certainly a great error in this calculation, and I must endeavour to find it out, and I shall be glad now you have the whole before you, if you can assist me in it.

Wedgwood would not have been so distressed had he realised that his fundamental principle in assessing the cost of production of the ware was a *minimum*, according to his breakdown of the four groups of items, rent, wear and tear etc. The selling price was a ceiling or maximum price, which as a capitalist pottery owner he expected to receive, when selling his wares, so as to make a profit. Wedgwood had anticipated a difference of some sort between the cost price and the selling price, of course, but he was shocked to find such a large difference between the two.

The fault in this arithmetical or statistical effort to find out the cost price in relation to the selling or market price, was that Wedgwood had omitted many items from his costing. He had not put down any items for his own wages or salary for superintendence of the works, nor the expense of his chemical experiments or his research. Besides, he had omitted many other items of overhead expenditure – such as heating and lighting of the factory premises and so on.

Then, Wedgwood had not realised that the selling price was often a fictitious or fancy price, having no basis in costs or items that could be calculated. It was at best sheer guesswork, especially for the decorated wares that Wedgwood classified as ornamental. The prices for goods sold in Wedgwood's showrooms and sales department were selling prices fixed arbitrarily by the manufacturer, something like the fantastic, unpredictable prices at Christie's or Sotheby's auction rooms for antiques or objects of art. The selling prices were what the market would fetch, or what the customer was prepared to pay. In other words, the fixing of the prices of much of Wedgwood's ornamental wares was to 'charge what the traffic would bear'. This is what Wedgwood and Bentley did with their ornamental vases. They continued to sell them at fancy high prices unrelated to the actual cost of production (whether or not that could be calculated exactly). Then, if they failed to sell at that fictitious price, they dropped the price and endeavoured to sell them at reduced or cut prices.

Some of the problems emerge in the Wedgwood–Bentley letters as early as 1770: 'By the enclosed account, it appears that the expense of our manufactory for one year was £1,802.4.8. Value of Produce £5,755.12.10. This account is very exact on the whole, but we cannot make it agree with its facts. It agrees with the small vases very well, but those we sell at 2 or 3 guineas do not appear to cost us one tenth of that money.' Wedgwood promises: 'I will in future, give you my opinion upon the prices of new articles. Firstly, I fear you will find a guinea and a half, too great a price for the pyramid flowerpots to sell any quantity, and we can afford them for less. Suppose you charge the Niobe 15/- (instead of a guinea and a half), if you think you can make an alteration without giving offence'. (This is a typical example of charging 'what price the traffic can bear'). Bentley, in charge of the London showroom, realised that for a certain class of customer the prices fixed by Wedgwood were too high, and beyond their reach; but for wealthy, aristocratic clients prices were hardly ever considered to be too high. Bentley had been pressing him[1] to sell cheaper vases, for other markets,

[1] 22 March 1772

as well as at the London showroom. Wedgwood replied: 'We will try to make some middle teapots, for Bath, Dublin, Liverpool and London, but as to cheap vases, I am afraid of danger here. Would it not be better to sell our seconds?' Here we see that Wedgwood is rather apprehensive of spoiling the market for high-priced vases, and therefore prefers to push inferior seconds at lower prices. It is really surprising that a business man like Wedgwood had not yet learnt the doctrine for effective and progressive salesmanship — to sell at lower prices the increasing output of mass production, and still maintain the quality of the product. Though Bentley, as a merchant at the selling end of Wedgwood's business, knew the limit to which customers would or could go for these wares, he still did not succeed in convincing Wedgwood to reduce the price of his vases. On 11 April 1772, he wrote Bentley: 'I have been thinking over the subject of *cheap vases*, and am persuaded you may have a range of shelves for that purpose, without injury to the sale of your *dear* vases.' But the cheaper priced vases were to be seconds quality.

The paradise of high prices, or the highest prices, was soon to prove a false one. Later, on 23 August 1772, Wedgwood saw the folly of too high a price. He wrote to Bentley: 'We have now upwards of 100 good forms of vases, and at one half the expense we have hitherto done.' Then he finally admits the value of lower prices as a good sales policy, and continues: 'The "Great People" have had their vases in their Palaces long enough for them to be seen and admired by the Middling Class of people, which class, we know, are vastly, I had almost said, infinitely superior in number, to the "Great." And though a great price I believe at first was necessary to make the vases esteemed ornaments for Palaces, this reason no longer exists. Their character is established and the middling people would probably buy quantities of them at a reduced price.'

Even for the rich customers, he admitted in another letter to Bentley, the prices of some of his vases were too 'salty' — 'The Grecian Vases we have, are sadly too dear, they do hurt us here, whenever we tell the price.' Wedgwood was really admitting that what modern economists call 'a saturation point at certain prices' had been reached as far as vases were concerned. Because of the large number of vases left on his hands unsold at the original high prices, Wedgwood wrote to Bentley on 18 June 1773, suggesting that customers be tempted to buy them 'at a round discount', i.e. by reducing the original price.

The trouble that Wedgwood had in fixing the price for his historic dinner service shows how much guesswork went into its calculation. In 1773 he estimated it would cost between £1,000 and £1,500. In April, he told Bentley it would cost between £3,000 and £4,000. It is true these were estimates at different stages of progress with the service. But Bentley finally computed the cost of production to be £2,410. 10s. 5d., while the price at which the service was sold to the Empress was £3,000.

Even as late as 1790, when he sent the famous Barberini Vase on tour with his son Josiah and his nephew Byerley, through Holland and Germany, Wedgwood had not solved this question of pricing his wares. The original Barberini Vase that was displayed on the tour failed to secure enough subscribers to purchase it for £50. Then, as a result of the publicity it later received, 20 were subscribed for, at £50 a piece. Writing to his son on 14 October 1790 Wedgwood said: 'I do not yet know what to say about the price. I have tried 5 more since you left us, but not one near so good as that you have. So unless we are more successful, £50 is too little to save us from loss. Perhaps it would not be amiss to say this to some of the Noblesse.'

This charging of high prices, which too often were a subjective estimate of what the public would pay, was often a short-sighted policy, and a short-lived one. It was only successful to a certain point with a potter like Wedgwood, because of his highly inventive mind in ringing the changes with a succession of ornamental and fancy wares – vases, seals, heads, flower-pots, or some other novelty. Periodically he was forced to dispose of them at a reduced figure.

Wedgwood had great difficulty in deciding what to charge for his Queen's yellow or cream table ware, which he originally sold as a service to Queen Charlotte, after whom he called it 'Queen's ware'. He writes Bentley: 'And now as to the price of this ware, whether they be deemed dear or not, I cannot say *but sure the Great Personage, they are for... can afford to pay for them* ... but I would rather not fix a price on them.' Later in 1778, Wedgwood wrote Bentley, 'Our potters have lowered their prices for they sell near 10 ins. dishes at 2/- per dozen wholesale. We are persuaded that the diminuation of our sales in London, Liverpool and abroad is owing chiefly to the very great difference between the prices of our Queen's ware, which is no longer the choice thing it used to be. Every shop, house and cottage is full of it, and other people's wares. *Without lowering prices very considerably, we shall not be able to continue our business or even sell up our enormous stock.*'

PROBLEMS OF CREDIT

Wedgwood appears to have fixed his prices for wares at first for cash sales in London. Where credit was allowed, he added so much to the cash price, as revealed in a letter to Bentley on 18 July 1766. The amount added to the cash price depended on the standing of the customer, or his 'credit'. In other cases, Wedgwood appears to have followed the practice of the potters who signed the 1770 Agreement referred to earlier, and allowed 5 per cent. off for ready money. In the case of sales abroad he tried at first to treat them as cash transactions through the London showrooms and warehouse, acting on the principle that they were retail sales. But, as time went on, he had to sell wares on credit even to the gentry and nobility. The same applied to his wholesale transactions. At first, he insisted on cash, but inevitably these orders were followed by an increasing demand for long-term credit. It is true that in these long-term credits, he was often covered by Bills of Exchange or by some guarantor named by the creditor. The high prices charged by Wedgwood for his wares encouraged customers and clients to ask for credit, or to refuse to purchase. Cash sales were high when he first opened his London warehouse, but soon credit sales predominated. Wedgwood certainly allowed a good deal of credit in his pre-Bentley partnership. He wrote his brother John on 2 August 1765: 'I have this year sent goods to the amount of £1,000 to London, all of which are owing for, and I should not care how soon I was counting some of the money.'

On 6 February 1769 he wrote Bentley from London: 'I have been a warehouseman today, whilst Cox and Swift have been collecting and they are now returned with six shillings and sixpence.' In March 1769, still in London, Wedgwood wrote Bentley: 'We continue collecting and collecting, but we get very little money. Mr. Swift has received but about £250 in all, and he has done nothing else but collect since he came to town. I must either collect in my debts, hire money or take my place amongst the whereases.' Writing later to Bentley again in London on 4 February 1770, Wedgwood says: 'I paid upwards of £12,000 at Burslem and nevertheless am as poor as a church mouse. I have set Mr. Swift to see what is become of the goods and the money. Pray do not let good people escape you without paying their bills. I shall be set in the stocks if you do. Collect, collect, my friend, set all your hands and heads to work. Send me the L'Argent, and you will see wonders. Collect £3,000, aye £3,000, not a farthing less will satisfy my architect for the next year's business, so you must either collect or take a place for me in the London Gazette.'

In this letter, Wedgwood recalled his mythical motto: 'I sell for ready money only you know!' Of course, it was a myth and nothing more than a business formula. Still, it was an ideal to aim at, and it served now and again for him to spur Swift, Cox, Bentley and all his London staff to collect debts that had a habit of piling up, to the agony of Wedgwood at the factory end at Burslem and Etruria.

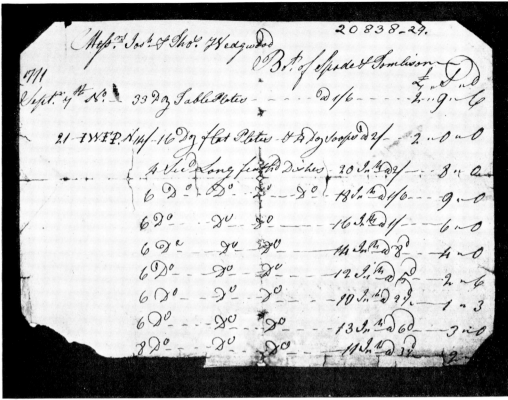

32 Documentary evidence of trading between Wedgwood and Spode

33 Josiah Spode's house, The Mount

34 A plate-maker and his jigger

35 The kilns

Matters did not improve after Wedgwood's day. In 1799, a statement prepared by Byerley to his partner Josiah Wedgwood II put the out-standing debts due to Etruria from London sales at £7,369. 18s. 6d. plus a sum of £4,857 to be written off – a legacy of the uncollected and bad debts of Josiah Wedgwood I.

The Account Books for 1800–1807 of Josiah Wedgwood II show the following figures for cash and credit sales in London:

Year	Cash Sales £	Credit Sales £
1801–2	3,988	14,825
1805–6	2,921	13,274

Nor was Wedgwood's firm the only victim of credit sales, as this table of sales compiled at another famous pottery firm in North Staffordshire – Thomas Minton – from their account books up to 1850, makes clear:

TABLE OF RECEIPTS AND CREDIT SALES AT MINTON'S POTTERY
1818 TO 1850

Year	A. Total receipts from Sales £	B. Credit Sales £	C. Wages £
1818		10,394	
19		12,670	
20		13,256	
21		14,154	
22		13,457	
23	24,369	13,528	
24	22,415	12,352	
25	33,342	13,702	
26	31,147	14,974	
27	38,429	17,831	
28	36,738	19,515	
1836	51,628	21,377	
37*	44,318	*19,483	21,633
38	51,134	23,155	22,685
39	53,988	25,791	22,953
1840*	56,934	*24,544	24,560
41*	48,485	*24,436	26,505
42	46,641	27,270	26,338
43	53,339	24,017	22,886
44	56,405	25,056	22,420
45*	56,362	*24,859	25,690
46*	57,272	*25,817	29,468
47*	52,520	*22,547	31,385
48*	53,933	*23,143	35,189
49*	58,134	*18,673	36,983
1850*	60,942	*19,637	34,907

With rare exceptions – in 1837, 1840, 1841, 1845–1850 (*) – the credit sales (B) exceeded the amount paid out in wages (C). Note also how receipts from all sales, with the exception of 1837, 1841, 1842, 1847 and 1848, all show a steady progressive increase from 1823 to 1850, when sales almost treble, while debts for credit sales increased by less than $33\frac{1}{3}$ per cent. from 1823 to 1850.

Why do credit sales figure so largely? Partly because pottery is so fragile a ware, especially the ornamental ware – vases, urns and so on – that it is impossible to sell it on sale or return terms, on account of the great risk of breakages in handling while in transit. Besides, merchants desiring to return unsold wares would never be able to pack crates or casks as efficiently as factory packers. Where creditors defaulted, as was the case with Du Burk at Amsterdam, Wedgwood had to auction off the unsold stock left, as it would incur a greater loss to send the unsold wares in crates back to London. Secondly, as suggested by the table of Minton's account of sales, it was probably because of the very high prices he charged for his decorated and ornamental wares that he had to allow such heavy credit. Conversely, it is quite as easy to argue that because of the heavy credit sales Minton (and Wedgwood before him) had to charge a high price for his wares.

Why is it, then, that potters such as Minton and Wedgwood were able to survive in spite of such heavy credit sales and debts, some of which we have seen had to be written off after Wedgwood's death by Byerley and Wedgwood's son? The Minton table recorded above supplies one cogent reason. Column A shows a mounting increase of output in production, enabling total receipts for sales to increase by 300 per cent, while debts increased over the same period by only $33\frac{1}{3}$ per cent. The increasing turnover of the factories, due to industrial developments, dwarfed even the increase in debts.

It must also be remembered that in the latter part of the eighteenth century credit arrangements for bills of exchange were not as developed and available for overseas trade as they became later, with the development of the telegraph in the first half of the nineteenth century. Nor indeed was banking developed sufficiently, in the latter half of the eighteenth century, to aid potters in the collection of their debts by means of cheque payments. Banks developed locally in the Potteries only in the second decade of the nineteenth century, when there was established in Stone a branch of the Midland, Liverpool and District Bank. The Boyle *Diary* quoted earlier, gives interesting details of his transactions with this bank, when he was a partner with Minton. Falkner in his book *The Wood Family* gives an interesting account of Enoch Wood's transactions with the local bank, the Burslem and Pottery Bank. There was a local merchant banker named T. Kinnersley, who discounted bills and made loans to local potters. Wedgwood transacted most of his business through Bentley's friend Hodgson, a merchant banker like Kinnersley, through whom Minton transacted his business, before he later transferred his account to the Manchester and Liverpool District Bank referred to by Boyle.

Shortage of coins (currency) for cash payment of wages was a problem in the eighteenth and early nineteenth centuries, till local banks were established. Even as late as 1811, we find that Josiah Wedgwood II had to write Matthew Boulton: 'I find it very difficult to get change to pay wages with. Recollecting that I have formerly had barrels of copper coin from your Soho mint, I beg to know if you will send any out. If you do, I shall be much obliged to you to order about £100 to be sent to me, and you will be so good as to draw upon me for the amount, or I will remit in any manner you please.' The following table shows consignments of penny pieces despatched from Soho to Wedgwood and Byerley, indicating their weight and value.

CONSIGNMENT OF COINS SENT FROM SOHO TO ETRURIA

Date	Casks	Conveyance	Weight	Value
June 5, 1806.	2	Canal	672lbs. 2ozs.	£67. 4. 0.
Mar. 28, 1807.	2	„	650 „ 3ozs.	£67. 4. 0.

These facts reveal the lack of banking facilities, or the absence of credit institutions with a supply of cash or credit instruments. But from 1825 onwards, as shown in cash books for 1825 to 1850 in Minton's archives, potters increasingly have dealings with banks in their sales transactions.

Among the Spode-Copeland archives is an interesting account of the savings bank established in 1834 by W. T. Copeland and Garrett. It encouraged employees to save, by paying $3\frac{1}{2}$ per cent. interest on all deposits over 15s. Then, as an additional encouragement for thrift, the pottery owners contributed a sum equal to the accumulated interest accruing to depositors who invested their savings for a term of three years.

From the picture of the growth of the potteries described in the previous 12 chapters I shall attempt, in the next, to draw certain conclusions about the economic evolution of the industry and to amplify the classification into stages of this evolution already advanced by other historians.

CHAPTER 13

Economic Stages of Evolution
in the Potteries

The historical school of German Economists, since Hildebrand Schmoller and List wrote their monographs, have attempted to classify the economic stages through which industry has passed, to reach the highly mechanized factory of the nineteenth and twentieth centuries. Carl Bucher in his book *Industrial Evolution* (1907), translated by S. M. Wickett in 1910, subjected the earlier writings to severe criticism. Later, the American Economist, Professor R. T. Ely has made a comparative study of all previous writers, who have attempted a logical classification of economic stages of evolution. Another American economic historian, Professor Day, in his *History of Commerce* has further contributed to this analysis. One of his students, inspired by his American Professor has raised the whole question by applying their analysis in particular to the factory system in England. This Fong did in his book on *The Triumph of the Factory System in England*, published in 1930. Fong attempts his classification of the successive economic stages in British Industry on the basis of the factory system, as revealed in the 1841 Census of occupations. In so far as Fong applies his general economic stages to the pottery industry from data collected in 1841, it is useful to set out his main conclusions concerning the pottery industry, as 1841 is near enough to the culminating date of this period – 1850. Fong's classification may be summarized under four heads. (1) The family-craftsman stage – consisting of members of a family, working in a peasant workshop. Many craftsmen had a by-employment. (2) The master-craftsman stage – where the master craftsman engages apprentices from outside his immediate family, and therefore has a greater workshop. A cash nexus appears in payments for service and training of apprentices, who may later work as journeymen for wages. (3) The merchant-employer stage, where the merchant employs apprentices and journeymen to make wares and products for him, as a merchant to sell. Fong is perfectly right in pointing out, that in his researches he never came across any example of the Merchant-Employer Stage. I shall return to this point later, as my researches point to a stage that can replace this one, which Fong failed to trace in the Potteries. (4) The factory stage, where the industrialist or capitalist manufacturer employs 'hands' in his factory to produce wares and products, which the factory owner sells direct to wholesalers, retail shops, or direct to customers from his factory or showrooms. How do these stages apply to the pottery industry? The small potworks before 1730 consisted of a small oven or firing shed attached to the homestead farm or croft. The people engaged in the actual potting-shop consisted of the father, with perhaps a son or younger brother, helping the master-craftsman. He was a handyman, who could throw clay on his potters' wheel, worked by a kick wheel or turned by a younger member of the family, or perhaps one of his women folk, who could be spared occasionally from household or farm duties. The master craftsman could turn the ware, he could 'stouk' handles on cups or mugs, and he could finish his wares ready for firing. He perhaps would produce wares for his own family and relatives, or he might make wares to sell at the local market town or at neighbouring fairs. He was not a full-time potter, for he had some other part-time work on his croft, or at an inn he owned, or possibly, like Dr. Thomas Wedgwood, he was also a barber-surgeon. These jobs other than potting Fong calls 'by-employment.'

The third stage mentioned by Fong in his general deduction, he terms the merchant-employer stage. He quite rightly concludes, that this third stage is not in evidence in the pottery industry at all, in complete contrast with the situation he traces in the textile industries of this merchant-employer phase of development.

Fong set this conclusion of industry in the following Table:

STAGES IN THE EVOLUTION OF INDUSTRY IN 1840 IN ORDER
OF IMPORTANCE

Industry	*First*	*Second*	*Third*
Pottery	Factory System	Craftsman System	Merchant-Employer System Nowhere found in Pottery

Note Fong's first stage, the earliest phase, has vanished by 1840 – the stage of Family (peasant) craftsman.

With the elimination of this non-existent third stage of evolution – merchant-employer, the gap must be filled by putting forward an alternative stage or phase. There did exist a real stage between the master craftsman and the factory stage. It was one where the master craftsman employed merchants to sell his wares for him, instead of the master craftsman selling his wares himself at fairs or markets.

The term I would suggest for this third important stage in the evolution of pottery manufacture is the employer-merchant stage. Earlier chapters record this important phase in the case of Wedgwood, Spode and Minton, as well as others selling their wares through Merchants in Liverpool, Birmingham and London, long before they established their own sales departments and show-rooms in London and elsewhere.

So the progressive evolution of economic stages in the North Staffordshire pottery industry, may be shown in the table.

TABLE OF STAGES

(a)	(b)	(c)	(d)
Family-Craftsman Stage	Master-Craftsman Stage	Employer-Merchant Stage	Factory Stage

In the first part of this book, then, I have attempted to show the development of pottery manufacture and distribution through the period of crucial change of the Industrial Revolution, 1730–1850.

These were years of crucial change, too, for the human beings involved – both pottery manufacturers and workers. And it is these changes the second half of this book describes.

PART II

MASTERS AND MEN

CHAPTER 14

Concerted Action

The Potteries of North Staffordshire are a concentration of factories within a compact area, about seven miles long by three miles wide. This enabled the potters to have close contact with one another on matters of common interest when occasion required.

Under the leadership of two of the leading potters – Thomas Whieldon and Josiah Wedgwood, the question of constructing a canal to serve the Potteries was first taken up.[1] Both were treasurers of the first subscription list for canal agitation. This voluntary association of potters was established as early as 1765, though it is only fair to point out that they joined forces with other individuals – landlords, coalowners and farmers. On the other hand, it must be emphasized that the leading spirits were potters, and among them, Wedgwood was pre-eminent. No potter by himself could construct a turnpike road or a canal, so leading potters co-operated, not only with their fellow potters, but also with other members of the community. The experience gained in this early association with landlords, financiers, politicians, coalowners and others in transport ventures, at inland navigation general assemblies (as the canal shareholders meetings were called) was an excellent training for potters to learn to associate, for more strictly pottery industry affairs. As Bowden says in his *Industrial Society in England in the Eighteenth Century* – 'The history of these early organizations of great industrialists is in many cases extremely obscure, and it is difficult in some instances to distinguish between informal or temporary groupings for concerted action in specific cases, and formally constituted bodies for exerting continuous influence on economic policies.' Bowden, though excellent on cotton and iron masters of Manchester and Birmingham, has little evidence of potters' organizations, except for the activities of Josiah Wedgwood.

The first evidence of concerted or collective action amongst potters is found in a letter from Wedgwood to Bentley on 14 February 1767. It refers to a letter from a partner of Chaffer, china manufacturer of Liverpool, about a higher duty

[1] See Chapter 8

on china. Chaffer had written to Sir W. Meredith, the Liverpool M.P., and to his fellow Liverpool potters asking for their support for a higher duty. Wedgwood writes: 'I am afraid our Pottery [i.e. group of North Staffordshire potters] will not be persuaded to think themselves so much interested in getting higher duty laid upon foreign china. . . . My brother is trying what he can with them, and I shall sense the account of his labours.'

Probably the views of potters on duties and prohibitions would be obtained casually, when some of them met at one of the many Navigation or Trunk Road Committees. But by 1773 the consultations became more organised: 'Our potters had a sort of General Assembly the last week to consider a reduction of their prices and came to a resolution *nem con* to lower them 20%, and I find that our Society and the whole Pottery abode by this decision.'[1]

This General Assembly (or association of potters) antedates by four years the Midland Association of Ironmasters formed in 1777. This informal type of gathering of potters for consideration of specific matters was meeting in 1775. Wedgwood writes: 'I did not sign the American petition handed about here for several reasons. The chief was that we had very lately petitioned as a body of Staffs. Potters, and I think as we have in that and other respects distinguished ourselves as a particular body of men (though not corporate), it will be right to continue our applications, when they are proper to be made at all in the same mode.'[2] But soon the business was to be formally established.

The first reference to a definite corporate committee of potters is found in a letter from Wedgwood to Bentley on 7 February 1776. Because of its historical importance, it is worth quoting in full:

My dear friend would receive a letter yesterday by Mr. Byerley, in his official capacity as Clerk of the Committee of Potters, with their thanks to Lord North for his kind attention to the interests of our Manufactory, and their opinion that lowering the duties upon foreign European Porcelains and Earthenwares, in return for much indulgencies as his Lordship can obtain for our Manufactories may be of considerable advantage to our trade and cannot injure it in any respect. But, they hope it is not intended to lower the duties upon Asiatic Porcelains, as we can have no motive or expectation of receiving any reciprocal advantages for that measure from our East India Co., but on the contrary, it would be the most effectual step, which could be taken to prevent our future improvement or any further attempts to rival that beautiful manufactory.

Having by 1776 established their corporate body the potters tackled three main groups of problems: supplies of vital raw materials for the pottery; protection and keeping secret processes and methods of production of wares; and relations between manufacturers and their employees.

In an earlier chapter[3] mention is made of a meeting of Potters called together

---

[1] Wedgwood to Bentley 14 April 1773   [2] To Bentley 14 November 1775   [3] Chapter 3

at Moreton's-on-the-Hill, to receive reports from Wedgwood and Turner on their return from Cornwall, after the fight in London against Champion's Bill from 1774–1775. After this meeting Wedgwood tried to get the 'Committee of Potters', with Tom Byerley as their Secretary to institute an 'Experimental Research Works' – but 'Our experimental work expired in embrio last night. We could not settle the question whether the partners in Company should pay separately or jointly.[1]

Fortunately I discovered in the Wedgwood Archives at Etruria a minute book of the North Staffordshire Committee of Potters (with corroborative evidence of its activities in Wedgwood's 'Commonplace Books' and other documents) giving details of the preliminary steps taken at the first meeting of this 'Committee of Commerce for the Manufactory of Pottery.' In the opening pages of the minute book are the following words: 'Great inconvenience having been felt in this Manufactory in several recent instances for the want of a Standing Body, invested with powers to act as occasion required in the conduct and protection of its Public Interests and concerns. A general meeting of the manufacturers was held at the Etruria Inn, on Thursday the 11th Nov. 1784.' This paragraph is followed by a list of 13 potters, with Wedgwood heading them as Chairman. Then follows: 'The expediency of forming a Committee of Commerce to watch over and conduct the public interest and concerns of the manufactory upon a plan similar to those already adopted by many other commercial bodies in this Kingdom was taken into consideration, and having been weighed and considered, it was unanimously resolved "That in the opinion of this meeting that it is expedient and will be highly advantageous in this Manufactory to establish such a Committee".'

There were at least three such 'Committees of Commerce' outside the Potteries, at Birmingham, Manchester and Edinburgh. In the minutes for 30 November 1784, a resolution read that 'The Chairman [Wedgwood] be desired to communicate the proceedings of the former meetings and this, to the Committee of Commerce at Birmingham and Manchester.' Then on 6 October 1786, it is recorded 'That Mr. Wedgwood laid before the Committee a letter received from the Chairman of the Edinburgh Chamber of Commerce and Manufacturers.'

This minute book of the Potteries Chamber of Commerce antedates the minute book of the Manchester Chamber of Commerce, which dates from 1794–1801. The Birmingham Commercial Society, though founded in 1783, a year earlier than the Potteries Chamber of Commerce, unfortunately has no minute book extant.

[1] Wedgwood to Bentley December 1775

At the adjourned meeting of the Potteries Committee of Commerce held on 18 November 1784, the enlarged body passed unanimously the eight resolutions submitted as a basis for the constitution on regulations for the Society. Among these was the rule for an annual meeting to be called. The Committee to consist of 21 members, 14 drawn by lot from among the potters, who would later elect the remaining seven members or their substitutes. Later annual meetings would elect the above seven by ballot. All records were to be kept in a minute book accessible to all members. The last resolution empowers six members, one of whom is William Adams, a close friend of Wedgwood, to wait upon the principal potters, and invite them to the next meeting. The joint secretaries of the Committee of Commerce were Messrs. Sparrow and Caldwell, Solicitors of Newcastle-under-Lyme.

The success of this canvass for members by Adams and his colleagues is revealed by the record attendance of 35 potters at the subsequent meeting of the Chamber of Commerce on 30 November 1784.

The potters' Chamber of Commerce discussed the supply of raw materials, protection of manufacturers from foreign (overseas) potters, and expansion of trade and commerce abroad. On 22 February 1785, a resolution points to 'the expediency of appointing an agent at the places where clay is raised, to superintend the getting of the same and to prevent any but such as is of proper quality from being sent.' Flint stones are the next item of consideration after clay: 'The meeting having also taken into consideration the present competition in the purchase of flint stones and the mischiefs attending it, and the advances occasioned in the price of the material — recommend it to the Committee to consider whether some mode cannot be adopted to remedy these evils.'

The question of clay and flint stones came up for discussion again at a general meeting on 21 December 1785. It was resolved to ask Mr. Fanshaw of Stoke to go to Devonshire to find out about the clay question. On flints 'it was agreed to send some person to Liverpool and Preston to see where the injury was done to them before they arrive here'. Mr. Fanshaw reported to the Committee on his visit to Devonshire at the meeting held 27 January 1786, and it was fully confirmed that the Pottery had been very greatly imposed upon for many years past in the purchase, freight and weight of the article.' Everyone present at the meeting agreed 'in the opinion that the late concessions of the clay factors were by no means adequate.' It was 'determined that no concessions they made, or will make, could be sufficient to induce us to renew our correspondence with men, who had so basely forfeited every claim to any confidence in them.' At an adjourned meeting held at Hanley on 7 February 1786, 'The clay business was taken into consideration when Messrs. Chatterley, Heath and Shelley were requested to take a journey into Devonshire to lease some clays and settle other matters necessary for the better processing of that material.'

The potters had three worries: First, the possibility of potters' tools and machinery being exported. Secondly, the possibility of secret pottery processes and formulae being stolen by spies and taken abroad; and thirdly, the real danger of pottery workers emigrating and being employed by rival potters abroad.

At a meeting on 27 January 1786, Wedgwood, from the chair, read a letter from the Secretary of the General Chamber of Manufacturers of Great Britain,[1] stating that he had received information from the Commercial Committee at Birmingham of their intention to apply for an Amendment of the Act (25 Geo. 3, Cap 67) for prohibiting the exportation of tools and implements. 'The General Chamber will be happy to receive any information it may be in the power of this Society to communicate on the subject not only as it may relate to the manufacture of metal, but any other unprotected branch, and also a list of such Tools, Implements and Utensils in our manufacture – to prevent foreigners from obtaining from this country.' The later minute records: 'That our Secretary be instructed to represent that the Committee of Potters – have taken the said letter into consideration and request to have Potters' wheels and lathes for plain, round and for engine turning inserted in the list, for prohibiting the exportation of tools.'

As shown in an earlier chapter[2] potters spied into one another's processes. They obviously could and would not take any joint action to prevent this. But foreign manufacturers spying on British potteries was quite another matter, which called for prompt action. So on 24 August 1789: 'Josiah Wedgwood from the Chair read a letter from the Searcher's office at the London Custom House, dated 20 August. It stated that various articles for exportation had been stopt on suspicion of their having been collected for the establishing a manufactory of earthenware at Copenhagen and very politely offering permission to inspect the same.' Wedgwood also read a letter from Byerley, his London Agent: 'On receipt of the above notice, Byerley and a Mr. Neale went to inspect the articles. They found single specimens of earthenware made in this country, biscuit pitchers, plates with enamelled borders and plain, numbered and the prices on them. Some pitchers with trials of cobalt, clay and lead, manganese etc. About a dozen fine lawns, such as are used in the pottery, which collection appeared to have been made with no other view than to convey information to manufactories abroad.' Wedgwood read further that: 'There was a large bound manuscript

[1] See Chapter 15 for an account of this body   [2] See Chapter 2

book in the Danish or German language full of drawings of different machines and engines. The Commissioner would seize and destroy such articles as the manufacturers on examination should deem improper to be sent abroad and that the foreigner to whom they belong is a Dane by name Ljungberg.'

The Chamber of Commerce decided 'To request that the said volume be detained and obtain permission to have it translated and examined by manufacturers . . .' and expressing thanks to the Commissioners for their attention. At the next meeting of potters on 20 January 1790, Mr. Byerley gave an account of the correspondence with various Chambers of Commerce relative to the detention of the tools and the translation of the MSS. book obtained by the Commissioners. This discovery of spies in the Potteries made Wedgwood and his fellow potters more careful about the admission of foreign visitors to Etruria and other establishments.

But an even more serious matter was emigration by pottery employees. At a meeting of the Committee of Potters held on 16 July 1790, Wedgwood, as Chairman, laid before them a letter from a G. Buckley of Baltimore in North America to a Newcastle solicitor. The letter dated 15 January 1790, referred to Mr. Buckley's friend in New York who had prevailed on him to write the letter asking the solicitor friend to find 'one good turner' and 'a good moulder', as well as one to superintend a pottery, 'one who understands every branch of the business and the constructing of kilns. . . . To such a one he will give 100 guineas and pay his passage.' Then follows a copy of the letter from Abraham Wilson dated 7 December 1789: 'Sir, I have lately erected works for the purpose of carrying on a manufactory of white and cream coloured earthenware. Hearing that you are an expert workman at the moulding business I write you to come to New York by the first opportunity that offers. I will pay 10 guineas for your passage and will allow you one guinea a week for your wages for the space of 2 years. If you are pleased with your situation, and I with your performance, you shall be kept in employ as long as you please.'

Wedgwood had long before 1790 devoted a good deal of attention to this question of emigration of pottery hands. As early as 2 March 1765, he had written to Sir William Meredith M.P.:

The bulk of our manufacture is exported to foreign markets – the Continent and N. America. This trade to our colonies we are apprehensive of losing in a few years, as they have set on foot some Potworks there. They have an agent amongst us hiring a number of our hands for establishing a Potworks in S. Carolina, having got one of our insolvent Master Potters, there to conduct them. They have material there equal if not superior to our own. As the necessaries of life and consequently the price of labour are daily upon the advance, I make no question, but more will follow them and from their brother artists.

Julia Wedgwood in her *Personal life of Josiah Wedgwood* gives more details of
this emigration of workers and names the master potter referred to in the letter
above as a Mr. Bartlem. He had been offered a government subsidy to encourage
the manufacture of pottery in Carolina.

Earlier, Wedgwood had to stem the flow of pottery workers to France.
He countered the efforts of French pottery manufacturers to persuade workmen to leave Britain by publishing one of his most vigorous pamphlets. He
published in 1783 *To the Workmen in the Pottery on the subject of entering the
service of Foreign Manufacturers*. It was a plea containing some frank warning,
and some threats and penalties. Wedgwood in the opening paragraphs of his
pamphlet, gave a lurid description of the suffering of those hands who emigrated
to the Colonies referred to above. He stressed the ordeal of crossing the Atlantic,
and the further disasters on arrival at Carolina. 'The promised work was
abandoned and only one person returned to England.' This one, William Ellis
of Hanley, informed Wedgwood on his return that 'workers never received half
the promised pay – a guinea a week and their keep'. Wedgwood described in
detail 'the fate of eight emigrant workers seduced by these tempting offers, who
were reduced to begging their bread in the streets of Philadelphia'.

After this historical retrospect of the disasters of emigrating to America in
1765, Wedgwood then devotes the latter part of his pamphlet to the danger of
emigration to France in 1783. Wedgwood referred to 'the efforts of a George
Shaw, a deserter, who ventured after a 10 years exile to set foot in a country
where his life was forfeit as a decoy duck for a pottery in France'. Wedgwood in
most trenchant words described the duplicity of this Shaw, as agent for French
pottery owners. Then he passes on to play on the emotions and feelings of would-
be emigrants, referring to the suffering from home-sickness in a foreign land.
'A disease of the mind peculiar to people in a strange land, a kind of heart sickness and despair with an unspeakable longing after their native country not to
be described, and of which no one can have a just idea, but those who have been
under its influence. Most travellers have felt it in a greater or less degree; many
have died of it and those who have recovered declare it to be worth death itself.'
From this dark picture of fear, Wedgwood passes to a passage appealing to the
patriotism of pottery hands:

Would it have no weight with you to think that you were ruining a trade which has taken the united
efforts of some thousands of people for more than an age to bring to the perfection it has now attained –
a perfection nowhere else to be found – an object exciting at once the envy and emulation of all Europe?
But they will ever be harmless to us whilst we are true to ourselves. For Englishmen in arts and manufactures, as well as in arms, can only be conquered by Englishmen. The enemy must first gain over some
traitors and renegadoes among ourselves, before they can obtain any decisive advantage.

Wedgwood becomes rhetorical: 'Is there a man among you then, who will stand forth and acknowledge himself to be that traitor to his country and fellow workmen? Who will openly avow, that for the sake of a paltry addition to his wages for a few years, he would betray their interests and wantonly throw away into the hands of foreigners, perhaps of enemies, the superiority we here laboured for and obtained?'

Wedgwood closes his pamphlet by quoting in full two Acts, imposing fines of £500 against anyone who should induce either workmen or manufacturers to leave this country. The fact that still in 1790 the Committee of Potters were forced to discuss the problem of emigration of pottery workers proves that Wedgwood's early efforts in 1765 and later in 1783 to stem the emigration tide had not been very effective.

After Wedgwood's day, and particularly between 1830 and 1850, the North Staffordshire Pottery Trade Unions openly advocated emigration of pottery workers and actually prepared elaborate colonization schemes to finance and assist workers wanting to leave the Potteries. The anti-emigration Acts of the Georges had become dead letters, and during the early decades of the nineteenth century trade union organization had become a power in the open, after the failure of the Combination Acts.

The increase in the emigration of potters and their workmen from North Staffordshire to U.S.A. can be traced in the researches of Edwin Attlee Barber recorded in *The Pottery and Porcelain of the United States*. After making a passing reference to Bartlem's emigration to America in 1766, Barber states, 'Not till 1769 was there any serious attempt to manufacture fine china on this side of the Atlantic.' Quoting as his authority Watson's *Annals of Philadelphia* he writes, 'A china factory was also erected in Prince St., near the present navy yard to make china at a saving of £15,000.' Barber unearthed some advertisements of these early American potteries. He quotes a Boston (Mass.) pottery advertising on 16 October 1769, 'Wanted immediately at the New Factory in New Boston, 4 boys for apprentices to learn the art of making Tortoise Shell, Cream and Green colour plates, dishes, coffee and tea-pots, cups and saucers and all other articles in the Potters' business equal to any imported from England. Any persons inclining to bind such lads to the aforesaid is desired to apply to the factory.'

Barber quotes in full the announcements of the proprietors of the Southwark (Pa.) China works, their new venture in white china ware 'warranted equal to any imported from England in goodness and cheapness'. He also quotes an interesting document relating to a lottery ticket, entitled 'New Castle Lottery

36 Placing the ware in the oven

THE
POTTERS' EXAMINER,
AND WORKMAN'S ADVOCATE.

" GOD, AND OUR RIGHT. "

No. 7. Vol. 1. SATURDAY, JAN. 13TH, 1844. *Price One Penny.*

No. 23. Vol. 3. SATURDAY, MAY 3RD, 1845. *Price One Penny.*

37 *The Potter's Examiner*, 1844

– for the encouragement of the American China Manufacture. This ticket enables the bearer to such prize as may be drawn against its number, free from any deduction'. Alas, this lottery scheme did not save the pottery, for it closed down in two years.

The first emigrant craftsman mentioned is James Lycett, who belonged to a family of potters in Stoke-on-Trent. He established a stoneware pottery at Norwich, Connecticut, in 1780. He claimed his grandfather built kilns for the Spode works, when the first porcelain was made there in 1800. His father and uncle came to the United States in 1849. Barber also mentions the Ohio Valley Pottery, belonging to John Hancock, who came from Staffordshire in 1828 and at first erected a pottery at S. Amboy. (N.J.) In 1829, Hancock sent to Stoke-on-Trent for his wife and son Frederick to come to America, bringing with them two turners – one from Minton's Pottery named Bernard Houston and another, as well as a thrower, C. Harrison. On the arrival of these extra workmen, Hancock had his pottery finished and commenced to produce yellow ware. Barber adds, 'John Hancock was a potter of large and varied experience having served an apprenticeship at Etruria with Josiah Wedgwood'. James Clewes operated the extensive pottery at Cobridge, Staffordshire, from 1820–1829. 'It is not generally known that after the closing of his big English works in 1829, he came to the U.S.A. and took charge of a pottery at Troy (Indiana) which was selected because of its favourable situation on the Ohio River.' Later 'Mr. Clewes returned to England, where he died in 1856, at the age of 70. He was a remarkable manufacturer in his day, and at one time ammassed considerable wealth much of which he subsequently lost.'

Barber mentions the sad case of George Walker, the son-in-law of W. Billingsley, an artist, who first painted for Spode and other potters in North Staffordshire. He established a famous pottery at Nantgarw, S. Wales, where he died. George Walker left Nantgarw and established a pottery at West Troy making teapots. 'Alas, he died poor', says Barber.

Fortunately, Wedgwood recorded in detail, in his commonplace book the steps taken by him on behalf of himself and his fellow potters to protect, and where possible expand their markets, as early as 1773, ante-dating the formation of the Potters' Committee of Commerce. Wedgwood reports of his meeting Lord Rochford about the new French Treaty with England on Commerce, and presenting a memorial on behalf of the 'Manufacturers of Earthenware in North Staffordshire'. The memorial says, 'They therefore humbly hope that their manufacture will be thought worthy of some attention as a national object in the present Treaty of Commerce.' Later at a meeting on 30 November 1784, correspondence was read acknowledging the receipt of the Memorial by the Rt. Hon. W. Pitt and the Marquis of Carmarthen – the latter pledging 'to the utmost of my power to promote the advantage of so valuable a branch of our commerce'. Then in December 1785 Mr. Eden, the Minister in charge of the Bill, invited a delegation from the Potteries to meet the Privy Council. Wedgwood 'was requested to take that trust upon him'. The minutes of the Potters' Committee later record the discussion over the terms of the treaty 'in which it was stipulated that 12% duty *ad valorem* be imposed on Porcelain, Earthenware and Pottery imported into each country'. They were invited to send persons to attend the Lords of the Committee to describe and rate the articles to be imported. At a meeting held 6 November 1786, the potters decided after hearing a report from Wedgwood and his two fellow delegates to forward a further memorial to the Commissioners of Customs pointing out the difficulty in classifying wares to be imported and their prices, and suggesting a 'duty *ad valorem* on the invoice would be the simplest and most equitable and best mode in every respect'. This memorial was despatched on 19 October 1786, signed by Wedgwood, Warburton and Neale, the delegates.

It is important to note that in all these Treaty of Commerce negotiations the Potters' Association acted without the mediation of the National Chamber of Commerce. It was successfully accomplished by the skill of Wedgwood, aided by two fellow potters, and the political pull of Lord Gower, and some of Wedgwood's close political friends in Liverpool and the Midlands.

CHAPTER 15

The National Chamber of Manufacturers

From the outset, Wedgwood and the other potters in their newly-formed Committee or Chamber of Commerce decided to enter into correspondence with similar bodies in Birmingham, Edinburgh and Manchester.

As early as 1784, the Chairman of the Birmingham Chamber of Commerce, Samuel Garbett, a close friend of Watt and Boulton, had written to Wedgwood about a projected Government tax, which Birmingham manufacturers opposed on the grounds: 'That the population and riches of this kingdom, essentially depend on its manufactures and taxes laid upon them are impolitic. Property acquired by trade and manufacture is a fit object of taxation, but not the manufactures themselves.' In a further resolution against the tax they stated, 'It tends to depress or crush the ardour of invention and those adventurous attempts after every improvement and new discovery, to which many of the British manufacturers owe that superiority which they have attained.'

So, the Birmingham manufacturers decided: 'that in order as far as it lies in us to counteract the opinion, which has long prevailed, that manufactures are proper objects of taxation, it has become necessary to correspond with the Commercial Committees and eminent merchants and manufacturers in different parts of the kingdom in order to represent such particulars to the Government respecting exports to foreign countries and to the manufactures which are established there, as may be thought most effectual for the protection of British manufactures in general.'

The resolution went on: 'And also to represent that the mines of coal, iron, copper, tin, lead, calamine and clay, together with manufactures very much contribute to the rank this country bears among nations. It is essential for persons to form some mode of corresponding in order to remonstrate against injudicious taxes.' Unfortunately, during the early decades of the eighteenth century, the only method of influencing the Government open to manufacturers was that of petitioning or memorializing the Government, as Wedgwood did with the support of his fellow potters on the Champion Bill and later on the commercial treaty with France. Wedgwood's watchfulness and his personal standing with prominent politicians and statesmen in both Houses of Parliament gave a certain amount of protection and immunity to the pottery industry.

But Pitt's Fustian Tax was imposed on the cotton industry, in spite of the frantic efforts of the Manchester Chamber of Commerce to get support from Glasgow manufacturers, as well as the Birmingham Chamber of Commerce. As Bowden states, 'They were treated with a humiliating condescension . . . but under the new conditions hostility was thereby aggravated and the tendency towards general united opposition was given powerful incentive.'

There is a consensus of opinion amongst such writers as Bowden, Mantoux and Redford in their accounts of the history of the General Chamber of Manufacturers, that Wedgwood had taken a prominent part in its initiation and later progress – but coupled with a sharing of the credit 'with Birmingham and cotton manufacturers.' Ashton, in his *Iron and Steel in the Industrial Revolution*, says Bowden gives too much credit to the cotton manufacturers, and tries to restore the balance by emphasizing the part played by the Birmingham manufacturers.

But so little had been written about the rise of the General Chamber of Manufacturers, till Bowden dealt with it, that much that has been written before and since Bowden is open to revision and revaluation in the light of fresh evidence. Other evidence shows the vital part played by Wedgwood in the formation of the General Chamber of Manufacturers with the loyal and consistent support and approval of his potters, through their Chamber of Commerce in North Staffordshire.

The idea of a Society of Manufacturers in Britain germinated in Wedgwood's mind in connection with the need to combat the emigration of pottery workers, as early as 1783. He sent James Watt a copy of his 'Emigration' pamphlet, referred to in the last chapter, and on 30 January 1784, Wedgwood acknowledged Watt's comments in the following letter:

Etruria.

Dear Watt,

I thank you for your kind letter of the 28th and am most pleased to find the little thing I wrote to my brothers in the pottery, has met with your approbation. The subject seems of sufficient importance to employ an abler pen, and I wish it may be taken up amongst you [referring to the Birmingham Committee of Commerce, of which Watt and Boulton were active and leading members], for it is far from being exhausted. With a little assistance from gentlemen in the alteration of one of our laws and a Society formed out of the more powerful manufactories in different parts of the island more of the evil emigration might be prevented.

(Signed) Jos. Wedgwood

The last sentence gives the 'germ' of the General Chamber of Commerce of British Manufacturers expressed by Wedgwood to a fellow manufacturer,

Watt in Birmingham, where one can be sure Watt would discuss the idea or project with his colleagues Matthew Boulton and Samuel Garbett, and other Ironmasters of Birmingham. This idea later developed into a positive scheme by Wedgwood, who had been in London, as a delegate from the Potters' Committee of Commerce to the Privy Council, regarding the Irish Treaty. This can be confirmed by quoting the following letter from Wedgwood to Matthew Boulton, discovered in the Boulton M.S. Westwood Collection Assay Office:

Maidenhead, Feb, 21, 1785.

I go by Birmingham as you desired and will endeavour to see Mr. Garbett and one or two more at the hotel. I mean to recommend to them the measure of a Committee of Delegates from all the manufacturing places in England and Scotland to meet and sit in London all the time the Irish Commercial affairs are pending. This strikes me as a measure, which may be productive of very beneficial effects, principally in forming and cementing a commercial bond, which may be of great use upon others, as well as by the present occasion.

This letter clearly sets out the proposal to set up a piece of new machinery of a national character to enable industrial capitalists to deal with the Government of the day on issues affecting them. Though prompted by the desire to oppose the Government on this specific question of the Irish Treaty proposals, Wedgwood distinctly suggests 'the machinery could be set in motion and of great use upon others, as well as by the present occasion.'

When Wedgwood returned to the Potteries from Birmingham on 22 February he called a meeting of the Committee of Commerce. Here in the minutes of that meeting of Potters, we read for the first time of the proposal to form a National Chamber of Commerce.

Wedgwood reported, 'That he had conversed with many of the principal manufacturers from Birmingham and other places on the subject, who had agreed to send a delegate from their respective manufactories in order to form a meeting in London to watch the progress of this business in Parliament.' Then the minute continues, 'And he therefore recommended it to the consideration of this meeting, whether it will not be advisable to send a delegate on the part of this manufactory to act in concert with the delegates from others in a business of so much national importance.' Inevitably, the Potters selected Wedgwood to represent them at the London meeting of the General Chamber of Commerce.

The preliminary gathering of delegates from the various manufactories took place on 7 March 1785 at the London Tavern, Bishopsgate Street, to consider the Irish Treaty proposals. John Wilkinson, the Ironmaster presided. Julia Wedgwood erroneously says that Wedgwood presided at the meeting. What she really meant was that Josiah Wedgwood was the Committee Chairman, negotiating the treaty proposals with the Privy Council.

This meeting adjourned till 10 March, when Sir Herbert Hackworth presided. It unanimously agreed: 'It is the opinion of this meeting that a probable means of producing such an opinion and free intercourse would be the establishments of a Chamber of Manufacturers in London to watch over their interests at large as one aggregate, to communicate and correspond with the several Committees, which are or may be established in different parts of Great Britain.'

Other resolutions deal with officers suggested for such a Chamber, and the election of a standing committee to draw up proper regulations and to transact such business and affairs as could not conveniently be delayed from the time of one meeting of the Chamber to another. Wedgwood was elected the Chairman of the standing committee, and they planned to meet on 14 March to draft the rules. But the situation regarding the Irish Treaty became so critical, that Wedgwood called a special committee at the London Tavern on 12 March. They had no time to discuss the rules at this meeting, so Wedgwood called the meeting to meet again to discuss draft rules. The minute relating to this meeting held on 14 March, states, 'That they received many letters from various parts of this kingdom approving highly of the institution of a Chamber of Manufacturers of Great Britain, and offering suggestions for its future regulations, but the business of each day had pressed so hard upon the Committee that they have not yet been able to prepare any digested state of particulars for the consideration of the meeting.'

The above report of the Select Committee meeting of 14 March with Wedgwood in the Chair, was actually presented by Mr. Silvester from Manchester in the absence of Wedgwood, at the next General Meeting at London Tavern, where Matthew Boulton presided on 22 March.

Both Bowden in his *Industrial Society in England* in his account on the General Chamber of Commerce, and Redford in his *Economic History of England*, state that 'the plan for the new Chamber was presented by a Manchester delegate'.

They are wrong, for no plan was ready for the 14 March meeting, the last referred to by Bowden and Redford. I have been unable to trace any minute relating to meetings of the General Chamber of Commerce after the above held on 22 March. However, I have been fortunate enough to find in the Boulton archives the minutes of the standing committees presided over by Wedgwood, and so can trace the story of the proceedings of the meetings of the select committees presided over by Wedgwood, in their attempts to present the draft rules of the General Chamber, by quoting relevant reports of progress contained in various letters Wedgwood wrote to Matthew Boulton, from a period beginning 29 April to 31 May 1785.

The first letter is dated 29 April 1785.

10 Grt. George St.

Dear Boulton,

Mr. Russell, the soapboiler, and two of his friends have deceived me very much today. He promised to attend the Committee and assist to prepare and sign a petition. I got the materials — a lawyer and a skin of parchment ready, but they have made some excuse. The iron people have found it out, that they shall be ruined and are to meet us in a body at the General Chamber tomorrow.

Jos. Wedgwood.

In a second letter, dated 1 May, Wedgwood reported to Boulton the proceedings of the General Meeting held on 30 April.

Sir Herbert Hackworth opened the meeting with a very handsome speech in praise of the institution, exhorting us to continue as we had hitherto done, detached from all party views. At the conclusion of his speech he called upon me, as Chairman of the Committee to lay before them such matters prepared for the consideration of the meeting, upon which, I first produced some regulations for the Society. These took us near 2 hours in debating. The principal difficulty was to fix upon the meaning of the term 'manufacturer'. The Manchester gentlemen seem to have it fixed in their own mind that a calico printer was not a 'manufacturer'. I found the debate was not likely to be soon ended, and that it grew rather warm.

These difficulties of definition were left for each Chamber of Commerce to settle amongst themselves on Wedgwood's recommendation.

Wedgwood wrote to Boulton on 29 April: 'The iron people here have now found out that they will be ruined and are to meet us in a body at the General Chamber tomorrow. We now sigh daily for the amendments of the Iron petitions, and some good men to speak to them.' Two days later Wedgwood wrote: 'I am extremely sorry Mr. Garbett is not coming. For myself I have only one plain simple line of conduct to pursue. I have promised those who sent me hither to do my best to prevent the Irish Resolutions passing into law. I have done so hitherto, and will continue in the same course, though I am even left to do so alone.'

A worse blow was to follow for Boulton himself withdrew from the fight, which led Wedgwood to write him, 'The loss our cause maintained when you left us, will not early be retrieved.' Boulton probably withdrew as the result of pressure from his partner James Watt, who sent Boulton on 31 March a sharp letter: 'I find myself quite unequal to the business now lying behind, and wish you were at home and direct your attention solely to your own, and to Boulton and Watt's business.' This was an extraordinary letter, as Watt had earlier written a pamphlet circulated by the General Chamber entitled, 'An answer to the Treasury paper on the Iron Trade of England and Ireland'.

Wedgwood was deeply disturbed at the defection of the Iron Masters of Birmingham, as he shows in his letter to Boulton: 'The Minister is using every engine to prevent persons who are likely to be injured from coming forward. The gentlemen of the Iron Trade, who promised to attend our meeting yesterday, did not one of them make their appearance.' Then Wedgwood really hits out at some of the defectors: 'The principal glover of this town has a contract under the Government, so he cannot come. The buttonmaker makes buttons for His Majesty, and he is tied fast to His Majesty's Minister's buttonhole. In short, this Minister has found so many buttons and loopholes to fasten them to himself, that few of the powerful manufacturers are left at liberty to serve their country.'

Having got this off his chest, Wedgwood proceeded to plead: 'Here I cannot help expressing my wish, which shall be once for all, that my good and worthy friends Garbett and Reynolds would see the great call of their country in the light that it surely deserves, it would be 50 times more effective than the call of any house I am acquainted with here.' In a later letter on 5 May to Boulton, Wedgwood writes: 'Mr. Crawshay (of S. Wales) the great iron merchant, has expressed his surprise, that neither Wilkinson nor Reynolds, nor any of the Iron Masters were in town to give evidence. If all our labour is at last thrown away I must, with many others, attribute it to their standing aloof.'

Wedgwood despatched a letter to his friend Wilkinson on 6 May: 'I cannot sufficiently assure you how much surprise it strikes in every quarter, that no one has been heard at the Bar of the House for so important an article as the iron trade.' The same theme is followed by Wedgwood in still another plea to Boulton on 7 May. 'If the iron masters had been true to their cause and to their country, this business might be put off the whole session'——'You cannot conceive how things approach a crisis, and how this extreme backwardness in the first town of manufacturers and the first manufacturers in iron in the kingdom distresses us.'

The final letter dated 14 May from Wedgwood to Boulton, shows how deeply Wedgwood felt the withdrawal of the Birmingham Chamber of Commerce from the fight. Their defection exasperated him to the point of risking a break in a lifetime of friendship with Boulton, as revealed by the following extract:

I will venture to say to you, who know the difficulties which delegates are laid under, when a necessary confidence is not reposed in them. . . . This is written in great haste and in confidence to you, but personal considerations weigh so little with me compared with the great cause we are embarked in, that I leave myself in your hands and am with the greatest regard and every good wish to you and yours.

Jos. Wedgwood.

The aloofness and desertion of his Birmingham ironmaster friends disturbed Wedgwood much more than the half-hearted support from the cotton manufacturers, who came to talk matters over at the General Assembly, but took no decisive action, when they discovered that the Fustian Tax was to be repealed.

The minutes of the Potters' Chamber of Commerce reveal that all through the trials of the General Chamber of Manufacturers in London, the potters stood by their leader and representative, Wedgwood, in his fight against the Irish Treaty proposals. At their meeting on 21 December 1785, the Potters recorded their unshaken faith in the General Assembly and its potential future.

With respect to the General Chamber of Manufacturers, here the different branches of manufacture in this island, have a natural and necessary connection with one another and ought to unite their counsels and endeavours for the protection and extension of their mutual interests. The General Chamber of Manufacturers appears excellently calculated for that purpose. By the wisdom and well-timed exertions of the gentlemen who compose it, a most alarming danger which threatened the whole body of our manufacturers at once, and which no single branch could have withstood, has already happily been averted.

Then follow three resolutions which show the potters' loyalty:

(1) That this meeting approves of the above-mentioned institution and so long as it continues to be conducted for the purpose of watching over the manufacturing interests of the Kingdom, it shall have their hearty concurrence and support.
(2) That we recommend the Chamber to proceed in the same line of conduct, which it has hitherto observed, regardless of either allurements or menaces, that may tend to divert it from the main objects of its pursuit.
(3) That the thanks of this meeting be given to the Chairman, Mr. Wedgwood, and that these resolutions be printed in some of the London and County papers. It was resolved that this meeting enter into a subscription for defraying the expenses already incurred by the General Chamber, and likewise an annual subscription for its support. Also that the Committee be requested to collect the donations and subscriptions of such of the manufacturers of this neighbourhood, as are not now present. Upwards of 100 guineas were subscribed before the gentlemen left the room.

Wedgwood came in for a good deal of abuse from Irish politicians and aristocrats. One nobleman declared that should more of Wedgwood's ware come to Ireland, if the public did not break it, he would. But, though Wedgwood and his supporters from the Potteries failed to defeat the proposals of the Irish Treaty in Parliament, despite persistent petitioning and lobbying, they won their fight in the end, for Pitt had to admit, by 1786, that the negotiations with the Irish Parliament had failed.

There were other victories. Wedgwood had the satisfaction of knowing that through the activities of the General Chamber of Manufacturers, the iron-masters had secured the withdrawl of the threatened taxes on coal, iron and copper, while the cotton manufacturers benefited by the withdrawal of the Fustian Tax. Further, the potters staved off any proposal to tax pottery wares, during Josiah Wedgwood's lifetime and after. The threatened tax on porcelain and earthenware did not materialize until 1811. Wedgwood and the Potters' Chamber of Commerce on 14 February 1785, had strongly supported the Birmingham Chamber of Commerce in their opposition to the imposition of the tax on iron, coal and copper – raw materials so vital to the ironmasters of Birmingham. As Boulton put it pithily in a letter, 'Let taxes be laid upon luxuries, upon vices, and if you like, upon property, tax riches when got and the expenditure of them but not tax the means of getting them – of all things don't cut open the hen that lays the golden eggs.' Last, but not least, the General Chamber of Manufacturers lived through the 1785 turmoil and defections of individual Chambers of Commerce, and took on a new lease of life in 1786.

In 1786 the Government proceeded with its preparation of the Anglo-French Treaty. As a result of an invitation from Mr. Eden, the Commissioner in charge of the Treaty, the Potters' Chamber of Commerce appointed Wedgwood as their delegate on 7 February 1786. The minute immediately preceding his appointment read, 'A letter from the General Chamber of Manufacturers was received . . . ordered that they are sensible of the necessity there will be from the various commercial treaties now negotiating, for the continuation of their exertions, and that they may depend all the support from the manufacturers in this neighbourhood.' The Birmingham Chamber of Commerce of Iron Manufacturers was also in favour of the General Chamber continuing its functions over the negotiations relating to the French Treaty.

Encouraged by this support, Wedgwood took up the cudgels on behalf of the French Treaty. He was greatly helped by having a most sympathetic Minister in charge of the Treaty. The latter had even converted the Prime Minister, Pitt, to respect and to make full use of the Provincial Chambers of Commerce, as well as the General Chamber of Manufacturers, in framing the terms.

On 18 February 1786, Wedgwood wrote quite hopefully to T. Walker of Manchester, inviting him to join in the activities of the General Chamber. Wedgwood had not realized the depth and intensity of Walker's political opposition to Pitt and his party, as an anti-Pitt Whig. He was repudiated by his own Fustian Manufacturers, who along with their other Cotton Manufacturers in the Manchester Chamber of Commerce, had supported Wedgewood, his fellow Potters and the Birmingham Chamber in the French Treaty negotiations.

I have found no trace of any reply from Walker to Etruria in response to Wedgwood's letter. But what we do know from the *Manchester Mercury*, 6 March 1787, is that the New Committee of Fustian Manufacturers agreed with the French Treaty, and repudiated Walker, who had violently attacked Lawrence Peel in a meeting of the Manchester Manufacturers. Walker opposed his Manchester colleagues and as the head of the Whig Party in Manchester, became the leader of the opposition to Pitt and his Government. He attended the General Chamber of Manufacturers in London on his own account and rallied an opposition Group. He was a capable speaker, and at the meeting worked up a majority consisting of smaller manufacturers of the older types of industries, outside those from Manchester, Staffordshire and Birmingham.

Wedgwood wrote Boulton: 'You have seen by the public papers the discussions which rend our Chamber almost asunder and the disgrace it is brought into by the weak and undigested, unfair reports and resolutions they fabricate. . . . I have gone as far as to stop them being deliberated at the Committee tonight. If Walker comes here in one of his warm moods, I have my doubts for I stand almost single to stem the tide and the circulation of such stuff, as could disgrace any meeting.'

Wedgwood asked Boulton to send him a letter on behalf of the ironmasters approving the action of the General Chamber Committee, which Boulton did at once. Similar support was forthcoming from the Potters' Chamber of Commerce, and the Manchester Cotton Committee, who disagreed entirely with Walker. Wedgwood's state of mind relative to Walker's conduct in disrupting the London meeting of the General Chamber is revealed in his letter to Boulton on 23 February 1787: 'I am quite wearied out with the nonsense of some, the pirtness and abuse of others. If I am not supported from the country soon, either by letters or some of the members arriving at the Committee, I must quit my post for I have been buffeted and teased beyond human endurance.'

He was greatly cheered by a letter from James Watt on 26 February 1787, which read: 'I am sorry to see by the public papers that there are two opinions in the Chamber of Manufacturers about the Treaty with France. As your opinions coincide with my own, I also assure you that Boulton, Garbett and I believe all the town of Birmingham are of the same sentiment. I was present at a public meeting with about a 100 of the principal inhabitants, merchants and manufacturers, where success to the Treaty and a perpetual peace between Britain and France was drunk and followed by three hearty and unanimous cheers.' This spontaneous support greatly heartened Wedgwood, and he decided not to quit his post as Chairman and chief inspirer, guide and virtual guardian of the General Chamber of Manufacturers. This decision he conveyed to his friend Boulton in a letter: 'Some of my friends say "Let the Chamber go to the Devil". I say "No". We may want it hereafter. It should be new modelled (about which I shall be glad to consult my friends in Birmingham), but not demolished.'

These plans were later discussed by Wedgwood and his Birmingham friends, as well as with his Potters' Chamber of Commerce, which sent a resolution to this effect to Mr. Nicholson, the Secretary of the General Chamber, suggesting a new charter for its reorganization.

But in the turbulent atmosphere created by Walker and his rebellious following, such a reorganization was impossible. In fact, Wedgwood and his supporters decided that the only thing to do was to let the General Chamber lapse, as the only way open to them to freeze out Walker and Co. Wedgwood writing his political friend, Mr. Eden, on 16 June 1787, sums up the situation almost poetically and pathetically, 'The Chamber of Manufacturers sleepeth for the present, but may be awakened at any time, when its services are called for.'

This decision not only effectively purged the Chamber of Manufacturers of the self-appointed delegates, like T. Walker, but it also enabled Wedgwood and his supporters to put into operation an alternative scheme for manufacturers, suggested by Watt: 'The idea now started, but not in any way fixt is that the Union of the Chambers of Manchester, the Ironmasters of Birmingham, Sheffield, the Pottery, Nottingham and such others as are in the neighbourhood to meet at Manchester, Birmingham, The Potteries etc., either in rotation, or as may be convenient and . . . to have nothing to do with Londoners except on particular occasions'. Truly this was a 'strike' or 'lock-out' by the Provincial Chambers of Commerce against the 'Londoners', led by Walker in the revolt that ultimately wrecked the National General Chamber of Manufacturers.

I have found no trace of any meetings held by the Potters' Chamber of Commerce between 1 November 1786, and 16 February 1789. There is a similar gap in the records of the Birmingham minute book, from 1787 until 1790. The Manchester Chamber of Commerce was dormant during this period. Unfortunately, the minute book of the Potters' Chamber of Commerce ends on 17 July 1790, and I have failed to trace any further records of correspondence with neighbouring committees of commerce. The first reference to any united gathering of neighbouring chambers of commerce is found in Helm's *History of the Manchester Chamber of Commerce*: 'In 1796 delegates from Manchester, Liverpool, Leeds, Halifax, Birmingham and Leicester met to consider the confiscation of property in Southern Europe.' No delegates came from the Potteries, which is explained, probably, by the fact that after the death of Wedgwood in 1795, the Potters' Chamber of Commerce also 'was left to sleep', like the General Chamber of Manufacturers.

Bladen suggests that 'the French Treaty killed the General Chamber of Manufacturers'. The French Treaty was never the *cause* of the break-up of the Chamber. It might be better described as the *occasion* of the break-up. The General Chamber did not die from any external cause. There was no one single cause of failure; there were many. The failure of this grandiose scheme for a national organization of manufacturers is to be sought not in a foreign outside cause, but in the inherent internal weaknesses of the organizations composing the General Chamber. The nascent and separate provincial chambers of commerce were too young and inexperienced to venture on a national body in 1785. It was only kept alive by the strategy and personality of Josiah Wedgwood. The provincial chambers did not have sufficient community of interest to fuse their forces into a national unit, in spite of his generalship and inspiration. The rising industrial capitalists of the new factories of the Industrial Revolution had taken on too big a national task, too gigantic an effort, with their too small and short-lived experience with local organization. They were attempting to erect a top-heavy national institution, before they had laid firm enough foundations, through strong local chambers of commerce. Almost an exact parallel may be drawn regarding the failure of the General Chamber of Commerce after 1786, with the failure later, during 1830–1834, of the Owenite national organization of trade unions. A good, strong, sound national organization of employers or employees can be built only on a solid structure of well-knit local units. The General Chamber of Manufacturers died or 'went to sleep' as Wedgwood put it, because it was really a premature organization. It was nevertheless the offspring of great industrialist or capitalist employers like Wedgwood, Boulton, Watt, Garbett and Sir Herbert Hackworth, to name a few. When such giants of industry and great personalities were criticized, attacked and abused by smaller capitalists, even when united temporarily by a Thomas Walker, the National General Chamber could be dissolved or 'sent to sleep' by the 'big businessmen'.

But, looming through the short-lived existence of the General Chamber were the disruptive influences of political party clashes and animosities, with their noisy slogans and party war cries. The Walkerites really wrecked the General Chamber, through their party political tactics. This party-political strife spread as a disease later to send even the provincial chambers of commerce to sleep.

The meeting of the Potters' Chamber of Commerce held on 4 February was much disturbed by the speech and actions of a Mr. W. Fernyhough, who was a kind of 'local' Thomas Walker. The potters at their meeting of 16 February passed the following resolution: 'It is the unanimous opinion of this meeting that this body of manufacturers having never yet taken a part or come to any public resolutions upon mere political questions, they deem it expedient not to do so upon the present occasion. The Committee highly disapprove of the proceedings [of the 4 February Meeting] and agreed to abide by the unanimous resolution of the first meeting, not to interfere as a body of manufacturers in questions merely political.'

Unfortunately, the potters took sides in this Fernyhough episode. The pro-Fernyhough group included Josiah Spode, a Church member, and on the other side, in the anti-Fernyhough group was Josiah Wedgwood, leading the majority of his fellow potters on the Potters' Committee. Perhaps a little sectarian religious animosity entered into the rowdy meeting on 4 February. The Rev. Mr. Fernyhough was a curate at St. Peter's Church, which Spode attended, while Wedgwood was a prominent Unitarian, and a supporter of Wesleyanism in his day. However much Wedgwood and his fellow potters tried to keep politics out of the agenda of their local Potters' Chamber of Commerce, it was inevitable sooner or later that individual potters would be involved in party-political controversy.

Josiah Wedgwood II was the first potter to enter the lists in a Parliamentary contest, for the Newcastle-under-Lyne seat. It was one of the 'rotten boroughs', which by leave of the freeholders belonged to the Duke of Sutherland. Wedgwood was unsuccessful as a candidate, when he polled only 374 votes as a Whig, against the successful Tory candidate Edmund Peel, who polled 746 votes, while a second Tory candidate had 463 votes. After the contest Wedgwood sent the following letter to his employees at Etruria on 2 May 1831:

To the workmen employed at the factory at Etruria,

I am desirous of expressing to you my feelings on hearing of your liberal contribution to the fund for defraying the expenses of my contest for the representation of Newcastle. If it had, on my part, been merely an effort for the gratification of my personal ambition or vanity, your generous support would have raised my gratitude, but I believe that your donation is a testimonial of your approbation of the Reform proposed by H.M. Government, and I am most happy to be united in the furtherance of this cause with a body of men so intelligent and so upright, as from long and intimate experience, I know you to be. Nor do I doubt that the very honourable men who have supported me in this contest without expense to me, will have much pleasure in the knowledge of your being associated with them in the support of a measure on the success of which depend the maintenance of our unrivalled constitution and the peace and welfare of our Country.

But your donation has given me a satisfaction which is purely personal. You and I well know, that in the long run our interests agree – but it may often have appeared to some of you, and must sometimes have been the case, that in taking care of my own interest I have not been sufficiently regardful of yours. Now your unsolicited, unexpected and free gift is a proof, that my conduct during the very long period of our connection has been such as, on the whole to have obtained for me your esteem and regard, which I prize as among the most valuable of my possessions.

Josiah Wedgwood.

In this very frank letter, the industrial capitalist confesses that in the long run his interests are those of his work people, despite lapses, where the owner probably has placed his self-interest before that of his workpeople.

But in the next Parliamentary contest for the newly created Borough of Stoke-upon-Trent, after the passing of the Reform Bill, Josiah Wedgwood headed the poll as a Whig candidate and a senior member for the new Borough. John Davenport, a fellow potter, was the successful junior member, as a Tory. One of the defeated candidates, as a reformer, was George Miles Mason, while the other defeated candidate was R. Edensor Heathcote, a local landowner. This time Wedgwood headed the poll with 822 votes as compared with 232 votes cast for the defeated reformist potter Mason. On the retirement of Josiah Wedgwood, in 1835, R. Edensor Heathcote succeeded him as the successful Whig candidate, and Davenport was returned as a Tory M.P.

In the later General Election of 1837, two pottery manufacturers headed the poll, a new candidate, W. T. Copeland with 681 votes as a Conservative and Davenport, as a Junior M.P., polling 670 votes as a Whig candidate. W. T. Copeland, son of William Copeland, the London Agent of Josiah Spode, had become sole owner in 1833 of Spode's original factory, which had been considerably augmented and at that date was one of the largest factories in the Potteries. He represented Stoke-upon-Trent as Conservative member from 1837 to 1852, and was re-elected from 1857 till 1865.

Another prominent potter represented the Stoke-upon-Trent Borough from 1874 till 1880. As a Tory M.P., he was the head of the Minton Pottery factory, one of the largest factories, not far from Copeland's pottery. Coming later still to the twentieth century, Mrs. Ronald Copeland, the wife of one of the direct descendants of W. T. Copeland of Spode's Pottery, was elected as a Conservative M.P. for Stoke.

Thus, we see that willy-nilly the Pottery's industrial capitalists were forced to enter politics in the early nineteenth century, when as a result of the Reform Act of 1832 they were enabled to defeat the former land-owning Members of Parliament. But when the potters entered Parliament some were Whigs, others, Tories.

This direct entry of potters as M.P.s into Parliament is probably the real reason for the decline of the General Chamber of Manufacturers. Direct pressure on the Government of the day, through their M.P., as representing the rising industrial capitalist, was more effective than the slow, painful process of indirect political pressure, often ineffectual, exerted by the General Chamber of Manufacturers, which had caused such heartache to Josiah Wedgwood I.

The failure of the 'General Chamber' has led traditional writers on the period of the Industrial Revolution, to assume that the Master Potters' local organization also ceased to exist. This traditional view is probably based on the negative evidence, that no minute book has been discovered relating the proceedings of the Potters' Chamber of Commerce after 30 March 1790. There may be such a minute book in existence, but as yet unearthed. Still, as we shall prove later, there is plenty of contemporary evidence that the potters did meet collectively as a Chamber of Commerce or Chamber of Potters.

A copy of the minutes of the Weaver Navigation in Cheshire, shown me through the courtesy of Mr. Shirley, the Secretary of the Navigation, records that 'On 9 September 1800, a meeting of Manufacturers of Earthenware in the parishes of Stoke, Burslem and Wolstanton was held at the Swan Inn, Hanley, with Mr. Keeling in the Chair.' The minutes of this meeting record several resolutions dealing with the proposed Anderton Lift constructed to join the Weaver to the Trent and Mersey Navigation. A guarantee was given that the trade would amount to £1,500, and it was signed by 21 firms.

The threatened taxation of other industries than cotton and iron in 1811 rallied the Potters' Committee once more into action, as this letter from the Spode-Copeland MSS. Collection shows:

Sir,

The committee earnestly request your attendance at a *General Meeting of the Manufacturers*, at the Swan Inn, Hanley, at 11 a.m. on Monday 27th inst., punctually to meet Mr. Caldwell and Mr. Spode, and to express the grateful sense of the Manufacturers for their services and of the important assistance they have received from many distinguished characters on the occasion of the proposed Tax on Porcelain and Earthenware.

Your obedient servant,
Josiah Wedgwood, Chairman.

Roe-buck, Newcastle, May 24, 1811.

In due course Josiah Spode sends an acknowledgment on 21 October 1811, in which we see this expression of gratitude had been acted upon.

My dear Sir,

I duly received your note for £105 voted by the Manufacturers for a piece of plate, and I feel greatly obliged to the Committee, and particularly yourself for your polite attention on this business.

I am, My Dear Sir,
Josiah Spode.

To Josiah Wedgwood Esq.

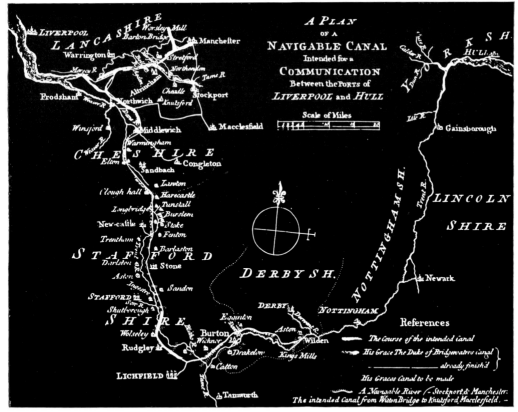

38 Sketch-map showing the Trent and Mersey Canal

39 The Greyhound Inn, Stone; headquarters of the Trent and Mersey Canal Committee, of which Josiah Wedgwood was Treasurer

40 Wedgwood plaques at Tsarskoe Selo Palace, Leningrad

41 The Duke of Bridgewater

42 James Brindley, the Duke of Bridgewater's canal engineer and adviser

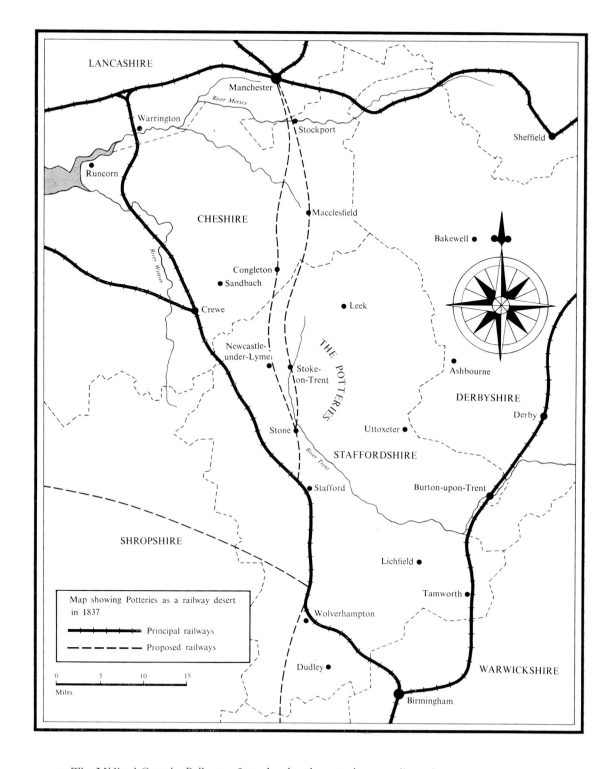

43 The Midland Counties Railway, 1837, showing the potteries as a railway desert

This Committee or General Meeting of Potters kept a vigilant eye on political and Government affairs affecting their trade, as shown by the decision to send a deputation from the Committee of Potters to attend the various Committees, dealing with the Orders in Council on America. We discovered the following letter, dated 7 May 1812, in the Boulton-Watt archives. It reveals that Josiah Wedgwood II was as keen on deputation work on behalf of his fellow potters, as his father.

To Matthew Robinson Boulton,   London, 7 May, 1812

    I am here with a deputation from the Potteries to attend the Committees on the Orders in Council. I have just been writing to Watt to urge his coming up to give his most valued assistance, and to tell him that the evidence already given has produced great effects. I do not know what applications have been made to you, but you will excuse the liberty I am taking in expressing my conviction of the very great advantage that would accrue to the cause, if you would be induced to co-operate with the deputation now in town... If we have not you, we want our "right hand". Deputations are here from Birmingham, London, Sheffield, Leicester, Hinckley, Wolverhampton, Kidderminster, and Bolton, Stockport, Rochdale and other districts are expected.

                                               Jos. Wedgwood.

Josiah Wedgwood II, like his father before him, was disappointed by the refusal of Matthew Robinson Boulton to join in a deputation. His excuse was that, 'My state of health has obliged me to decline all active interference in public discussion', but perhaps his real reason for declining to join is contained in the latter part of his letter: 'The distressed state of our Manufacturers cannot admit of a doubt, but how far depression can be attributed to the encitement of the Orders in Council, or how far the repeal of them would restore our lost trade, I am by no means competent to give a decided opinion.'

Josiah Wedgwood's reply to Boulton on 26 May 1812, stressed the anxiety felt by the potters of the injurious consequences of the Orders in Council on their trade with America. He says: 'The object of the witnesses at the Bars of the two Houses has been to make Parliament acquainted with the facts. A case has been made out of the misery occasioned by the suspension of the trade with America, as the immediate result of the Orders in Council.'

In the general atmosphere of depression during the American and French Wars, the potters were anxious to avoid any extra burden imposed by pending costly factory legislation, contemplated by the factory reformers. So in 1816, we find Josiah Wedgwood appearing on behalf of the Potters' Committee, and before a Committee of Inquiry into 'Children employed in manufactories'. In a reply to Sir Robert Peel, who asked him, 'How did you come into possession of your information?' Wedgwood stated:

RSP M

I received it from Mr Ridgway, who undertook the office of Secretary, at a General Meeting of the Manufacturers, who met to consider what they understood to be the provisions of the Bill. [Wedgwood then reported] This meeting [of Potters] came to a resolution that, with respect to the manufacture of Earthenware such legislative enactment was not necessary, and that it should by all means in their power be opposed being applied to their manufactory. . . . It was also settled at that Meeting, that some manufacturers should attend here for the purpose of giving information as to the condition of children in the manufactory of Earthenware.

After this Committee of Inquiry of 1816, the Government set up a Select Committee to deal with the rise of combinations amongst workmen and the question of exportation of machinery. The terms of reference of the Select Committee on 'Artisans and Machinery' were 'To inquire into the exportation of machinery and into the state of the Law and its effects so far as relates to the condition of workmen and others to raise wages or to regulate their wages.'

In the reports of the Parliamentary select committees of 1824 and 1825 there is no record of delegates of the pottery manufacturers attending any of these inquiries. The potters did hold a meeting in 1825, for Ward in his *History of, Stoke-on-Trent*, states, 'In September 1825 a Committee was formed for the promotion of measures calculated to benefit the general trade of the Potteries.' Ward gives no further details. Whether they met to discuss prices, marketing of wares or problems relating to wages (for since Peterloo in Manchester even the workmen in the Potteries had shown a good deal of restlessness) – is a matter of conjecture. The Report of the 1825 Inquiry into the Combination Laws (*Parl. Report*, 1825, Vol. IV, p. 437) contains a list of communications received, petitioning for an alteration in the 'Combination Laws'. This list includes five communications from Potteries at Newcastle, Burslem, Hanley and Fenton. Probably, these five potters consulted with the meeting of potters, referred to by Ward, and sent in individual communications. This was done so as not to involve the potters collectively, as the Potteries were an industrial area lying between the turbulent industrial area of Manchester with its Peterloo incidents, and the South Staffordshire Coal and Iron District, with its continuous conflict between masters and men, both of whom openly combined. The potters were wise not to meet in too organized a fashion or to express themselves too definitely and prominently on the Combination Laws. A strike of the pottery workers took place in 1825, after two pottery workers' unions were formed in 1824. Warburton quotes press reports in the *Pottery Mercury* of 30 March and 17 August 1825, and also in the *Staffordshire Advertiser* of 2 April 1825, that the pottery manufacturers met the men and discussed with them their grievances, which concerned prices and sizes of wares. Warburton calls this meeting of potters a 'Chamber of Commerce'. In the local newspapers in Staffordshire for the year 1825 and 1826 (e.g. *Pottery Mercury*, 31 August, 19 October, 14 December 1825, and 1 February 1826) the body of potters meeting is specifically referred to as a 'Committee or organization representing Potters', and formed as such officially in August 1825 as reported in the *Pottery Mercury* in that month. It was this body of potters that Wedgwood was referring to in a letter he sent in reply to one from W. T. Copeland. Copeland had asked Wedgwood for his support in opposition to the Bill introduced by Mr. Lyttleton in the House of Commons, for the purpose of compelling potters to make certain sizes.

Wedgwood's reply was curt, but it was obviously backed by the power of collective action by his fellow potters, 'I have received your favour and I must decline to take any part in opposition to the Bill in question out of deference to the wishes of a great majority of the manufacturers.' Further, it is safe to assume that, with the general agitation and industrial unrest that took place after the Combination Acts of 1824–1825, and the campaign conducted personally by that fiery supporter of workers' combinations, Robert Owen, the Chamber of Manufacturers in the Potteries would be anything but dormant or dead.

A later publication than those quoted above was published by the Chamber of Commerce of Potters, called *The case of the earthenware manufacturers in Staffordshire, with some account of the late Turn-out, its origins, proceedings and termination 1836-1847*. This describes in detail the general character of the Chamber of Commerce. It is referred to in Boyle's excellent article in the *Royal Statistical Journal*, 1839, dealing with the 1834–1836 strike or turn-out, as it was then called.

Thus, it can be said definitely that the Chamber of Commerce was in almost continuous existence from the early days of Josiah Wedgwood in 1775, through the vicissitudes of the Irish and French Treaty deliberations of 1784–1786, and when called for, from 1790 to 1824–1826 and on to 1830, after which the Chamber of Commerce came to action in 1826–1837. Although I have been unable to trace a copy of the minutes of these successive gatherings of the potters in general meetings, Chamber of Commerce, or Chamber of Manufacturers, or some such title, between 1790 and 1836, this is no proof that the potters did not meet as a body. In fact, the first minute book since 1790 I have been able to discover, giving records of the meetings of Potters, is that recording the activities of the Chamber of Commerce in 1851. This is still being continued to record the deliberations of the present North Staffordshire Chamber of Commerce.

CHAPTER 16

The Wage-earner Emerges: 1730 to 1824

During the early decades between 1730 and 1760, the outstanding aspect of the pottery industry was its small-scale character, with its paternalism and intimate personal relationship between the master potter and his journeymen and apprentices. The apprenticeship system prevailed, particularly from 1730, until it decayed as a system in the early decades of the nineteenth century. The Government, under pressure from the manufacturers, repealed the apprenticeship clauses of the old Elizabethan Statute of Apprentices, by its Act of 54, George III, Cap. 96. Apprenticeships lingered on as a matter of form a little longer, with merely nominal fees when an apprenticeship indenture was signed.

In the early decades following 1730, individuals were taught the art and 'mystery' of pottery according to the varying terms of a legal document or indenture duly signed, binding the apprentice to a master potter. An apprenticeship document, dated 23 August 1731, bound Aaron Wood to Dr. Thomas Wedgwood for a term of seven years, but the document apprenticing Josiah to his brother Thomas Wedgwood was for a term of only five years. There was a further difference in the terms of these apprenticeship documents; the father of Aaron Wood 'shall provide for his son all sorts of apparell, whether linen, woollen or others, also meat, drink, washing and lodging' – then in return Dr. Wedgwood shall engage to pay in the first, second and third year of his apprenticeship the sum of one shilling weekly, and in the fourth, fifth and sixth year the sum of 1s. 6d., and in the seventh and last year, 'the full and just sum of 4s, and over and above the weekly wages aforesaid give yearly one pair of shoes'.

The indenture of Wedgwood with his brother stipulated that Josiah had 'with him as an apprentice to dwell, continue and serve . . . and the said Master . . . will also find and allow unto the said apprentice meat, drink, washing and lodging and apparell of all kinds, both linen, woollen and all other necessaries, both in sickness and in health'. Apparently, Josiah received no money from his brother, but merely his keep.

There was one other difference between the two indentures. Aaron Wood was to learn 'the art, trade, mystery and occupation of a potter, that is to say turning on the lathe handling and trimming'; one notes the absence of any reference to 'throwing on the potter's wheel'. Wedgwood's indenture on the other hand reads 'Josiah Wedgwood doth bind himself to learn his art, mystery, occupation or employment of Throwing and Handling'.

The indentures of apprenticeship were a burden to aspiring apprentices of poor parents, who were often asked to pay a premium. There are not many of these early indentures extant. But there are records of such apprenticeships in Thomas Whieldon's 'Memo Book', which contains the following interesting note about Josiah Spode: 'April 9/1749.

'Hired Siah Spode to give him this time to Martelmas next 2s3d or 2s6d if he deserves it. 2nd year 2s9d, 3rd year 3s3d. Paid full earnest 10d.' A variant of the above note is that relating to a contemporary of both Spode and Wedgwood – Daniel Greatbatch. 'Hired Daniel Greatbatch. If he tries hard, is to have 2s/4d, and if good work, 2s6d.' And again, he records hiring a girl to decorate ware: 'Aug 24/1752.

'Hired little Bel Bloor to learn to flower, 1st year per week 1s, 2nd year 1s3d, 3rd year 1s6d.'

Whieldon has several 'hiring' records in his Memo Book.

June 2/1749   Hired a boy of Ann Bloor for treading ye lathe, per wk, 2s0d.
Aug 29/1753   Hired Westabys 3 children per wk 4s0d. paid earnest 6d.

On pages 70–74 of Whieldon's 'Memo Book', we have a long list of hirings of skilled adults or journeymen.

					s.	d.
Hired J. Austin	for placing white per wk				5.	6.
„ W. Keeling	„ handling	„	„		6.	0.
„ W. Cope	„ „	„	„		7.	0.
„ Low	„ making slip	„	„		5.	3.
„ E. Simpson	„ turning	„	„		8.	0.
„ Siah Spode		„	„		7.	6.
Earnest				£1.	11.	6.
Paid in part					16.	0.

Some of the hiring agreements were recorded showing payments in kind, for example:

Paid 1 pr stockings 3s6d.
To give a new shirt at 16d per yard
To give him a pr. shoes each year
I am to give him an old coat or something about 5/- value

This payment or gift in kind, as a kind of bonus, may have been a legacy of the indenture or apprentice's agreement. It may also be a foreshadowing of the later introduction and spread of the truck system, which led to great abuses in the early nineteenth century.

A typical journeyman's indenture was that of Aaron Wood, whose apprenticeship indenture we noticed earlier. The terms of years for six days work, plus an earnest of 10s. 6d. to be paid on the eleventh day of November. The journeyman must not be away from work more than two weeks in any one year. The penalty for breach of the agreement was the forfeiture of £10.

When Wedgwood employed his cousin Thomas, as a journeyman, his agreement was less formal. It read: 'Memo of agreement between Josiah Wedgwood . . . potter and Thomas Wedgwood journeyman, now living in the City of Worcester, potter. The said Thomas Wedgwood engaged to serve Josiah Wedgwood as a journeyman from the 1st of May 1759 to 11th Nov– 1765, and is to receive of said Josiah Wedgwood £22 of lawful money for every year's service.' The natural promotion for a trained journeyman was first to be made a foreman, or even a top foreman or manager. This was the case with Aaron Wood, who became foreman at Whieldon's works. Josiah Spode became foreman or manager of John Turner's potworks at Stoke, which Spode later purchased. Joseph Poulson, a journeyman potter at Spode's, became a manager of Spode's works, and later a manager of Minton's pottery, when both left Spode's employ. Later Poulson became a partner with Minton at his factory as a Master Potter.

As already noted many apprentices, journeymen and master potters succeeded in establishing in due course the ownership of their own potworks, first on their own and soon with partners. This was the case with Aaron Wood, Josiah Wedgwood, Spode, and many others. But not all qualified journeymen potters and master potters had the opportunity to become pottery owners. It required capital or someone with capital, prepared to become a sleeping partner, while supplying part of the capital to set up a pottery. If one belonged to a wealthy family or married into one as was the case with Wedgwood and Spode II, the setting up of one or more pottery factories was a fairly easy matter. The more these family concerns of potters developed and succeeded, the less was the opportunity for a small master potter to succeed in competition with them — unless, of course, he could borrow money from some banker or landlord to finance the venture.

From a list given by Wedgwood in his Commonplace Book, it seems there were 84 master potters and partners owning pottery works in 1783. These by

1790 had increased to 125. The number of apprentices and journeymen, who had completed their terms of indenture and qualified as journeymen craftsmen or master-potters, during that interval of seven years was much more than 41, the difference in the increase of pottery owners. Wedgwood records that in 1790, he employed 60 apprentices, while the number of hands, including journeymen craftsmen, women, oddmen, clerks totalled 282. Towards the latter decades of the eighteenth century, it is evident that where journeymen craftsmen did not find means of being promoted foreman, managing foreman or manager of a department or of the whole pottery works, they had to content themselves with being journeymen craftsmen, paid a day wage or, as was increasingly done, paid by piece-rate. The prospects of becoming a master-potter owning his own potworks had become very dim, as it required a large fund of capital to run a highly mechanized factory in the latter decades of the eighteenth century, and the situation became more difficult still in the nineteenth century. The most that some of the best journeymen craftsmen could hope for was to be put on the staff as 'salaried' personnel. In one of Wedgwood's Ledgers, for the years 1793–1795, there is an entry, 'W. Greatbatch, Etruria wages = £157.13.8. (£150 ½ years salary)', and on page 45 there is an entry, 'W. Wood on a/c of wages, say salary = £113.2.0.' This salary status probably carried certain privileges or 'perks', not open to a mere wage-earner.

From the moment Wedgwood decided to expand his business by building a new factory at Eturia, he was faced with a continual labour shortage. Once he set up Etruria, he later tried to establish his decorating and enamelling factories at Chelsea, under the supervision of Bentley. We find him complaining bitterly of his inability to get sufficient hands. He was short of painters, polishers, lapidaries, vase-makers, printers, modellers, carvers etc. At one stage, he was so distressed over the problem of getting a suitable supply of artists, that he contemplated setting up a house, as a colony for artists.

The demand for vase-painters was such in September 1769 that Wedgwood wrote Bentley: 'You say you can sell a waggon load a week [of vases]. If you sell that quantity in the season, you must have a waggon load of painters to finish them . . I repeat again you shall not want vases, it must be your and Mr. Croft's care to collect and make painters.' Wedgwood was not particular as to where Bentley obtained his painters. 'Perhaps, you may get some better hands from the Fan-painters, if that business is carried on now or from the best Coach and House-Fresco painters.' Wedgwood received a letter from Bentley advising him to hire more painters in Staffordshire. Wedgwood replied: 'Aye, but trade is as good with others, as with ourselves, almost everybody wants hands. Palmers have given it out that they want a dozen handlers. Hollins near as many, so that there is scarcely a hand to be hired.'

So desperate was the labour position in the Staffordshire Potteries that Wedgwood drew on centres as far afield as Liverpool and Birmingham. He turned down workers from Birmingham, as they wanted too high a price. He wrote Bentley on 11 November 1769 'Such hands for [painting] borders may be got cheaper from Liverpool, or from the Delph works at Lambeth.' He succeeded in getting some painters from Liverpool, for he wrote Bentley on 3 February 1770, 'Do you want another hand for painting figures – a Mr. Robinson late of Liverpool?'

The supply of painters was not forthcoming, so Bentley resorted to advertisements for them in the press. As Wedgwood wrote almost in despair again, on 29 April 1790: 'We must have painters, the life and soul of our business depends upon them. . . . How you may speed with your advertisements.'

Bentley's assistant Mr. Crofts introduced into the Chelsea works the technique of chalking outlines of designs on vases, which could be easily filled in by 'dilutees' and not trained painters and artists. Another device Wedgwood used for decoration was the employment of a printer to print outlines, which could be filled in by 'dilutees'. Wedgwood wrote Bentley on 21 February 1770, 'I have had a person with me to offer himself as a printer. I hope you can get two or three plates engraved or etched for him to try his hand with some of the vases, for we shall never get a quantity done without some such operation as printing or stencilling.'

Wedgwood was elated with this technique of enrolling dilutees to help with the decorating of vases etc. On 22 December 1770, he wrote Bentley, 'It is hard but then it is glorious to conquer so great an Empire with raw, undisciplined recruits. What merit the General must have, who achieves such wonders under such disadvantageous circumstances. The Glory & Honour my friend is yours. To add still to your Boys, I send two more recruits on Monday, Barratt & Glover. They walk it to London, and I allow them 12s each besides their wages.'

Wedgwood uses the metaphor 'General' for the employer and the term 'Recruits' for his employees. He wrote better than he knew. For that was what the discipline and regimentation of the manufactory meant at this period to the apprentices, journeymen and master craftsmen, who saw the workrooms and workbenches flooded with these raw recruits, untrained dilutees and fresh hired wage-earners.

Wedgwood wrote Bentley on 30 October and 19 November 1769: 'We have not got 30 hands here, but I have much ado to keep the new ones quiet. I do not know what I shall do with them. We have too many fresh hands to take in at once, though we have business enough for them, if they knew how, or would have the patience to learn, but they do not seem to relish the thoughts of a second apprenticeship. I have been an Etruscan and dined at the works every day, and preparing to make such Machines of the Men as cannot err.'

Then again on 19 May 1770: 'What is become of your scheme for taking in girls to paint? You observe very justly, that few hands can be got to paint flowers in the style we want them. I may add nor on any other work we do. *We must make them.* There is no other way.'

On 23 May 1770, Wedgwood returned to his early idea of a school for artists. 'I have a waking notion that haunts me very much of late, which is the beginning of a regular drawing and modelling school to train artists for ourselves.'

Wedgwood hesitated to develop this 'waking notion'. He knew what un-manageable material artists were. He confessed to Bentley 'I have enough to do to make the Pots and manage the Potmakers, though I would rather man for man, have to do with a shop of Potters than Painters.' Josiah Wedgwood II did not seem to be able to manage painters at Etruria much better than his father, to judge from the following extract from a letter to him on 25 May 1789. 'On going down to the works tonight, I find that all the painters & John Steel who is to come to work tonight, left work at 4 or 5 o'clock. Some disgust at printing I believe is the cause.' On receiving a reply from his father, Josiah Junior wrote on 29 May 1789, 'I had said to the painters just what you now direct me to do, that printing would be their best friend.'

Even the amiable Josiah Wedgwood Senior at first would not allow his artists the liberty of inscribing their name on their artistic products, be they heads or busts modelled solely by them. This is revealed in a letter to Bentley 22 December 1777: 'I cannot resist the temptation of shewing my dear friend our new Shakespeare and Garrick, though they are not so well fired, as they should be. You will see by looking under the shoulder of each, that these heads are modelled by William Hackwood, but I shall prevent his exposing himself again, now I have found it out.' Wedgwood, who liked to express his own individuality in so many ways, was honest enough to tell Bentley his fears about Hackwood's possible reactions: 'I am not certain, that he will not be offended, if he is refused the liberty of putting his name to the models, which he makes quite new, and I shall be glad to have your opinion upon the matter. Mine is against any name being upon the articles, besides 'W and B' [Wedgwood and Bentley], and if you concur with me, I shall manage the matter with him as well as I can.'

Wedgwood would have to tread warily with William Hackwood, who was his best modeller in Etruria, and was considered the senior modeller and artist among his employees. One would expect Hackwood to stand out for his rights as an artist, and a very skilled one, to be allowed to add his signature to his artistic production, as was the case with painters and their canvasses. However, Hackwood did not win outright; Wedgwood compromised, and allowed Hackwood to sign all his future products with his initials 'W.H.' It is on record by Falkner in his *Wood Family of Burslem* that William Wood, the son of Aaron Wood, got even with Wedgwood by deleting the imprint 'Wedg' from 'Wood' and substituting his initial 'W' before 'Wood'. Professor A. H. Church, in his *Josiah Wedgwood* condemns Wedgwood for this niggardly attitude to his artists. On the other hand, J. C. Wedgwood, in his *History of the Wedgwood Family* states, 'that there was no complaint from the artists on this score'. Professor Church sums up the artist's complaint thus, 'Individuality was lost. The workmen became parts of a well ordered and accurately adjusted machine. The marks of human handiwork became unrecognisable.'

Wedgwood was in a sense the victim of the Industrial Revolution, a captain of industry, even though he was the creator to a large extent of his factory and its output. It was no easy task to run a pottery factory of the magnitude and complexity of Etruria, supplemented by its Chelsea decorating and ornamental works, as well as the useful works at Burslem. As Wedgwood indicates in a letter to Bentley 3 February 1770, 'To keep 150 hands of various professions and more various tempers is no easy task.' How much more difficult this became, when the hands reached nearly 300!

Wedgwood's dealings with the wage-earning journeyman and other employees were very unhappy at times. There were almost endless rows, repeated revolts, threats of discharges. After failure of coaxings, at one time there was a 'fracas' at the factory, as Wedgwood put it in a letter to Bentley on 6 February 1773.

The artists, when ruffled by the restrictions of factory conditions on their art, could either escape from it by selling their services and art elsewhere from their own studio, or accept a position on the staff at an agreed progressive salary. The wage-earning employees – craftsmen, artisans and others had no escape from the wage status. Their only form of protest in the latter part of the eighteenth century was to revolt. Only in the early decades of the nineteenth century were they able to stage a strike collectively, in 1824, which proved abortive. It was only after the repeal of the Anti-Combination Acts of 1799–1824 that the wage-earners of the pottery industry were able to come out openly and defiantly on strike, as they did in 1834–1836.

The law in the eighteenth century, with its respect for apprentices' agreements and journeymen's indentures, prevented the workers from taking united action against irksome factory conditions relating to low wages, long hours and other features of the industrial system, with its infiltration of machinery and mechanical processes. The legal penalties for breaking faith with the master of the pottery factory, in the case of apprentices and journeymen, were heavy enough to deter individual or collective action in most cases. But the increasing tendency of the master potter to 'hire', with its correlative to 'fire' when deemed necessary, led to an increasing opportunity for the individual, disgruntled rebel to join hands with some fellow-rebel and stage an open revolt or a 'fracas'.

The number of hired wage-earners was often increased by a number of apprentices, whose indentures were not signed or properly executed, to judge from this letter to Wedgwood from his son Josiah on 25 May 1790:

We are so situated with respect to our apprentices that I find it necessary to consult you. Finding that some of the apprentices played whenever they pleased. Tom sent word, that they should not play without their master's leave. Six of them seem determined to do as they pleased. Some exertion of authority seems necessary, and yet, they are not apprentices, in which the terms of the Act have been exactly complied with. Some are not indented, others are not executed. It is exceedingly unpleasant to pretend to an authority one cannot fully establish. Would it not be proper to have fresh indentures? If nothing, I should think it much better to discharge them, than to have a set of nominal apprentices, who are not bound by the rules of apprentices.

The bigger the manufactory grew, ultimately becoming a more or less mechanized factory, the less did the journeymen and craftsmen have a say in the general conditions of work and employment. The factory's size, its machinery, its processes, its length of day, its succession of shifts, overtime, night-work if necessary, the time to work and to play was dictated by the owner, as revealed in the strict Factory Rules recorded in Wedgwood's 'Commonplace Book'. The workers might make some feeble protest and grumble – but they had to put up with it in the eighteenth century and early decades of the nineteenth century. Many took to drink as an escape from the oppression and often tyranny of the factory. As early as 1765, Wedgwood wrote to Bentley on 7 August, 'I am teased of my life with dilatory, drunken, idle, worthless workmen.' Throughout his partnership with Bentley till his death in 1780, Wedgwood had many bitter complaints to make about the intemperance of his employees. Combined with this intemperance was the desire to yield to wanderlust. Wedgwood wrote Bentley on 6 December 1767, 'The man I mentioned to you from Derby will do us no good. He told the man he worked along with, that he would stay about a month here, would then go to Liverpool which would complete his tour over all the works in England, then he would embark for

America. He has been drinking three days, and I have ordered him off, that he may proceed upon his intended tour.' To show that this type of migrant employee or bird of passage was not exceptional, we quote from another letter to Bentley on 28 August 1770, 'We have three Liverpool hands. They have drunk half their time here.' Wedgwood was also troubled with drunken workmen in his London factory at Chelsea. He wrote Bentley on 25 March 1776, 'The bearer is the packer, I mentioned in a former letter. I believe him to be perfectly honest and sober. I have warned him of the danger from Thomas Mear who I told him was a drinking man.'

Wedgwood in his correspondence with Bentley has left on record several occasions when his workpeople rebelled or revolted against his system of running the factory. He realized that often the period of the open rebellion was preceded by subterranean uneasiness and dissatisfaction, indicating that trouble was brewing. The main causes of the revolt was invariably dissatisfaction with wages paid, whether on a day or weekly basis, or latterly on a piece-rate basis. This attitude of the workers was to be expected, when journeymen or master craftsmen found themselves removed from the former close personal contact with their workshop master-potter of earlier years, and treated so cavalierly, as mere pottery 'hands', to use Wedgwood's own phrase for them. When their day or weekly wage rate was attacked or not reviewed progressively for a rise, with the progressive and increasing output of the factory, the employees felt they had a real grievance.

Particularly so was this felt by those put to work on piece-rates. Their number increased rapidly, whilst those on day-wage declined. This change over to piece-work rates explains a good deal of the psychology of the workpeople. Piece-rates were settled arbitrarily by Wedgwood, or by his manager, foreman or workshop boss. There was no negotiation, no consultation between the employee and the boss. A figure had been worked out by the pottery owner, or his works manager, his foreman or workshop boss. The price offered was the same throughout the factory for an article or job done. It struck at the roots of the personal character of the settlement of pay originally between master and man, when a personal chat between the apprentice or the journeyman and the master-potter before, or at Martinmas, was the rule or tradition.

The fixing of a piece-rate for a job done or for an article produced was in itself a one-sided process. The industrial capitalist or pottery owner had it all his own way in fixing it for the piece-worker, with a fiat, 'Take it or leave it' or 'This is my price – you can take it or your discharge'. We have seen how the master-potters, as early as 1771, had organized informally to settle the prices of their wares to be sold on the market. The workpeople on the other hand had no organization of any kind to protect them in their day-wage or piece-rates. The Combination Laws were against them forming a union. They could see how their master's business kept expanding and thriving. They saw the pottery owners amassing wealth as they believed at their expense as journeymen and craftsmen. The meteoric rise of master potters such as Wedgwood, Spode and Minton was witnessed by many of their journeymen and master craftsmen, who had originally worked and been trained at the bench, when they were apprentices. They felt they were not being given a fair deal, and that Wedgwood cut prices on piecework or unreasonably refused to give a progressive increase in their day or weekly wage rates.

In the Wedgwood-Bentley correspondence, the first indication of an impending rebellion or revolt over a cut in piece-rates occurs in a letter of 22 July 1772:

Every day I have battles of various kinds and orders to fight my way through. This morning all the men at the ornamental works were assembled to meet me, on the outside of the gates at 6 o'clock in order to expostulate with me about their prices, some of which I had told them before I left home, were exorbitant and must be reduced. Others they had fixed, whilst I was away, which I thought more exorbitant. I told Daniel (Greatbatch) on Saturday, they must be reduced and he must sit down in earnest and work a day or two on each article. I should point out to him, and to show the men to their conviction, what they could be done at.

The men obviously refused to take orders from his 'lieutenant' Daniel, and insisted on seeing the 'General' himself. Wedgwood continued his letter:

Upon hearing this from Daniel, they determined not to begin work on Monday morning till they had settled with me, for they did their very best, worked late and early etc. – just in the strain of the painters at Chelsea. On my asking them the reason of their assembling together, they told me they did not choose to begin work till their prices were settled. I talked to them about a $\frac{1}{4}$ of an hour, and after producing several instances of their extravagant charges, I told them we could make a new sett of hands, which they must be sensible was in my power to do, rather than submit to give such prices. . . I told them a list of prices was making, but of all the articles with the present prices, that when that was done, I should fix the prices. They should have their choice, either to work at them or get a better place. If they choose to settle to their business till the prices could be fixed, it was well, but if they found themselves rather inclined to play, we could spare them a day, a week or a month. That, if they meant to frighten me into measures by assembling together in that way, they were very mistaken in their measures. I had no more to say to them, and they might better walk into the workshops or go home, as they thought proper. One of them a young fellow seemed to take the lead for the rest, talked very pertly and asked, 'Why I would not turn him away, if I did not like his work' I told him I did not act so light by any servant, I employed, who was willing to do his duty, as he seemed to act up by his place. The reason, that I had not parted with him before was my hopes, that he would as he had often promised me to do better, but as I was not convinced, that he would rather leave this place than mend his work, he was perfectly at liberty to leave our place. This stopped his mouth, and seemed to have a good effect upon the rest, for they all went quietly to their work and there the matter rests at present.

But Wedgwood was mistaken if he thought that by brow-beating a revolt of his ornamental employees by the 'take it or leave it', 'I'll hire and fire you' attitude he had suppressed all revolts at Etruria. He records in a letter to Bentley on 27 October 1772: 'No sooner is one disagreeable event subsided a little, but others succeed to keep my mind and body too upon the fret. . . . A combination of our servants at the useful works exists to have their own prices, which are exorbitant ones or to leave us. The ring leader, who was to try the experiment with us yesterday after several consultations amongst ourselves, insisted on having his own price or his discharge. Our Thomas Wedgwood, as we had agreed, gave him his discharge. He took his discharge and is gone and I think more will follow him.'

This discharging of so-called ringleaders did not solve the trouble either at Etruria or at Chelsea. On 3 February 1773, Wedgwood writes Bentley: 'I have had some Fracas with our workmen of late, which has vexed me a little.' He reported that Holland, the fireman that he had trained, had left him to start as a hawker. He left, when there was an ovenful of ware in the oven, because Wedgwood refused, what he termed 'unreasonable demands of his respecting oven-work and other matters'. Wedgwood wrote after the fracas 'Holland returned, asked pardon and promised to be very good. But, as he returned, two more are gone from the useful work, both handlers, which will inconvenience us, if they do not return again soon'.

As early as 18 April 1770, Wedgwood had written a strong letter to Bentley to resist demands for higher wages claimed by painters at Chelsea. One of his men at Chelsea, a painter, had asked for £1. 4s. a week. Wedgwood wrote:

Our treatment of this disorder to which painters are more liable, I think, than other men, will have its consequences, if we absolutely refuse this man's demands and turn him off or let him go about his business. Instruct Mr. Rhodes [Bentley's manager at Chelsea] that unless I can have the useful ware enamelled upon moderate terms in London, I am determined to have it done in the country [i.e. Staffordshire] where I can have hands in plenty at 12/- or 14/- a week, the disease may perhaps be stopped in its first stage, but if his demands are at all complied with, it is sure to spread and infect every soul we employ. . . . I am therefore for parting with this man at all events unless he chooseth to be good and continue upon the terms he as at present engaged for.

Wedgwood used the lever of low wages at Etruria to keep wages low in Chelsea, in spite of the higher cost of living in the Metropolis.

The constant reminder to Bentley in Chelsea and his son in Etruria, that wages must be kept static or permanently fixed, or worse still, should be pruned and cut-down, leads me to think that Wedgwood firmly believed or was even obsessed by his theory of a wages fund being fixed, as though it were an immutable law of the eighteenth-century economic system. He resisted most strenuously any individual claim for a rise, as revealed in a memorandum, written to Wedgwood by his son. 'James Lilly, the clay beater, who has now 11/6 per week wishes to know, whether you will allow him to stay at 12/-. He says he has worked 20 years with you, and it is very hard, that you should now differ about 6d. per week.'

Wedgwood probably argued that as an employer of hundreds of wage-earners or hands, if he yielded in the one instance, he would be inundated with demands from the mass of his employees. This attitude is revealed in one of his letters to Bentley. 'I observe what you say respecting Hutchins, and if there were no other consequences to be apprehended from raising his wages per week, there would not be much in it. But I apprehend that Wilcox and the other hands will follow his example, if he succeeds, but it may be better to risk these consequences, than to part with Hutchins.' Wedgwood adds, 'Would his working piece work be a better plan?' and he ends by suggesting to Bentley, that he should squeeze more output for increased wages, whether by wage or piece-rate. 'You may tell him, that you have observed he has not got so much work out of his hands, and that if he has more money, he must do more work for it. . . . I believe he would be content to work some over hours for it.' The idea that his employees merited a share of the prosperity enjoyed by the firm was foreign to Wedgwood's mind. Even though he made a distinction between the wages he paid some of his employees and his more generous payment of salaries to his foremen, managers and supervisors, their weekly payments were entered as 'wage say salary', in his books.

Even in the case of what Wedgwood considered generous remuneration, he expected in return almost the allegiance a feudal lord expected from his vassals. The idea of any salaried staff member ever wanting to better himself by seeking another job, upset Wedgwood as much as an assembly of workmen demanding new piece-rate prices or a rise in wages. This is brought out in a letter from Wedgwood to Bentley on 28 December 1769. 'I think Mr. Croft does not use us very well, and I admire in you, what I fear I could not have imitated, though I believe it was right – I mean your patience with him. He's not pleased with our behaviour to him! Why, if he had been a Nabob himself, we could not have behaved with more respect to him. And between friends, I believe that is the very thing which has spoiled him. . . . I believe our engaging him at the rate of £200 per annum, and making a companion of him has turned his head.'

Wedgwood showed a one-sidedness in his conception of the liberty of the individual. He did not consider that the individuals, once engaged as wage-earners or salaried members of his staff, had the right to leave his employ, unless he discharged them. Yet, as we have seen from numerous examples, he took away workers from other employers in Liverpool, Derby or Chelsea. This sense of ownership of his workpeople and employees was undoubtedly a relic of the domestic relationship that once existed in the workshop stage of the master-potter with his journeymen and apprentices. It was an extension of the paternalism of the peasant and family handicraft feature of the early pottery stage of the industry, which Wedgwood knew from about 1740 to 1750.

This parental right of an employer over his workman explains a good deal of Wedgwood's indulgence in threats and a desire sometimes, if he dared, to go further in meting out punishment. Writing Bentley on 19 August 1772, Wedgwood wrote: 'I observe and lament your want of plates and ware to enamel, but could not possibly do more, than we have done. Our men will go to the Wake's one day, if they were sure to be carried to the D——l the next. I have not spared them in threats and I would have thrashed them right heartily, if I could.'

These extracts from Wedgwood's own correspondence may well show him in a less favourable light than do some of his biographers – Meteyard, Smiles and Jewitt. Nevertheless, taking Wedgwood as a type of the rising and successful industrial capitalist of the eighteenth century master-potter, the picture could not be otherwise. While admitting that Wedgwood was an outstanding personality with extraordinary gifts as an organizer, as an artist too, he really was no exception to the class of employers produced by the Industrial Revolution in his treatment of his workpeople. Because of his success as a wealthy business man, and the great social contacts and power he achieved, he may have taken a more dictatorial and, at times, tyrannical attitude towards his employees individually and in the mass, than some of his less wealthy contemporaries.

Because of their central geographical position, midway between Manchester, the 'Cottonopolis', and Birmingham, the 'Metalopolis' of the Midlands, the Potteries were a favourite halting place for the 'political reform' orators to pitch their tent. 'The epidemic of political reform was extremely rife throughout the nation from 1817–1819', says Ward, the Potteries local historian. Ward in his *History of Stoke on Trent* shows no sympathy with the orators: 'Some itinerant orators from a distance, who were afterwards prosecuted for sedition declaimed against the burden of taxes, the corrupt state of the Representation, the stagnation of trade occasioned by the bad measures of Government, and the poverty and oppression of the labouring classes. . . . Attempts were made to form political Clubs to carry the views of the Reformers into effect, but most of the manufacturers and respectable inhabitants stood aloof from these Associations.'

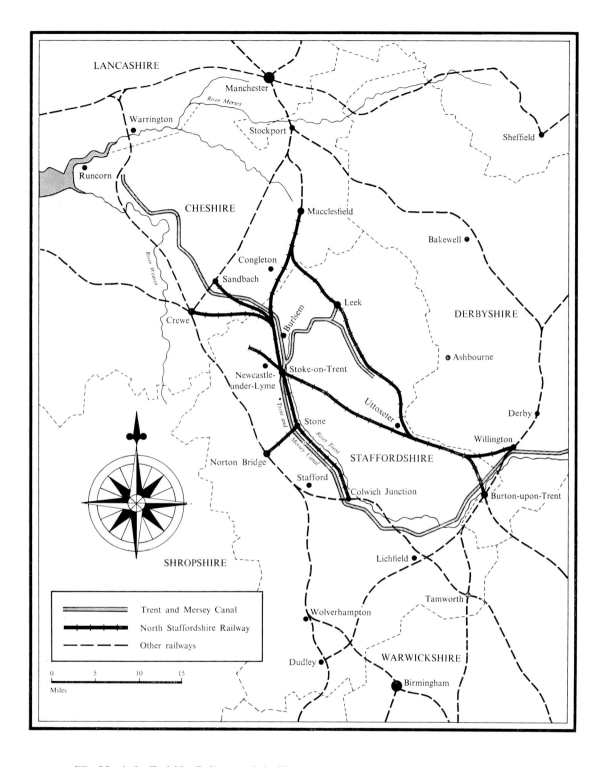

LANCASHIRE

Manchester

River Mersey

Warrington

Stockport

Sheffield

Runcorn

CHESHIRE

River Weaver

Macclesfield

Bakewell

Congleton

Sandbach

Burslem

Leek

DERBYSHIRE

Crewe

Ashbourne

Newcastle-under-Lyme

Stoke-on-Trent

Uttoxeter

Derby

Stone

River Trent

Willington

Trent and Mersey Canal

Norton Bridge

STAFFORDSHIRE

Stafford

Colwich Junction

Burton-upon-Trent

SHROPSHIRE

Lichfield

Tamworth

Trent and Mersey Canal

North Staffordshire Railway

Other railways

Wolverhampton

0   5   10   15

Miles

WARWICKSHIRE

Dudley

Birmingham

44 The North Staffordshire Railway and the Trent and Mersey Canal

45 Joseph Priestley, Wedgwood jasper medallion

Ward was very indigant in his account of the actions of these itinerant 'demagogues', as he terms them. As a thriving local solicitor, he belonged to 'the respectable inhabitants', and later made a name for himself as a prosecutor of these 'demagogues' before the local magistrates. He writes: 'The demagogues however affected to excite no ill feeling among the working classes towards their employers, but the tendency of their levelling doctrines, whatever they might profess, could hardly fail to produce such a result. We do not expect to be contradicted in asserting that from the excitement of that period may be dated whatever political fervour the operative classes in this District have since manifested, as well as the combinations of Trades Unions, by which they have since greatly injured themselves and inconvenienced their employers.'

Ward showed a strong bias and indeed venom against trade unions and these itinerant speakers who fanned the flames of discontent amongst the working or labouring class of the Potteries. He does quite rightly connect this political-reform-agitation epidemic in the Potteries from 1817–1819 with the definite industrial activity amongst the pottery wage-earners, and their early efforts to form an organization or trade union. Ward is more correct in his assessment of the influence of this contemporary political reform propaganda on the movement to attempt the establishment of trade unions in the Potteries, than later local writers specializing in the history of the Pottery Workers' Trade Union movement.

Political events had oppressed the pottery workers long before the culminating Corn Law of 1815. The whole country was disorganized and disturbed by the conditions following the American War of Independence and the French War against Napoleon. One of the first effects of these wars was to create a shortage of food, with a great increase in the prices of necessities. The first section of the community to feel the pinch of war or post-war conditions then, as now, were the poor ranks of wage-earners. The only form of protest by the oppressed pottery workers was to riot.

The discovery of a letter in the Wedgwood archives which, from their account of the riot Miss Meteyard, Smiles and Ward have obviously not perused, enables fresh light to be thrown on one incident in particular.

Josiah Wedgwood II sent this letter to his father on 7 March 1783:

Dear father,   Etruria.

The rioters, who were at Newcastle came here from Burslem, Hanley etc; to follow a boat laden with corn, flour and barley, which I believe was going to Manchester. I think they had notice of it from our works. There were several 100's of men, women and children, who followed it to Longport. There a man jumping into the boat, the boatman cut the ropes and with a knife struck at the man. Immediately, half the mob cried "Put him into the canal", which they certainly would have done, if some gentleman had not interfered. Then they brought the boat in triumph to this place and lodged the contents in the crateshop. This was between 3 & 5 o'clock this evening. About 7.30 p.m. 4 men came up to the house and asked for something to eat and drink, as they were to sit up and guard the corn flour. John went to them and told them a great deal. My mother followed and said some more and then they went off. But, I don't know whether they will come back or not. It is now 8 o'clock breakfast time March 8th. They are all quiet, and I hope they will continue so. The men did not come again last night.

I am your dutiful son,
Josiah Wedgwood.

The details of the riot at Etruria by Eliza Meteyard (ii, 472–473) must have been related to the one occurring after 8 March, when she states Josiah Wedgwood was at Etruria himself – probably arriving some time after the receipt of the above letter from his son. Meteyard concludes her tale of the riot at Etruria as follows:

The boat had meanwhile gone on its way, but it was followed to Longport, seized and brought back to Etruria, and with another boat, which had just come up to the locks was rifled of its contents. These were sold at such prices, as the mob pleased. An endeavour was made to give an air of justice to this daring act, by handing over the proceeds to the Captains of the boats, but the real spirit of the rioters was shown in the attempt to rifle and fire several houses and to do other mischief. For a time the works seemed threatened, but Mr. Wedgwood, who was fortunately at home despatched messages to Newcastle and the result was the speedy arrival of a company of Welsh Fusiliers, and a detachment of the Staffordshire Militia, under the command of Major Sneyd.

The Riot Act was read and the order given to charge, but the mob, as cowardly as it was ignorant, fled in all directions. There can be no doubt that this wise show of resistence at Etruria saved the adjacent towns from widespread ruin . . . Two men were subsequently arrested. . . and both executed.

John Ward, commenting on this execution, states that 'The Government were alarmed at the popular disposition to tumult and poor Barlow [one of the executed] became a victim to public safety more than to the heinousness of his crime.'

Miss Meteyard states that 'Wedgwood, as soon as tranquility was restored to the district endeavoured to enlighten the rising generation around him as to the folly of looking to such outbreaks for a redress of social wrongs'. The contents of Wedgwood's 28-page pamphlet called *An Address to the young inhabitants of the Pottery* (published by J. Smith in 1783), not only reveals what Wedgwood thought about the riot, but also clearly shows that he was fully aware that his own workpeople were involved in the tumult.

Wedgwood opens his address: 'My young friends. This difficulty of knowing what to decide upon, and the chances of judging and acting wrong are greatly increased, not only by the unsettled state of the mind in the midst of riot and tumult, but more particularly by seeing your friends and relations and perhaps even your parents taking the most active part in the disturbances. I therefore address myself, particularly to you, because when you are placed in these unhappy circumstances, seeing those who have fed and protected you from infancy are very forward in promoting such disorder. . . .'

What motives led Wedgwood to plan this pamphlet? First, he was deeply disturbed by the discontent of the inhabitants of the Potteries, many if not most of them concerned in the riot being elderly people, probably many of them wage-earners in Etruria – the largest pottery at the time in the Potteries. Secondly, he was well aware of the economic evils that formed the background to the riot, as revealed by the logic or line of argument in his pamphlet – the high prices of provisions, the large number of provision dealers in the area, the poverty of the poorer classes. Wedgwood's remarks on these questions were to say the least naïve and unconvincing, if they had been addressed not to 'my Young Friends', but to some of his elderly employees. His view of the high prices of provisions was that they were due 'to the hand of providence'. His reply to the charge of too many middlemen and dealers handing provisions was to point out what a necessity in society middlemen were.

Reading between the lines of pages 8 and 9 in the pamphlet, one cannot escape the conclusion that Wedgwood was troubled in his own mind about his own action in calling in the military to put down or quell the rioters, for he strongly defends the powers given to civil magistrates to order soldiers to industrial areas during a riot or tumult. Probably he had come under criticism from some of his own workpeople for calling on the military forces to quell the disturbance at Etruria. Wedgwood's reply to the charge that the rich had not relieved the distress among the poorer inhabitants was simply, that he had not been made aware of this distress. This reply would be treated with cynicism, if not contempt, by many of his own employees, whom we have seen earlier often complained to him about low wages and their rising cost of living. Certainly Wedgwood's final paragraph – 'when you labour under any real grievance, make your situation known in a peaceable manner to some magistrate near you, or to your employers, and I have no doubt of your meeting in this way with speedy and effective redress' – would resound as being a piece of sheer hypocrisy to many of his wage-earners, whose direct appeals to Wedgwood himself on genuine wage claims had fallen on deaf ears and been contemptuously dismissed. As to approaching a magistrate, this was difficult, as the nearest magistrate to Etruria was eight miles away!

This riot at Etruria in 1783 illustrates the discontent and even despair of the pottery workers during the latter decades of the eighteenth century. The workers of the Potteries were without a Parliamentary vote or representation, as well as being without a corporate organization or trade union to express any protest on their behalf, to remedy the situation. Social conditions got worse after 1783, when in addition to the War of American Independence, the ravages and after-math of the French Wars on the Continent were felt in England. On 22 September 1800 some of the pottery manufacturers themselves joined with the inhabitants to protest against the high prices charged by dealers for corn and provisions – social conditions so vividly exposed by the rioters, that Wedgwood had asked the magistrates to call out the soldiers in 1783.

Conditions in 1800 were so bad that even a large employer of pottery labour like Enoch Wood took the initiative among his fellow inhabitants in Burslem to deal with the distress. But the situation was worse in 1815. The Hammonds state: 'The war [in France] then added special complications to the struggle for a standard of life, into which the working classes were thrown by the revolutions in industry. The working classes, who suffered as wage earners from all the disorganizing forces, suffered as consumers from two causes – the course of the Currency and the Corn Laws. The former led to an immense inflation of prices, which was a catastrophe for the working classes'.

Prothero states 'that from 1811 to 1813, when wheat reached 126 shillings, one fifth of the price was due to the currency muddle'. Professor Nicolson in his *History of the English Corn Laws*, states, 'After 1815, and especially towards the end of the Corn Law Period, the influence of the Corn Law was becoming real and serious.' The Hammonds, summing up, state: 'The war and the Corn Laws brought great distress and misfortune to the people of England . . . there were landlords, who were enriched by the Corn Laws, and if some of the manufacturers were ruined, many fortunes were made during this period.'

It was during this depressing period that the pottery workers were prepared to listen even to those whom Ward called demagogues and orators, especially from 1817–19, and up to 1824.

The Public Record Office in its files of Home Office Papers 1816 to 1820 has original letters and reports from civil magistrates, generals commanding troops, M.P.s, manufacturers etc., which throw great light on the political ferment in the Potteries. These were the troublesome years of Hampden Clubs, Union Societies, and the harangues of itinerant orators like Hunt. A letter dated 25 January 1817 (which was attached to a notice calling special constables to meet, found in the H.O. files) reads:

Sir   Post-Office, Newcastle,
  Late last night was posted upon the walls in Burslem, 3 bills calling a meeting in Burslem for a
Reform. The bills were all written by one man, and the names of the Club – Wm Massey. The members

of the Club met at Massey's 'George and Dragon', Burslem. The moment these bills were discovered, the principal gentlemen of Burslem met. They sent letters to Lord Talbot and asked the magistrates round here to meet at Burslem. The writer of the letter then reports 'the Swearing in of nearly 300 special constables'.

Later Lord Talbot from Ingestre writes Sidmouth:

I am just returned from the Potteries, where the meeting was held today for the Parliamentary Reform. There did not appear to be the smallest indication of a disposition to riot in the numerous assemblings to hear the Manchester Orators. I think nearly 30,000 were assembled. . . . I did not call out the Military, who were in readiness at Newcastle to march at a moments notice. I am of the opinion, that the Manchester Speakers were kept within proper bounds from the knowledge that the magistrates were prepared to check any popular disturbances. [Concluding, Lord Talbot said]: The Gentlemen of the Potteries did express some doubt as to the result of the measures of the disaffected in establishing a Hampden Club, of which there are already 500 members, subscribing 1d per week, for the purpose of distributing seditious publications. I hope some measures will be devised for the abolition of this Society.

The year 1818 was fairly quiet, and free from disturbance, probably for reasons given by Sir James Lyons in a letter dated 19 February 1818, H.O. 40/7. 'In the Potteries, there are no traces of disloyalty and the propect of an abundant harvest has silenced every expression of discontent.' But the year 1819 brought its crop of trouble in July. Letters from Sir John Heathcote and the Marquis of Stafford (H.O. 40/4 and 40/5) asked for the movement of troops and the raising of volunteer corps in the Potteries to meet with 'the proceedings of the disaffected'. The Home Office was alarmed at news of 'pikes' being discovered in the Potteries, which was a vital industrial link with Birmingham, famous for its repeated riots, and Manchester, with its 'Peterloo' massacre in August. Local magistrates and the Home Office suspected that the Potteries might become a strong link with the radicals. Lord Sidmouth on 20 October 1819 reported to Lord Dartmouth that 'pistols of a particular construction' had lately been manufactured in Staffordshire 'for the use of Radical Reformers'. On 20 December 1819, a John A. Prowse of Hanley wrote to Lord Sidmouth giving evidence of propaganda emanating from the Union Reading Rooms, being circulated in the Potteries.

Throughout 1820 the Home Office was kept busy tracing the truth or otherwise of the allegations made by two deserters of the Coldstream Guards, named Hayley and Clarke, who swore on oath that they had attended Union meetings in Hanley, and stating that a man at Wetley Rocks had a store of pikes underground there, and also a store of grenades hidden in a pit at Hanley. These two deserters may have been spying on union meetings, or concocting evidence to mitigate any punishment they deserved as deserters. In file H.O. 40/15, there are letters from the Mayor of Manchester to Lord Sidmouth reporting a union meeting of delegates in Manchester on 7 December 1820 'to ascertain its strength throughout the kingdom and to infuse fresh vigour by assurance, that a crisis is approaching.'

On 12 and 16 December 1820 the H.O. received two letters from a respectable Anglican Tory, J. Tomlinson, – 'depreciating the practice introduced by certain parties in the neighbourhood [the potteries] of taking their workpeople to public meetings, as an overawing force, and the clamour and disorder, which had existed, in consequence. No person of respectability who is friendly to the Government will think of attending in future, whilst this order of things continues.' Then in his second letter, Tomlinson gives the news, that 'The person who headed the Radical meeting at Hanley last year was a leading character today. It is said that the workmen attending were allowed their wages or money for liquor by their employers, who chiefly belonged to the New Connexion of Methodists.'

After 1820, the H.O. files contain little data about the Potteries of North Staffordshire, but there is ample evidence of disturbances in the mines and ironworks of South Staffordshire over wages and the evils of the truck system, prior to the passing of the repeal of the Combination Law in 1824. The workers of the North Staffordshire Potteries delayed their action over wages and other conditions of employment, till after 1824, when the Government wisely passed an Act to repeal the Anti-Combination Acts of 1799 and 1800.

CHAPTER 17

Trade Unions

The Pottery workers in the North Staffordshire area responded almost immediately in 1824 to the favourable circumstances permitting the legal organization of trade unions. This local atmosphere favourable to trade union organization was only possible because of the legislation introduced by the 1824 Act, repealing the old Combination Acts of 1799 and 1800, and the changes in attitudes towards trade unions, nationally, which accompanied it.

There is no sign in the Blue Books, reporting the Committees of Inquiry of 1824 V. 51(21) and 1825 IV 437, of any evidence in their 400 pages of information from the pottery manufacturers. The explanation, probably, is that at that period the pottery manufacturers lacked a leader like Josiah Wedgwood, for his son Josiah had retired from actual business to reside in the south of England. It is possible too, that as the pottery manufacturers were divided politically into Conservatives, Whigs and some Radicals, it was realized that it was hopeless to oppose the trade union organization that followed the agitation by reformers and itinerant orators. On the other hand, although I have been unable to find any early minute books or official trade-union records of the pottery workers' unions during this early period 1824, there are other sources of information. These are the files of the local press – *The Pottery Mercury*, *The Staffordshire Advertiser*, and the *Pottery Examiner* (which was really a trade union publication) – all containing valuable reports of trade union activities. During the period of the 1834–1836 pottery workers' strikes, the manufacturers published pamphlets exposing the strikes, and hostile to the trade unions, which are of great interest. Then, many of the Chartist pamphlets and journals report a little of the trade-union activities in the Potteries. Also among the Robert Owen MSS. at the Co-operative College, Manchester, there is correspondence between Robert Owen and leaders of the trade unions in the Potteries. From these varied sources can be traced the development of trade union organization among the pottery workers, first in the locality of the North Staffordshire Potteries, and later, nationally.

During 1824, the first year when trade unions were free legally to organize workers, we find two unions for pottery operatives: first, the union of clay potters – the larger organization catering for throwers, turners, handlers, hollow ware pressers, plate and saucer makers – and, secondly, the printers' union, for those engaged in decorating the wares made by the craftsmen. There were a number of pottery operatives left unorganized for various reasons:

those engaged in the preparation of the clay – the slip-makers;

those engaged in the decoration of wares by hand, mostly women and young girls; and

those engaged in the final process of fixing the wares – the kiln or oven-men.

The slip-makers were few in number in any factory, mainly supervising water-driven mills or steam-driven machinery. In some of the smaller pottery factories, there would be no slip-makers employed, for the slip would be purchased in bulk from potters' millers ready-mixed. The female decorating hands consisted of some married women or young girls, who were considered as being outside the scope of trade unions, which at this early period were considered a realm for male workers only. The kiln or oven-men were just a few in number on the pot-bank, and they were mostly engaged in contract work. As such, they had no incentive to join any trade-union organization.

The clay potters listed above were engaged in making pottery wares with assistance of machines, wheels, lathes or mechanical devices for moulding and casting. These operatives were engaged in processes which Josiah Wedgwood admitted in the 1816 Inquiry had power applied to turn the wheels or lathes. This application of power-driven machinery on the pot-bank meant a greater output of wares. Hence, here was a motive for employers to cut down piece-rates, because of the increased output per employee. If the employees would not accept this lower piece-rate, then the employer would introduce younger workers to operate the mechanical devices.

The union of pottery printers, when mechanical transfers were introduced to decorate wares found that, as copper-plate printers, their rates of pay were reduced. They had a long tradition of organizing their workers, as apprentices and journeymen, in 'works chapels'. Here, the introduction of machinery (often power-driven) and the extreme mechanization of their craft, drove them to be among the first to organize as a trade union in 1824.

Boyle in an article on 'The Strike in the Potteries 1834–1836'[1] states that the purpose of the Clay Potters' Union in striking in 1824 was to obtain an increase in piece-rates, the abolition of the truck system of provision, and the regulation of the sizes of wares.

[1] Royal Statistical Society Journal Vol. I, 1839

The truck system was unpopular in North as well as in South Staffordshire, where the miners in particular suffered from its iniquities and incidence. Small master potters were in favour of its abolition, for in the hands of large pottery manufacturers it could be translated into a substantial element in the costs of production. Because of the political agitation of 1817–1820, the abolition of truck had been very prominent in the propaganda of the itinerant orators. There was strong support for its abolition even among middle-class and upper-class radical employers in the Potteries.

The strike in March, 1825, was only partially successful. The employers only agreed to abolish the truck system, and to promise that they would endeavour to standardize sizes of wares. The question of the revision of piece-rate wages was deferred till 8 July, as the result of the March strike. In fact, the pottery employers caused further delay by postponing their meeting till 27 July. This delay led to a revival of the strike at several factories. Some small increase in wage rates was obtained at a few small pottery factories where lower rates had prevailed. Boyle states that the union paid out £3,000 in strike pay, and completely depleted its funds. He also states that while the strike continued 'the well-known commercial panic of that year occurred, which frustrated the strikers' endeavours, and work resumed at the factories at the same wage rates or lower prices, than those previously paid prior to the strike'.

More important than the commercial panic of 1825 in the collapse of the strike were the following: first, the strike affected only a few of the employed craftsmen – the clay workers – which enabled some of the larger employers to introduce 'scab' labour from the ranks of other operatives not members of the union, as well as using female labour excluded from membership of the union; secondly, the union's demand for higher wage rates was Utopian, in the light of the reduction in prices of provisions in 1825; thirdly, by linking their wage demands with the abolition of truck and the standardization of sizes of wares, the pottery workers enabled the employers to claim that they had met most of their demands, by abolishing truck and promising to standardize and rationalize the sizes of wares. This enabled the employers to defer any decision on the demand for higher wages. Fourthly, the union precipitated the strike of 1825 too soon after the passing of the 1824 Act (abolishing the Combination Act), before they could accumulate a large fighting fund for strike pay; and finally, some of the strikers diverted the strike from their fight with the employers, by starting a co-operative pottery to manufacture wares. If the strike was premature, the venture into a co-operative production of pottery was more visionary and premature still.

In a report in the *Staffordshire Mercury* in October 1830, J. Boyle, on behalf of the Pottery Chamber of Commerce declares: 'After the 1824 Union was dissolved, those who had been at its head, or who had actively promoted it, were viewed by the masters as individuals who would on all occasions be ready to execute a spirit of disaffection among their fellow workmen and take every opportunity of raising the price of labour. As a consequence, such parties had difficulty in obtaining employment, and some therefore left the district, while others took to different occupations.' Boyle adds, 'No more was heard on the subject of a Union for a considerable time.' Harold Owen in *The Staffordshire Potter* sums up the situation as follows: 'The Union, now deprived of its leaders, collapsed with the strike, and for the succeeding five years no attempt to re-organize any combination was made.'

Before 1824, the pottery union enthusiasts had received a good deal of inspiration to organize their union from the 'Philanthropic Society' or 'Philanthropic Hercules', with its headquarters in Manchester. Both the Webbs and Hammonds mention the activities of this so-called national 'Union' – the term 'national' was often used to describe any organization that operated over several localities, like Manchester, the Midlands and London. This 'Philanthropic Society' later merged with other political and radical societies that flourished between 1817 to 1820.

But, after the collapse of the 1824–1825 strike in the Potteries, the defeated employees came under the direct influence of the 'National Association for the Protection of Labour' – the N.A.P.L. emanating again from Manchester, with the famous Doherty as its Secretary. Boyle states: 'About 1830, two delegates from the General Trades Union [The N.A.P.L.] convened a public meeting to be held in the open air, at a short distance from the Potteries. The individuals harangued in a strain of great violence, they denounced all the masters, with one exception, as oppressors of their workmen and exhorted all the pottery workers to form a general union of the operative classes throughout the Kingdom, which could correct all that was amiss in the relations between master and servant, and give the latter a proper station in society.' After this class-conscious outburst, Boyle then concludes 'A short period after this occurred and probably consequent upon it, a Union of the Potters was formed.'

The Webbs give the impression that the National Pottery Union was organized forthwith, and affiliated to the N.A.P.L. This is not strictly true. The first meeting of the delegates was held on 8 October 1830, when no resolution was carried at all to form a National Potters' Union. The speeches made there led to a good deal of correspondence in the *Staffordshire Mercury* (30 October,

5 November, and 13 November 1830.) Then, on 15 November, a huge meeting was held outside the Potteries and speeches were made by Doherty, the Secretary, and three others. The press report described the orators 'as sincere men of moderate speech', a contrast to the biassed and distorted account by Boyle. A journeyman potter took the Chair, and a resolution 'to form a General Union of Potters, which was to affiliate with the N.A.P.L. was passed'.

After the public meeting, the local pottery workers set to work to implement the terms of the resolution. What they ultimately formed was not a 'National Potters' Union', as recorded by the Webbs, but a 'Local China and Earthenware Turners' Society', as reported in the *Voice of the People* on 5 March 1831.

This sectional, local China and Earthenware Turners' Society did not immediately decide to affiliate to the N.A.P.L. It decided to give financial support to the N.A.P.L., which appealed for funds, but 'the Society expressed a desire to be given time to consider the rules and regulations of the N.A.P.L., in order that every member thereof might be satisfied of the utility of such an institution', as reported in the *Voice of the People*. It was not till 28 February 1831 that the Turners' Society was affiliated to the N.A.P.L.

It is significant that the section of the pottery workers that responded to the appeal of the N.A.P.L. to reorganize themselves as a union, after the 1825 strike, was the highly mechanized section of turners, operating power-driven lathes. They were successful, as a society, as even the biassed Boyle admitted: 'This Union of the potters was formed, the effects of which were soon felt by some of the smaller manufacturers, who were paying a low rate of wages.' The support of the N.A.P.L. was persistent and strong behind the decision to set up the local turners' society. In due course, in August 1831, the first National Union of Operative Potters was formed, as reported in the *Staffordshire Mercury*, and at the same time, there is a reference to a separate organization formed for the potters' painters, as recorded in the *Voice of the People* 10 September 1831. As there appears to be no further reference to this separate sectional painters' union, we may assume it did not last long, and ultimately its members joined the 'National Union of Operative Potters' – the N.U.O.P.

This was the first national organization embracing all pottery operatives. It was also the first organization to extend its influence beyond the North Staffordshire Potteries to the out-potteries in other counties, establishing lodges where potteries were established outside Staffordshire. From 1830 to 1833 the N.U.O.P. consolidated its strength in membership and funds. It did not challenge the pottery manufacturers in their hiring agreements, nor attempt to achieve anything more spectacular than adjusting some truck abuses, still remaining, and settling some good-from-oven ware disputes. In fact, the union became so respectable and favoured that one manufacturer, according to the *Staffordshire Mercury* (15 June 1833), recommended 400 of his employees to join it. Another manufacturer wrote a letter to the same paper on 13 July 1833, publicly expressing his support and sympathy with the N.U.O.P.

A joint Committee of the union and the Chamber of Pottery Manufacturers met to draft a list of pottery selling prices, and a list of working piece-rate wages, as reported in the *Staffordshire Mercury* for 21 September 1833. This list was the forerunner of the famous 'Green Book of Prices', settled later in 1835. This list was approved after the second annual meeting of the N.U.O.P. held at Hanley, which delegates from the out-potteries of Bristol, Derbyshire, Newcastle-upon-Tyne, Swansea, Yorkshire and Worcestershire attended. Its strength was given then at 8,000 members, 6,000 in the North Staffordshire Potteries, and 2,000 in the out-potteries, as reported in *Crisis*,[1] 19 October 1833, and in a letter from a Mr. Wood to Robert Owen on 14 June 1834.

Before proceeding further to trace the progress and ultimate decline of this National Union of Operative Potters, we should trace the contacts of its officers and members of the board of management with certain prominent national figures of this decade.

The new policy connecting selling prices of wares with a revision of wage and piece rates was adopted in 1833. It must have emanated from a master mind in trade union organization, for it was an astute move, establishing a new set of tactics. There is only one conclusion one can come to: the mind behind this move was none other than Robert Owen. Boyle states: 'In 1833 Mr. Owen of New Lanark visited the Potteries, and encouraged the spirit of union among the workmen. He took every means of advancing his principles, and some of his most active agents of the Union were considered to be his followers.' In the Robert Owen MSS. collection at the Co-operative Union, Manchester, I discovered the following letter from an Owenite disciple, signing himself R. O. and reporting progress of his mission to the Staffordshire Potteries. 'A great point has been gained in this District by Union. The Union are now making a tariff of prices. The masters were at first highly indignant at this dictation from the mob. . . . There is no section of the country, where the march of intellect is making more rapid strides than this, and I will make public this solid proof of the disposition and ability of the people to look after their own interests.' Robert Owen gave full publicity to this information at the first Co-operative Congress,

[1] An Owenite journal

meeting a few days later. He described the potters as being far above other trades in intelligence, with the builders' trade organization next.

This encouraging report from his disciple in the Potteries stimulated Robert Owen to make a personal visit there. This he did on 4 October 1833, and it was reported in the *Staffordshire Mercury* on 5 October. There Robert Owen and his colleagues met Simpson, the Secretary of the National Union of Operative Potters, Pratt, a prominent member of the Union Board of Management, and a few other prominent and leading members of the N.U.O.P. Owen made a second visit to the Potteries later in October, and addressed public meetings organized in Hanley and Burslem, two local pottery centres in North Stafford-shire. These meetings are reported in the *Staffordshire Mercury* and *Staffordshire Advertiser* of 26 October 1833.

Pratt wrote to Owen after this second visit a letter dated 12 November 1833, saying, 'The seed you sowed when you were here has taken a deep root.' Then Pratt promised to report progress of the negotiations of the 'Grand Lodge' with the Master Potters. 'They, last Monday but one, sent for a deputation from our Lodge, to go to the Swan Inn. They would be glad if we would consent to the foundation of a Council consisting of seven Master Potters and six of our Lodge to meet at stated periods, in order to discuss little differences, which might arise betwixt the two parties.' Later, Pratt disclosed what he had found out about the master potters and selling prices. 'I will tell you how things are acting, (as they think without our knowledge). They have actually doubled the price of their ware, which has struck the dealers with consternation. This is the paltry expedient they have recourse to, in order to convince us that the extravagant demands which we made upon the time of the formation of the List, had led to a deprivation of Trade.'

Writing to Robert Owen after his second visit, T. Simpson, the Secretary of the N.U.O.P., stated: 'There is a great hue and cry against you, all the religious world, so-called, are opposed to you. This is very natural, and I fear it will do us much more mischief than any other subject.' But Simpson wisely and cheerily adds 'this is what the enemy says'. Whatever religious animosity was displayed to Robert Owen's views on God and sectarianism, his correspondence with leaders of the pottery workers, the propaganda of the Owenite Disciples, as well as his personal contacts with the officials and members of the Board of Management of the N.U.O.P. strengthened by his three stirring public meetings – all achieved two practical results. First, Owen and his missionaries inspired some pottery workers to venture on a Co-operative Pottery; and secondly Owen, through the medium of his missionaries, got the N.U.O.P. to join his Grand

National Consolidated Trades Union, which had taken up protests against the Tolpuddle martyrs' penal sentences. A large protest meeting was organized in Hanley, and presided over by Mr. Stacey, whom the *Staffordshire Mercury* calls 'the Grand President of the N.U.O.P. branch of the Grand National Consolidated Trades Union', in its issue on 24 May 1834.

The Webbs write of Owen's Grand National Consolidated Trades Union: 'The whole machinery of the organization was turned to the preparation of petitions, and the holding of public meetings. Cordial relations were established with the five great Unions – The Builders' Union, the Leeds and District Union, the Clothers' Union, the Cotton Spinners' Union, and the Potters' Union.' Warburton in his *History of the Staffordshire Pottery Union* states that, 'Owen wielded great power over the Union leaders, but it is equally true that he had more over the potters in the mass.' This was probably due to his power of oratory at the three public meetings that he held in the Potteries.

One may quite justifiably compare the influence of Robert Owen on the Pottery Workers' Trade Union organization with that of Josiah Wedgwood and his influence on the local Chamber of Commerce, his aspirations and strenuous efforts to establish and maintain the National Chamber of Commerce. Both organizations were short-lived and ultimately came to grief, but while they lasted they greatly influenced those associated with their efforts. Both Owen's and Wedgwood's ideas and plans created bitter dissensions, despite their strenuous efforts to assist with advice and inspiration to their respective organizations.

The two strikes of 1834 and 1836 were bitter battles in the struggle between the organizations of the pottery workers and their masters. Incidents in the struggle are described by contemporaries according to their particular, and often personal, points of view.

For example, the lawyer John Ward, in his *History of Stoke on Trent* writes:

The Masters were called to encounter a formidable combination of the workmen, to raise wages and prescribe regulations for their advantage. The operatives, by mandate from their Union Lodge, systematically 'turned out' in a mass from any manufactory where their Prices and Rules were not granted. This procedure greatly inconvenienced many of the Masters, and induced some to forgo that character, and submit to the dictates of their workmen. But the evil became so great at length, that nearly all the Manufacturers combined in their turn, held weekly General Meetings as Chambers of Commerce for upholding their interests and ascendancy, and completely closed their works for a period of several months, until the men were reduced to the necessity of returning to their labour upon the footing on which they stood before the disputes arose.

Boyle, in his account of the struggle, obviously speaking on behalf of his fellow manufacturers, sums up the issue of the 'turn-out' in a sentence: 'To encourage the proceedings of the Union would destroy the control of the Manufacturer over his business and expose him to constant, progressive annoyance.' Boyle knew this from experience, first as a partner in Minton's pottery during the 'turn-out,' and afterwards, as a partner in Wedgwood's pottery.

The Chamber of Commerce of the Pottery Manufacturers published in 1837 a 24-page pamphlet, giving, 'The case of the manufacturers of China and Earthenware in the Staffordshire Potteries.' After detailing their side of the struggle, they concluded their pamphlet with the words: 'Thus terminated a struggle as singular in its nature as unexampled in its duration. And for what has this enormous sacrifice been made? Not through any complaint of prices, not through want of employment, but through the proceedings of a powerful, organized Union, acting on the principles inculcated by Mr. Owen, and directed by a Board of Management invested with almost unlimited power, and using it for the worst purposes.'

But a pamphlet (published by Moore in Hanley in 1837) entitled 'Report of the important meeting of delegates in the Potteries on behalf of the Staffordshire Potters' (on 28, 29 and 30 December 1836) records the speech of a Mr. Richards, one of the pottery delegates. 'This is a contest of money against labour. Money which makes one man arrogant, the other a slave – a context in which money is endeavouring to lessen the price of Labour.'

Mr. Buchanan, another delegate, stated: 'I consider the arguments brought forward by the men perfectly satisfactory, those by the Masters are shuffling and evasive. Delegates, agitate your respective constituencies to obtain funds, for no battle of this nature can be won without. We must meet Mammon with gold.'

However fiery the speeches of these 40 delegates, the three-day Conference concludes on a most peaceful note. 'Thanks being voted by the Delegates to the Principal Officers, and to Delegates, and the thanks of the whole given to the Chairman, the meeting broke up as it had commenced, in the utmost order.'

Despite Boyle's bias as a pottery manufacturer, he concludes his account of the 1834–1836 strikes with the following compliment to the workers: 'No outrage was committed during the strikes, either on the person or property of any manufacturer. There were no tumultuous assemblages, nor indications of violence, and in this respect, due credit must be given to the operating workers.'

An examination of the Home Office files throws some light on the activities of the pottery manufacturers in their approaches to the Home Office and to their local representatives to get assistance in coping with strikes organized by the N.U.O.P.

A letter from the Home Office, dated 9 May 1834, stated, 'Viscount Melbourne desired to point out to the Magistrates the illegality of the delegates' resolution at the meeting held in the Sea Lion, Hanley, on 24 April.' An earlier letter dated 21 April to Col. Thorn, Birmingham, from the Home Office, read 'An application for troops to be moved to the vicinity of the Potteries in consequence of the alarm prevailing there.'

This official instruction to Col. Thorn from the H.O. is explained by an earlier letter, dated 19 April, handed in by Lord Talbot, who had received it from a pottery manufacturer. It read:

From some information received from Mr. Bourne, an active and intelligent magistrate, who is by no means an alarmist, stating that the Trades Unions are in activity in the Potteries, where turn-outs are daily ordered, and mostly obeyed without reluctance, I am induced to request your assistance and to beg for the protection of the masters, and the authorities of that District, that you will station some soldiers in that vicinity. Mr. Bourne says it is impossible to foresee what the consequences of the excitement may be. I therefore request that you will order a detachment of troop of horses to march into Stone, to be ready to afford the Magistrates assistance on Wednesday, should they require it. On the next day, I would recommend their marching to Newcastle, and remaining there, as long as you may deem it proper or convenient. Perhaps, another troop or a company of infantry might be stationed at Stone, within marching distance of the Potteries, in case of necessity.

Needless to add that Mr. Bourne was a successful master potter in Fenton.

On 11 July 1835 Earl Talbot ordered the cavalry to Newcastle-under-Lyme and posted a leaflet to Lord Melbourne announcing 'an intended procession of the Unionists in the Potteries'. But next day he reported 'Procession passed off quietly'. Lord Talbot wrote on 6 January 1836 to Lord John Russell, informing him of the tranquillity of the Potteries, and stating 'as long as the present prosperity will continue, there can be no apprehension of disturbances in that District, as trade being most flourishing'. This extract throws light on the astuteness of the trade-union leaders in the N.U.O.P., in pressing for a revision of wage lists at that time. Troops were removed on 8 January 1836, but on 22 October 1836 Lord Talbot wrote: 'I consider Newcastle would be the most convenient place near the Potteries for the stationing of a military force. But, if it is expected that both cavalry and infantry should be marched into the District, either Stone or Congleton might be sufficiently within reach of the cavalry, while the infantry might be quartered at Newcastle.'

In the same letter Lord Talbot says, 'Some time ago the Innkeepers and Publicans at Newcastle-under-Lyme memorialized the Government on the hardship, as they termed it, of having their stables occupied by the cavalry, which were billeted upon them.'

On 26 October notice was sent that a troop of dragoons were at Stone, ready for disturbance in the Potteries. On 14 November Colonel Thorn, in charge of the troops, reported to the H.O. he 'had sent directions for the detachment of the 7th Fusiliers at Stafford to march into Newcastle, in consequence of a representation that there were to be burnings in effigy today, that may break the peace, and that from the numbers of workmen out of employment, it will be necessary to be prepared.'

Two days later Colonel Thorn writes that at the request of the Magistrates he had 'marched the 7th Dragoons to Newcastle from Stone, as long as the difference between the Masters and Workmen in the Potteries remained unadjusted. I have requested these Magistrates not to move troops to Newcastle unless absolutely necessary, until they had sworn in special constables.' The curtain is drawn down on the military drama and invasion of the Potteries by troops in a letter dated 24 January 1837, from Lord Talbot: 'I have much satisfaction in being informed that the Potteries Union is dissolved.' This message was followed on 9 February 1837 by a curt note, 'Military unnecessary at Stone'.

Well might J. Boyle, as a prominent pottery manufacturer, compliment the trade union leaders and their followers on their good conduct of the 1834–1837 strike or 'turn-out', under such trying and threatening circumstances. As we have seen from the Home Office records quoted above, they were surrounded by hostile magistrates armed with Riot Act powers, watched on all sides by spies and tale-bearers from the manufacturers, and hedged in by posses of special constables and armed forces of Dragoons, Fusiliers and other troops.

Warburton records: 'After the 1836–1837 strike, little more was heard of the N.U.O.P. It was shattered by the struggle, and had come to an end.' The defenceless operatives, who endeavoured to keep the N.U.O.P. together, had to yield to the *force majeure* of the employers individually, and organized as a powerful group in their Chamber of Commerce. After the defeat of the N.U.O.P. the Master Potters introduced a system of deductions or rebates on previously agreed wage price lists. This grew to the dimensions of a grave scandal and led to a revival of trade unionism.

Trade union organizations are like soldiers, they never die, but fade away. Probably – as Josiah Wedgwood said of the General Chamber of Manufacturers – 'they go to sleep for a while'. The next mention of an active pottery trade union after 1837, refers to a federation of small branches or lodges of operative potters. It is called 'The United Branches of Operative Potters', having been born officially on 6 September 1934.

With the dissolution of the highly centralized N.U.O.P., it does not necessarily follow that all forms of trade union organization vanished overnight from

RSP O

the Potteries. The superstructure of 1837 broke up, but the constituent basic societies still remained intact and ready to function, when and where necessary.

There is evidence that this did happen in North Staffordshire, but more so in the 'out-potteries', where they did not suffer so severely from the repressive measures of the manufacturers, and the civil magistrates and military, as did the workers in North Staffordshire.

William Evans, the Editor of the *Potters' Examiner and Advocate*, in his issue of 4 January 1845, records: 'In all trade societies, the one great motive for combination is that of obtaining and conserving a fair remuneration for labour. This was the principle that actuated the potters of these Districts, when the first meeting of the present Society took place.'

In a letter to the *Examiner* on 29 December 1843 there was a report of 'a turn-out of ovenmen at Middlesborough', and in the *Examiner* of 20 January 1844, there is 'an appeal to all the "out-pottery" branches at Worcester, Coalport, Derby, Glasgow, Middlesborough and Llanelly, to collect and subscribe money to a fund to extinguish the debt of the "Old N.U.O.P." '

Even though victimized the pottery workers, black-listed and debarred from returning to their benches and lathes after the 'turn-out' of 1836 at various factories, could not be prevented from associating with their re-employed fellow workers, and associating actively with them in their lodge meetings at the various inns.

The new terms under which the pottery workers were re-engaged after the 1836 'turn-out' soon led to a desire and a determination to reorganize their dormant trade unions, so as to combat the evil system of 'allowance-off-wages'. This system compelled the workers to allow the masters to deduct 5, 10 or even 20 per cent. off the 1836 prices for piece-work, before the masters consented to re-hiring. Then another evil cropped up to rob the workers of a fair wage. The piece-work rate remained fixed, but the number per dozen wares or articles finished could be made 15, 20, 30 or even 36 to the nominal calculated 'dozen'.

William Evans reports in the issue of the *Examiner* dated 4 January 1845 the activities of the United Branches of the Potters' Society, which comprised a federation or fusion of the scattered branches containing flat-pressers, hollow-ware pressers, printers, slip makers, china makers, packers, handlers and turners. This federated new union did not include 'The Ovenmen and Throwers, two firmly united branches of potters that have no connection with the U.B.P.S.' Evans also, in the same issue, reports: 'That a deputation be appointed from the U.B.P.S., to wait on the Society of Painters and Gilders, to impress them that as they are about to dissolve their Society, the necessity and justice of their devoting their funds or balance in hand, amounting to £20, towards their share of the liabilities of the debt of the old N.U.O.P., owing mainly to the Sheffield Trade Union.'

This legacy of heavy debt from the dissolved N.U.O.P., was a millstone round the neck of the revived federation of the U.B.P.S. T. P. Simpson, the former secretary of the defunct and dissolved N.U.O.P., was one of the officials of the Debt Committee set up to liquidate the old debt, by collections from the branches of the new U.B.P.S. This federated organization of the U.B.P.S., by means of secret meetings, or under the guise of harmless friendly societies with very subdued and moderate programmes and policies, had kept a close watch on the activities of the master potters, since the dissolution of the Union in 1837. Though the Executive or Management Committee of the U.B.P.S. had little centralized power, since each federated branch was autonomous, it exercised great power through the medium of its trade-union newspaper – *The Potters' Examiner and Workmen's Advocate* (Fig. 37). Its Editor William Evans, an Owenite and a Welshman, wielded a powerful pen, and had a remarkable talent for composing telling editorials and open letters. He even contributed bogus signed and anonymous letters to indoctrinate his readers among the 2,000 members of the U.B.P.S. The pages of his weekly between 1843 and 1845 throw a good deal of light on the activities of the new union organisation.

For a time after 1843 the most important of these policies was an appeal to pay off the debt of the old N.U.O.P. There was owing in all a sum of £5,838 in 1837, at the collapse of the strike. Of this sum £2,084. 10s. was owing to the Sheffield Trades Union alone. Some of the younger apprentices of the new Federated Union in 1843 tried to renounce any responsibility for paying off any of the debt, which they claimed they had not incurred. The Sheffield Unionists were quite entitled to press their claim, as their members themselves in 1843 were suffering from a depression and an acute increase in unemployment. So when they received only £141. 19s. 11½d. to pay off the debt from December 1843 to December 1844, towards the £2,084 owing, the Sheffield officials wrote very acrimonious letters to the officials of the U.B.P.S. In fairness to Evans, he published all the letters as he received them in the hope of stirring up enthusiasm for a wiping out of the debt. But the Sheffield letters became so abusive towards the end of 1843, that even Evans blue-pencilled them. The Sheffield trades then resorted to forwarding their letters to the anti-trade union local press, the *Staffordshire Mercury*, which put an end to any hope of the U.B.P.S members clearing off any more of the old debt. Probably what angered the Sheffield Trade Unionists was not the mere trickle of funds raised to pay off their loan, but the fact that in the pages of the *Examiner* there appeared week by

week appeals by the Editor to raise a £5,000 fund. What this mysterious fund
was for will be explained in due course.

We have already seen that the new union was begun in 1843 to try to put a
stop to the allowance system of cutting down wage price lists. The editor of the
Examiner stated repeatedly that its policy would be to expose 'tricksters and
trucksters', as he called certain pottery manufacturers. If any complaints were
lodged by individuals at certain potteries, then the editor gave publicity to them
by a letter in the *Examiner*. He also followed this campaign by writing privately
to individual pottery manufacturers. A leading article was addressed specifically
to Alderman Copeland, M.P. for the Potteries, in whose factory 'allowances' had
been an abuse and a scandal. The smaller firm of Alcock & Co. is exposed in a
later issue. In the same issue, a firm in the 'out-potteries' at Rotherham is exposed
in another letter. If this type of press and private letter exposure did not stop the
pottery manufacturer from practising the allowance system, a 'turn-out' or
strike of the pottery workers was pursued, and even advocated by the editor
of the *Examiner*, and backed by the Chairman of the U.B.P.S. But both Evans
and Aaron Wedgwood[1] were God-fearing Christians, and condemned
force or militancy amongst the members of the Union, as can be seen from the
Examiner for 30 December 1843. There, they suggested that instead of a
'turn-out' to settle the issue of allowances, the matter should be settled by arbitration.

However cautious Aaron Wedgwood was regarding the use of local turn-outs
at selected establishments to put a stop to the abuse of allowances, he could not
restrain the editor of the *Examiner* from an all-out attack on the introduction of
the jolly and jigger machines, and the later menace of the steam-operated
transfer printer for decorating pottery ware[2]. William Evans out-Morrissed
William Morris in his contempt for machinery. He signed himself as 'one who
worked at the bench'. Judging from his bitter hatred of the new machinery of
this period – the jolly and the jigger, one may conclude that he was once a
flat-ware presser or a hollow-ware presser by trade. As a victimized worker, he
probably had to leave the bench after the 1837 strike, and later took up the post
as editor of the *Examiner*, which one assumes was an honorary unpaid post,
for he carried on a business as a bookseller at the same time.

Evans' tirade against machinery led to a controversy and correspondence
between him and Mr. John Ridgway, a large pottery manufacturer in Stoke.
They entered the lists in this literary encounter as 'Aristides' versus 'Mentor',

---

[1] No relation to the manufacturing family
[2] See Chapter 5

contributing anonymous letters to the columns of the *Examiner* on 7 September 1844.

But it seems that Ridgway had the better of the argument about machinery, to judge from the following extract:

Yet, you must be aware that ever since the commencement of the potting business, the mechanical powers have been in constant requisition. Is it not strange that you should represent machinery as being now first applied to thrown and turned ware? It is now I believe, about 30 years ago since Mr. Wedgwood had a large steam engine constructed on his manufactory and applied steam power, not only to thrown and turned ware but to many branches of his business, thereby displacing a considerable amount of human labour. Yet, I never heard that respected gentleman spoken of as an enemy of the working classes.

Earlier chapters have included evidence to support these statements about Wedgwood – and indeed, his contemporaries Spode, Minton, Keeling and Enoch Wood – and their application of power to pottery machinery. Despite this crushing reply by Ridgway in the *Examiner*, Evans persisted with his anti-machinery campaign, supported here and there with an occasional turn-out of pottery workers. The called-out men rendered unemployed were maintained from a special fund. This anti-machinery turn-out policy was urged by Evans to put a stop to machinery installed in some of the smaller pottery works. In other cases, Evans raised the anti-machinery issue when a large number of pottery workers were rendered unemployed as a result of the permanent installation of machinery. Evans' tactics led to more anonymous letters, and more anti-machinery leading articles in the *Examiner*. He was able to stop the installation of what he called 'the rolling monster' or mechanical steam printer installed at Venables & Co's pottery, where the men refused to operate it. But he failed to prevent its installation at two factories in the out-potteries at Stockton-on-Tees and at Newcastle-under-Lyme.

These articles of Evans in the *Examiner* did succeed in raising a real animus against the machine in part of the North Staffordshire Potteries, but he failed to stop the mechanization of pottery processes. His real outcry was against particular pieces of pottery machinery – the jolly and the jigger used by the flat-ware and hollow-ware pressers, of whom, we have strong grounds to believe, he was one of the dismissed pressers, following the 1837 strike.

An analysis of the membership of the United Branches of the Potters' Society will also enable us to see the real reason for Evans's anti-machinery campaign. The U.B.P.S. never claimed a larger membership than 2,000, but in fact it was probably less than that. The census of 1841 gives the total number of pottery workers as 15,158. Even if we include burnishers, enamellers, painters, gilders and printers in the decoration departments, these would make the total

17,847. If we exclude the overlookers, foremen and clerical members of the staff, we would reduce the 17,847 by 2,847, leaving the actual members eligible for membership of the U.B.P.S. as 15,000. So the 2,000 claimed as members by Evans in his *Art and History of the Potting Business* and in Warburton's *History of Staffordshire Pottery Trade Unions* would be less than 14 per cent. of all the pottery workers. Its lack of numbers was not its only weakness, but its quality or calibre was also undermined by the absence from membership of key workers like throwers, turners, ovenmen and painters. The bulk of the membership of the U.B.P.S. consisted of the two sections Flat-Ware Pressers and Hollow-ware Pressers. Their number was returned in 1844 as 674 and 864 respectively. This gives us a total of 1,538 out of a total membership of 2,000 in the U.B.P.S. So we can see that 75 per cent. of the Union membership consisted of these two sections. Hence Evans concentrated his attack on machinery – the jolly and jigger – that threatened the employment of flat-ware and hollow-ware pressers. Thus, he concentrated on two issues that would please the majority of his trade union members. Evans also attacked the 'rolling-monster' – the steam-powered printer – to please the transfer printers, federated to the U.B.P.S., but representing only a small minority in numbers, totalling only 470.

One of the first factories where Evans attacked the introduction of machinery was at Mason's Ironstone Pottery factory. It had a bad name as a 'slop-pottery' where workers were taken on only after consenting to accept the 'allowance' system of reduced wages. So Mr. Mason became a marked man, and the butt of unsigned letters and abusive articles from Evans' pen in the *Examiner*. Mason's factory was the first in which the Union staged a 'turn-out.'

Here are samples of Evans' leading articles:

Working potters are placed on the verge of a precipice, which is fast crumbling beneath them. A year, a month, nay a day, may topple them to the bottom, leaving them the crushed and hopeless victims of mechanical movements. C. J. Mason of the Patent Iron Stone Manufactory, Fenton, is in the possession of machines for the making of all kinds of flat-ware. A building is prepared for the reception of the machines, and the Patent Experimentalist is about to break the hopes of the working potters on the wheels of the Manchester Machinery. Hunger and cold, rags and despair, are hatching in Fenton for the operatives of this district. Who knows, if Mr. Mason be successful, but that working potters may still have the good fortune to witness their wives and little ones wasting their bodies in tending on large rattling engines, while the husband, the lord of the castle, is pining at home? What matters it to the manufacturers, if hearts are destroyed or homes made desolate so that Gold can be gained? Gold is the juggernaut of commerce. To give potency to this idol of capital, machinery is brought into requisition and the poor destroyed. Pottery working Potters beware!

The editor is not content with this for he returns to the attack again, the week after, with a signed article by 'Candour', entitled 'A few thoughts on Machinery':

The doom that has befallen the handloom weavers will befall the potters. Wherever machinery has been introduced, with a very few exceptions, to any considerable extent, misery and wretchedness, desolation and want, have been its constant attendants. It has been the cause of anarchy, riot and bloodshed, and has brought many an honest man to the gallows. It has made happy fathers wretched, it has assisted to people our penal settlements, and to fill our gaols and penitentiaries. Up then, Potters, and be doing! Now is the time! Machinery is your foe, your mortal enemy. Battle with it as you love your wives and children. Delay not a moment. Make haste. Make haste.

No Revivalist in his campaign against sin could rival Evans in his condemnation of machinery. In this campaign, he even tried to win over the small pottery owner to despise and condemn the use of machinery, as shown below:

We beg to call the attention of the Union and potters generally, to the steps which the Central Committee are taking to obstruct if possible, the introduction of mechanical appliances into any branch of our trade. In this labour of life against Profit, we hope to be assisted by all good manufacturers, but more especially, those of small capital, as with them, if machinery be successfully introduced their trade will be gone. They will not have means to embark largely in the purchase of machinery. Their trade will pass into the hands of those who can command their thousands of sterling, who can raise huge fabrics and stock them with every contrivance of iron and steam; who can scour the world with their travellers, and by the vastness of their operations, and their facilities for manufacturing to sell their goods at a price that would bring all small manufacturers to beggary. Let the Stocking Frame makers of Derby be remembered with fear, and taken as an example. Small potters will see it to their interest to assist in the steps we are about to take. If working potters go down, through the introduction of machinery, small pot masters must follow in their wake. There is a common grave for both, from which there is no commercial resurrection. The Moloch Capital will swallow up all but its keepers.

But despite this fury from the editorial chair of the *Examiner*, which instigated a few short-lived strikes or turn-outs at one or two factories, nothing very dramatic happened in the Potteries or the out-potteries. Evans himself got tired of banging his big drum against machinery, and soon started a new attack on unemployment, and offered a cure and an elixir of new economic life to all unemployed pottery workers through Emigration.

This new doctrine and scheme for the emancipation of all pottery workers, displaced by the introduction of flat-ware and hollow-ware mechanical pressers, was enunciated only a week after the final appeal to the Flat-Ware Branch. The clarion call came in a letter, signed by 'A Burslem Flat-ware presser'. 'Up men of the Flat-Ware Branch, and be doing! Do not be found sleeping at your posts, when the enemy is at your gates. It is no time for half measures. The day has arrived when the question is one of life and death. Shall mechanical appliances supersede your labour? Men of the Flat-Ware Branch! the War of science has commenced. Where will it end? There is no telling, until it has swallowed the whole manual labour of these districts in one widespread vortex of ruin.'

But the next issue of the *Examiner*, on 16 November, shows a change of tactics 'We are happy to find that the Central Committee of our Society are about to hold public district meetings of all branches throughout the Potteries, for the purpose of taking into consideration the most legal and efficient means of obstructing, if possible, the introduction of machinery into any branch of the Potting Business.'

This announcement was premature, for the publication of the 'most legal and efficient means of obstructing the introduction of machinery' was delayed till the issue of the *Examiner* on 7 December 1844. The scheme turned out to be almost a copy of Robert Owen's well-known Utopian Socialist or Co-operative Colonies.

As Harold Owen has given a very full account of Evans' Potters' Joint Stock Emigration Society in chapters iv and v of his book on *The Staffordshire Potter*, it will suffice here to quote extracts from the Manifesto, published by the Central Committee of the U.B.P.S., of which Evans was the literary mouthpiece.

£5,000 Fund

Working Potters, your crisis has now arrived. Mechanical appliances are now being introduced in your trade, the evils of which no one yet has the power to foretell. Will you then, Brethren in Union, support your Executive, in all that they may legally and constitutionally do to obstruct the introduction of this evil? We have every confidence, that all that we may do now to obstruct the introduction of mechanical power, the evil anticipated will be heartily responded to by every member of this Union. With this feeling, we have made a levy of a half a crown per man, throughout the whole of our Union, and this levy you will pay and you will pay it heartily and cheerfully.

Then the skilled draughtsman of this Manifesto — none other than Evans himself — unfolds the purpose of the levy.

This will be the first of 8 levies, which will be called for fortnightly, until the whole will be paid. The aggregate of these levies, we call the £5,000 fund, as we anticipate in this undertaking the assistance of 5,000 potters. The funds thus realised will be devoted exclusively to the one great object of obstructing the introduction of machinery in the pottery business. It will be invested for security in the 'Emigration Society.'

Evans unfolds the purpose of this Society:

Steps will immediately be taken to purchase 12,000 acres of land in one of the Western States of the American Union, on which it is intended to locate all those who may now or hereafter be injured by machinery. On the payment of the first levy, Mr. Mason's [pottery] hands will legally be requested to leave their employment, and to place themselves on the general funds of the Union. Should any other manufacturer seek to introduce machinery in our trade, there would be plenty of room for his [pottery] hands on our 12,000 acre estate.

What an optimist Evans was to expect so many hands to be displaced, as to provide his Emigration Society with 5,000 Colonists in this Eldorado of the West in the U.S.A.! He hoped, too, to gain financial support for his plan from the general inhabitants of the Potteries. He ends his Manifesto, 'Your tills are in danger, will you protect them? Grocers, Butchers, Drapers, Hatters, Publicans,

46 Earl Gower, jasper medallion

47 Queen Charlotte, Wedgwood jasper medallion

48 The Crateman ('peasant-craftsman stage')

49 Home and Pottery ('master-craftsman stage')

50 The 'Employer-merchant stage'

51 Factory and transport ('capitalist employer stage')

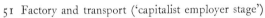

52 A plate from the set made by Wedgwood for Catherine the Great of Russia

Shoemakers, Tailors, in short, all who depend on the custom of working potters for trade, come from behind the counter, and defend the poor. To small manufacturers, we would say, you too are in danger.' Then he borrows a bit of Shakespeare to strengthen his appeal! – 'What a falling off is here, Othello's occupation is gone, and machinery is the victor.' The Manifesto concludes with an appeal to women:

To maidens, mothers, wives and widows, we say machinery is your deadliest enemy. It is a systematized process of slow murder. Women, you were made for higher duties than that of giant engines.

Your humble servants, The Central Committee U.B.P.S.

Talbot Inn, Hanley. Dec. 7, 1844.

Evans and his fellow trade unionists of the U.P.B.S. put forward emigration as an escape from the cogs and wheels of machinery. Alas, all he and his Emigration Society associates did was to provide a sweepstake for a few innocents to make a trip to the New World. As was to be expected, the strongest supporters of the sweepstake were the Hollow-ware Pressers Branch of the U.P.B.S. They became so enthusiastic, that they decided to devote half their branch subscriptions to support the Emigration Scheme. They even used their majority in the U.P.B.S., to devote half its funds to finance the Emigration Society. This was the beginning of the end. Soon the United Branches of the Potters' Society became almost identified with the Emigration Society. The membership of the affiliated branches other than the Hollow-Ware Branch declined, and the U.P.B.S. as such vanished as a trade union organization. Then in 1849 the Emigration Society itself collapsed, after it had sent its Fund Officers to found a centre called Pottersville in Wisconsin, U.S.A. The full story of the failure of the venture to open pottery works there, and the sad stranding of the few emigrant potters, is told in Harold Owen's book on *The Staffordshire Potter*. The failure of Pottersville was not the only calamity, for the Emigration Society at home in the Potteries was ruined and bankrupt; and worse still, the parent trade union organization, the U.P.B.S., that sponsored the Emigration Society, also perished. Through the courtesy of my late friend, Professor Fred Hall, M.A., of the Co-operative College, Manchester, I was able to examine a facsimile photograph of the framed Dollar note issued by the Emigration Society in the name of the Trustees and Directors of the Society.

Instead of machinery departing from the Potteries, Evans himself and his Emigration Society, with its sponsoring organization the U.P.B.S., made an inglorious exit from the scene. Even the *Potters' Examiner* ceased publication in 1848, when Evans changed it to *The Potters' Examiner and Emigrants' Advocate*. Alas, this ceased publication in 1851. Harold Owen, in his book *The Staffordshire*

Potter, comments on the Emigration efforts of Evans and his supporters: 'The net result of the Emigration Movement was merely to destroy all that had been accomplished, before it came into existence – the stopping of the allowance system with increases of $7\frac{1}{2}\%$ in the weekly earnings of the workers, the formation of friendly society, sick clubs and burial societies. The pottery workers had committed an act of suicidal folly in subordinating their Union (the U.P.B.S.) to the Emigration Society, which had fought a phantom.'

William Evans from his editorial chair was the chief spokesman of the anti-machinery campaign of the 1840's. But all his efforts ended in failure. More and more machines were introduced, despite the turn-outs and the propaganda against the 'jollies' and the 'jiggers'. Ridgway and Mason, the two large-scale pottery manufacturers, who had purchased Wall's Patent for his mechanical presser, installed them, despite Evans and the *Examiner*. The other manufacturers who may have hesitated to install the 'jollies' and 'jiggers' during the term of Wall's patent, unless they were prepared to pay a royalty for its use, only had to delay the installation of these mechanical pressers and rolling monsters derided by Evans, till the patent term expired. But, in the meantime, in many of the out-potteries, manufacturers had installed 'jollies' and 'jiggers', and used Wall's patent machinery, between 1844 and 1845.

Evans wrongly repeated in his *Examiner* articles that this 1844–1845 mechanization of the pottery industry was the first introduction of machinery and mechanical processes in the industry. His pottery trade unionists believed this to be true, because Evans repeated it so persistently in the *Examiner* – especially his own branch of the flat-ware and hollow-ware pressers.

Many writers since Evans have succumbed to the myth that it was only in 1844–1845 that machinery invaded the pottery industry. This then is the origin of this traditional heresy.

CHAPTER 18

Focus for Social Unrest

In his *History of the Chartist Movement* Julius West writes: 'Within a few years, working men had forced upon their attention the pros and cons of trade unionism, industrial unionism, syndicalism, communism, socialism, land nationalization, co-operative ownership of land, co-operative production and distribution, franchise reform, electoral reform, woman suffrage, factory legislation, poor law reform, municipal reform, free trade, freedom of thought, freedom of the press and many other ideas.'

Because of their national character, many of these ideas in ferment, when embodied in movements, and when expounded by missionaries and apostles like Fergus O'Connor and Thomas Cooper, were bound to influence a concentrated, populous industrial community like the Potteries. The various movements represented a growing discontent with the social evils of the time.

The discontent of the pottery workers was not born as a result of the oratory of itinerant 'demagogues', as suggested by John Ward in his *History of Stoke on Trent*. It arose largely from the industrial conditions prevailing in the Potteries. It was a favourite hunting ground for representatives of national movements, to seek recruits and to gain members and supporters of their particular cause and to secure mass public opinion.

We have already seen the pottery workers linked industrially with the National Association for the Protection of Labour, and later with the Grand Consolidated Trade Union, between 1831 and 1837. The defeat of the N.A.O.P. after their disastrous strikes, so enfeebled the potters that, from 1837 to 1843, they cut themselves adrift from any contacts with national organizations.

It is not until 1845 we find, from the *Northern Star* of 5 April and 2 August, that William Evans attends as a delegate from the pottery workers the National Conference of the United Trades, called by the London trades to discuss the formation of an association between the trade unions of the country. Probably, as a tribute to the personality and position of Evans, as Editor of the *Examiner*, he was elected the chairman of the conference committee elected to draft a scheme for the establishment of a permanent association.

As a result, two national organizations were launched: The National Association of United Trades for the Protection of Labour – the N.A.U.T.P.L. – to improve conditions of work in trades affiliated and to negotiate between men and masters, if necessary; and The National Association of United Trades for the Employment of Labour – the N.A.U.T.E.L., whose function was to find work for strikers, and thus reduce the burden on trade unions of financing strikers, when out of employment.

Almost immediately after the launching of these two national organizations, in which Evans took so much initiative, the *Northern Star* for 6 June 1846 reports that Evans failed to get his Central Committee of Pottery workers to affiliate to the National Association of United Trades for the Protection of Labour. To try to get the Central Committee members to affiliate, a Mr. West, the organizer of the N.A.U.T.P.L. visited the Potteries. Though he failed to win over Evans and his Central Committee, he succeeded in getting an active pottery member, Humphries by name, to become an active member of the National Association, and he later became the National Secretary. With Humphries, an original member of the Board of Management of the former N.A.O.P., Mark Lancaster, one of the old 'turn-out' victims, linked up with the National Association. We find in the *Northern Star* of 3 October 1846 that there were 150 paying members among the potters who had joined the National Association. These were mostly members of the smaller units of cratemakers, painters and gilders, salvaged from the wreck of the old N.A.O.P.

But, in spite of the efforts of Humphries as Secretary, the N.A.U.T.P.L. made little headway, as can be seen from the *Northern Star* from 3 October 1846 to 1847, partly because of the enmity and counter-propaganda of the Potters' Emigration Society, led by the militant Evans, but more, because of the depression in trade that set in during this period. The National Association itself dwindled in numbers and influence, and by 1851 had lost its importance as an industrial trade union organization. Thus came to an inglorious end the national organization, that W. Evans had described in his report in the *Potters' Examiner* issue of 5 April 1845, as 'Labour's Parliament'.

Though by 1850–1851, both national organizations and the local pottery trade unions were dormant, their non-militant spirit was kept alive, and enabled what Harold Owen[1] calls the 'Era of Arbitration', to be inaugurated, during the

[1] H. Owen: *The Staffordshire Potteries*

next decade. This was made possible by triumphs secured by the national political organizations.

Long before 1843, the master potters had succeeded in capturing seats in the reformed Parliament: Josiah Wedgwood II, Alderman W. T. Copeland (of Spode's old Pottery) and John Davenport. As a gain for the middle class, and members of the master manufacturing class, little interest was taken in the Reform victory by members of the working classes. But out of their disappointment, there emerged a political movement or a series of movements and agitations that had a direct appeal to the working classes, especially when roused by the oratory and propaganda of various political missionaries or agitators.

Disappointed though the working classes were with the Reform Act, they were forced to take an interest in three pieces of legislation, which led to a good deal of agitation up and down the country. These were the agitation against the Corn Laws, the agitation for a 10 hours Bill in Factories and the debates about the New Poor Law Act of 1834 and its subsequent administration. The main interest of pottery workers in Anti-Corn Law agitation was made clear before 1843. The Anti-Corn Law League would find the Potteries a favourable spot for its propaganda, but there is no local record in the press of its causing any specific action among the organized workers. As the 'Old Potter' remarks in his historical retrospect *When I was a child*: 'Even the resounding attacks against the Corn Laws excited little interest among the working classes, and so they gave little response. Betrayal and failure had made them sad and hopeless. There was a sullen passive reign of distrust among the people. The Reform Bill had disappointed them.'

The general apathy of pottery workers was such that we find very little interest, and in fact, no direct action or agitation taken over the 'Ten Hour Bill'. The only evidence is the action of William Evans in the *Potters' Examiner* of 20 April 1844, in devoting a leading article to Lord Ashley's speech on the Ten Hour Bill. Evans frankly states 'His Lordship's facts apply principally to the Cotton districts, but the same startling statements would apply equally as true to the Pottery Districts also. Nay! it is a matter of doubt or not whether the lives of potters are not shorter in the aggregate than those cited by Lord Ashley, relative to the Cotton districts. It had become a matter of curiosity to see an aged potter, who is in the daily practice of working in the clay. How requisite then, is it for every operative potter to seriously reflect on the poisonous nature of his employment, and to ask himself the question 'Is there no escape?' Evans leaves the question unanswered. But obviously he had in his mind Emigration to the City of Refuge in the West. The organized pottery workers, under his leadership and his colleagues, simply ignore politics and political action. All that mattered to them was the escape from the machine.

Some interest was shown in the New Poor Law. William Evans urged his members to select working-class representatives to the new Board of Guardians, in the *Examiner* of 26 April 1845. He opened its columns for correspondence, urging better and more humane treatment of the poor in the workhouses. The 'Bastille' as Evans called the workhouse, 'ought to be made more comfortable'. This complacent attitude to the political agitation in the country generally was not what certain national organizations and their leaders envisaged. Because of the general disappointment with the Reform Bill, and its subsequent Reformed Parliament, there grew up a strong movement for the so-called 'People's Charter' – the Chartist movement. Naturally, its leaders came to 'the Potteries'.

During the 1836 strike, organized by the then flourishing National Union of Operative Potters, the Union passed a remarkable resolution, which we shall see later contrasts very much with the attitude of the United Branches of the Pottery Society in 1843 and after. The resolution read: 'That as Fergus O'Connor Esq., has taken a very active part on behalf of the Staffordshire Potters in several large manufacturing towns in the British Empire, this meeting resolves by written communication, most respectfully to request him to use his best endeavours on their behalf in all large towns he may visit in the Kingdom.'

In 1843, the U.B.P.S. wanted to forget the 1836 strike and its militancy, and least of all did they want to bring the fiery Irish orator Fergus O'Connor back to the Potteries or to have any official contacts with him, as he had become the spearhead of the 'physical force' contingent of the Chartists. Whether they wanted him or not, O'Connor came to the Potteries, and addressed a meeting in the open-air at Hanley at Crown Bank on 19 August 1844. Nowhere in the pages of the *Potters' Examiner* is there reference to this meeting, nor a hint of any support of the Chartist movement, either by the editor or by the Chairman of the Union, Aaron Wedgwood. O'Connor spoke at the meeting of his favourite Land Scheme. During his address he poured ridicule on Evans' Potters' Emigration Society and their Utopian scheme. This led Evans to write an editorial in the *Potters' Examiner* defending his emigration plan. In a characteristic manner, Evans explained that as *The Examiner and Workmen's Advocate* was a trades organ, and not a political journal, 'it is not my intention to enter into a discussion of party politics'. Then he proceeds to disarm O'Connor by paying what might be termed a paper-tribute to O'Connor's Chartist principles. 'Let it not be understood that I entertain other than the most respectful feelings for the gentleman, and that I attribute other than the most disinterested motives to him in his laborious and laudable endeavours to improve the condition of the working population of this Empire . . . but I cannot allow the remarks made by him on 19 August relative to the Potters' Emigration Society, to pass without animadverting on the same, to the end that truth and justice may prevail, independent of persons, parties or papers.'

Evans then proceeds to enumerate six reasons why his emigration scheme to the U.S.A. is a sounder venture than O'Connor's Land Scheme. He pours contempt on the Owenite element in O'Connor's 'Home Colonization' scheme, which Evans states has generally failed with its ideas of self-feeding and self-supporting. Evans says 'we have had our [Owenite] Labour Exchanges and Co-operative Stores – *but where are they now?*' He is referring to Robert Owen's attempt to establish a Co-operative Pottery in 1834–1835, and his failures of Co-operative Stores and Colonies in Scotland and later, in Ireland. Evans continues with his tale of woe about Owenism – 'Alas! if all the crashed hopes, vexations and disappointments, consequent on these experiments of struggling labour could be laid before the public, what a frightful catalogue we should have.' Little did the Emigration enthusiast expect that ultimately in this catalogue his Potterville would appear, as well as O'Connorville and Ralahine!

Then Evans pours out his contempt for O'Connor's Chartism 'I believe O'Connor's patriotism carries him into an extreme of sublime folly, my notion of patriotism does not consist in seeing men wilfully and perversely remaining in the land of their birth to swell the ranks of starving mobs, to shout for liberty, when they may act for it, to have Poverty Demonstrations every day in the year with their rags and wretchedness, their death's hands, cross bones, coffins and tombs. No! There is a madness in this that may extend the sale of a public journal,' – a sly tilt at O'Connor's Chartist journal *The Northern Star*.

'Let it not be supposed from the remarks made here that I do not appreciate the value of Mr. O'Connor's political service in the cause of democracy in this country, or that I would not make a sacrifice to forward the great and important objects of which he is THE ONE GREAT PROMULGATOR. He and his objects had and shall have my most strenuous advocacy.' Then Evans qualifies his admiration with the proviso, 'But in giving this advocacy, I *will think for myself*, and should my thoughts differ from those of O'Connor, *I will express my thoughts*.'

It would be a mistake to conclude from these extracts from Evans' diatribe against O'Connor the Chartist, that the opposition of the United Branches of the Potters' Society was due merely to the personal differences between O'Connor and Evans, on the issue of 'Home Colonization' versus 'Emigration'. The opposition to Chartism in the Potteries went much deeper, and was more fundamental.

To explain the Pottery Workers' antipathy to the propaganda of the physical force section of the Chartists, led by O'Connor, it is necessary to go back a year prior to the foundation of the United Branches of the Potters' Society. These events are referred to locally as 'The Potteries' Peterloo', the Chartist riots in Burslem on 16 August 1842. The events that led to the Chartist riots, have been recorded by John Ward in his *History of Stoke on Trent* in his chapters dealing with the life of Thomas Cooper, and by 'an Old Potter' in his *When I was a child*, which gives a more sympathetic account of the riots than Ward's version. Both recall the savage sentences imposed on those arrested during the riots in Burslem. Fifty-four persons were transported, of which 11 were for life, 13 for 21 years, 9 for 15 years, 18 for 10 years and 3 for 7 years. 154 were imprisoned, of which 146 had to serve with hard labour. Compare these with the sentences on the Liverpool Chartist Rioters of 1842: only 11 men were transported and 115 imprisoned. One can imagine the effect on the mentality of the pottery workers of the terribly brutal sentences imposed by the judges at Stafford Assizes, after a trial that lasted from 1 to 15 October 1842.

Further, it must be remembered that the date on which the Potteries' Chartist riots took place, 16 August, was the anniversary of 'Peterloo', the slaughter of Chartists at Manchester. In addition, in the Potteries, there was a bitter miners' lock-out in operation. Ward states: 'A general stoppage of the Collieries and the workmen suffering from these privations, became the convenient and ready instruments of the seditious demagogues who had long been disseminating the deleterious doctrine of "The People's Charter", as the sovereign and sole remedy for poverty and all political grievances.' The miners employed by Lord Granville, and other local coal-owners, had been locked-out resisting a reduction in wages, for a period of 6 weeks. From the 6 August, they had tried to get all the colliers to come out on strike at neighbouring pits. At the time, there was no dispute between the pottery masters and their workers, but through this stopping all colliers in the Potteries pits, the pottery factories, so dependent on coal for firing their wares, were rendered idle. Add to this fact that the first two weeks in August are the Potteries' Wakes Weeks, when all the pottery workers take a week off and a week to get over the Wakes. The stage was set for a monster demonstration on 16 August, to commemorate the Massacre of Manchester – the Peterloo of 1819. Thomas Cooper had addressed a mass meeting, organized by the Chartists at Hanley on 14 August. He then addressed the miners on strike at Longton on 15 August where 8,000 miners assembled to hear him. Returning to address another meeting at Hanley in the evening, Cooper put forward a resolution by the Chartists for a general strike – 'that all work should cease until the Charter became the Law of the Land'. Cooper used all the rhetoric at his command to get the resolution carried. He then left Crown Bank, Hanley, where the crowd broke into a riot. The riot continued next day, and at Burslem a local Chartist named Ellis addressed a mass demonstration which had been reinforced by contingents of Chartists from Leek and Congleton. This then led to the fatal clash with the military. The Riot Act was read, and the firing commenced. The military fired into the mob, 'one man fell dead, another received a wound all but mortal and several others wounded, ran or were carried away, some of them are supposed to have died afterwards'. This is the account given by Ward. On a previous page he writes: 'The town of Burslem was fortunately prepared for a proper reception of the banditti – a troop of the 2nd Dragoon Guards, and a large body of volunteers had been organized as special constables.' He then closes the account, 'Thus was the authority of law vindicated and anarchy subdued at Burslem on the memorable 16th of August 1842.'

One can understand the animus of John Ward, a lawyer, when we learn that the rioters raided and demolished the Police Offices at Hanley, Stoke, Fenton and Longton, as well as burning down the houses of a lawyer and magistrates. The rectory at Longton was burnt to the ground. One can understand the raiding and demolition of the Police Stations, and the residences of those concerned with the operation of the Law, but one wonders why the rectory was burnt down. 'An Old Potter' perhaps has the explanation when he says 'The rioters were bitter against the parsons who ground them with tithes' as was the case a year later in South Wales, during the Rebecca Riots in 1843.

There is a tendency among contemporary writers of this period to blame the Chartist orators, as Ward does, or to blame the miners, as does 'an Old Potter' when he records: 'There was a marked difference between the pottery working people and the miners, who had invaded their towns from the outside districts, like a storm-flood. While having sympathy with them in their sufferings and wrongs, they were mutely appalled by their violence. The pottery people have not the grit, which makes revolutions, nor successful riots, nor even masterful trade combinations.'

But there are some facts to be explained away before one can accept such a clean slate, as far as the pottery workers were involved in these riots. One of the victims of the riots was Charles James Mason, whose house was gutted by fire at Heron Cross. We have already seen from the personal attacks made upon him by the editor of the *Potters' Examiner*, that he was the owner of the Patent Ironstone China Factory. He was exposed by Evans as one of the worst pottery employers where the allowance system was in operation. Worse still, in Evans'

RSP P

eyes, was Mason's introduction into his pottery of the much detested machine for flat-ware pressing – the jolly. From the records of the riot, and the trial of the arrested rioters, we know that the only master potter's house and property damaged was that of C. J. Mason. We also know from Boyle's *Diary* that Mason was the chairman of the Master Potters' Organization in 1834, at the time of the potters' strike. Further, it is known from the records of the Riot Commission at the Stafford trial that after the riots a large number of pottery workers were sentenced, as well as miners. So it is quite possible that some of these convicted potters, with memories of the early pottery strikes of 1834–1836, may have joined in the Chartist riots to get their own back on Mason, who had helped to break the strikes. On the other hand Mason, as a prominent pottery manufacturer, was probably personally interested in the local collieries, where the miners were locked out. He married Sarah Spode, whose family owned collieries in the areas where miners were locked out in 1842. We could well understand miners burning Mason's house during the riots even if the potters did not join them. The United Branches of the Potters' Society did not officially participate in or support the Chartists' action in any way.

RELIGIOUS MOVEMENTS

Although by today, religious and educational movements have become more or less separate in their organizations, during 1843–1850 and earlier, they were much more closely bound together. There was hardly any secular education amongst working-class adults or children. A good deal if not all the formal education of the children of pottery workers was carried on in Sunday Schools, as John Ward records. But it may help to look at them separately.

Ever since the days of John Wesley, the Potteries had been the scene of many religious revivals. Dotted about the Potteries today are many Methodist and other Non-conformist Chapels testifying to the impact of religion on the social life of the Potteries. The success of Wesley and Wesleyan religion in the district may be correctly explained by John Ward: 'The Clergy of the old school indeed, too generally, left the parishioners to find their own way to heaven, unless they would voluntarily put themselves in the way of hearing their weekly ministrations and learn from the formulary of the Church the pure and unadulterated word.' Ward writes of the followers of John Wesley in 1849, 'It would have vexed his righteous soul to have witnessed the schisms which have subsequently taken place among his professed followers.'

J. Aikin much earlier in *A Description of the Country around Manchester* said there was 'a great variety of sects in the Potteries, few places have so great a diversity of opinion on the score of religion as this'. This was written in 1795, only five years after John Wesley himself had written in his *Journal* of his visit to the Potteries on 28 and 29 March 1790, when Wedgwood was alive. These schisms were added to by the establishment in 1797 of the Kilhamites or Methodist New Connexion, that broke away from Wesleyanism. Then in 1808, there was a further split by the Primitive Methodists or Ranters, as they were called in the Burslem Circuit. Yet again, in 1836, there appeared another split called 'The Burslem Sunday School'. In addition to these sects, springing direct from Wesley's original organization throughout the Potteries, there were other Chapels of Dissenting Sects, the Baptists, Congregationalists, Quakers and Unitarians. Ward explains this proliferation of dissenting sects: 'Of the preponderance of the non-conformist bodies in the district, the reason is obvious. They sprang up spontaneously to supply the dearth of Church accommodation, and the lack of zeal or talent among the ministry of the Establishment.' He claims that even in 1849 'Although sects have multiplied, many thousands of the population can scarcely be said to be enrolled in any of their ranks'. It can, however, be shown that from 1834 to 1851 the leaders of the pottery trades unions were greatly influenced by religious thought and feeling. In fact, the pages of the *Potters' Examiner and Workmen's Advocate* under the Editorship of Evans, strongly supported by his colleague Aaron Wedgwood – the Chairman of the United Branches of the Potters' Society – reveal how steeped in biblical lore and illustration were the editor, the chairman and many leading trade-union members who contributed letters and correspondence to their union journal.

The Methodist Chapels, which had broken off from the Wesleyan parent church, had to train a corps of lay preachers. With their practice at delivering addresses or sermons at the Chapels on Sunday or at their week-night devotional meetings and Sunday Schools, they became powerful and convincing speakers and debaters. 'An Old Potter' says: 'These men – a cup-maker and saucer-maker, were engaged in discussion all day long' – presumably on Bible topics; Warburton states: 'Methodism was strong amongst the pottery workers, and even those who were outside its ranks were under its influence.' Many master potters were members of the New Connexion of Methodists. Tomlinson, a Tory lawyer of Stoke, in one of his letters to the Home Office on 12–14 December 1820 reported that 'The Methodists of the New Connexion were becoming more numerous, and worse still, in his opinion, they became Radicals, and appear to act as a body and in common concerns on these occasions'. As some master potters were Methodists, it is quite likely that they would favour the employment of pottery workers who were also Methodists, if only for their virtues of sobriety, temperance and thrift. Also an important point to remember is that the Methodist trade union leaders would probably have a great influence in negotiations with such Methodist pottery manufacturers.

The loyalty of the Methodist pottery worker to his Chapel was one of the best grounds for training for loyalty to other institutions to which he was attached, especially to his trade union. We see this in the case of both Evans and Aaron Wedgwood.

It was still true in this century of many of the leading officials and organizers of the Pottery Workers' Union, whom the writer met regularly in conferences and monthly meetings of the National Pottery Council during the inter-War years.

Where Chartists like the Methodist Capper gave full support to the Chartist movement even to the point of participation in open demonstration, they did at least counterbalance the non-militancy and toning-down of trade unionism, advocated by their leaders – Evans and Aaron Wedgwood. Warburton in his *History of Trade Unions in the Potteries* rightly sums up: 'Consciously or un-consciously, the force of Methodism must have greatly influenced the Potters' Union, and encouraged it along the path of respectability.' Faulkner in his *Chartism and the Churches* may be quite correct in his generalization about Wesleyan Methodism that 'it had lost the confidence of the intelligent working man', by the period of Chartism. This was only partially true of the Potteries area, where both Wesleyanism and Methodism had their left-wing tendencies, and produced rebels who, even when expelled from the Church or Chapel, made all the better rebels and leaders of movements for trade unionism, Chartism or Socialism. There was a Methodism in the Potteries with a special democratic stamp of its own, bred and moulded in a uniquely concentrated industrial community. Even today, the local Methodist lay preachers and their congregations point with pride to Mow Cop, the birthplace of the New Connexion and the Primitives.

WORKING-CLASS EDUCATION

It is only when one tries to analyse the early attempts at education amongst the working classes that one sees how inextricably interwoven religion was with the educational efforts. Ward sums up not only his own view as an Anglican Tory, but that of many of his contemporaries before and after the date of his book (1849): 'The facility with which a little learning is attained, may render the acquisition baneful, unless it is accompanied by the infusion of pure religious and moral principles. The subject of Education ought to be intimately connected with religion.' But Ward had to admit that though the education of the children of the working classes had been for nearly half a century assiduously cultivated in Sunday Schools connected with the Established Church and various Nonconformist bodies, it was more particularly by the latter. Seymour Tremenheere, a well-known Anglican ex-School Inspector and Inspector of Factories and Mines, in his 1844 Report is equally frank: 'In some instances too much zeal and earnestness has been manifested to provide for their spiritual wants, than for the education of the children. The Dissenting portion of the County of Staffs., have long been actively employed in this labour.'

The Sunday Schools organized by the Methodists in the Potteries provided an excellent training ground for older members, as teachers of juniors, and enabled many of the male teachers to become lay preachers and competent speakers at public meetings. The adult teacher became an avid reader of the Scriptures, and acquired a literary taste for religious literature, which could be later transferred to literature dealing with social and economic topics. This literary training and development produced the type of Methodist editor of the *Potters' Examiner*, and the good orator-Chairman of the Pottery Trade Union, Aaron Wedgwood. Some of these active Wesleyans and Methodists were actually master potters. An entry in Enoch Wood's diary in October 1804 shows him as manager of the Methodist Sunday School at Burslem, instituted as early as 1787. Enoch Wood and others who occupied pews in the Burslem Chapel, did not hesitate to help in the good work of Wesley, whom they had known personally. Then there is a letter in the Wedgwood MSS. regarding another Nonconformist Potter – a Unitarian – Josiah Wedgwood II, from Joseph Lancaster, thanking him for his generosity in subscriptions towards his Lancastrian Schools, and more particularly, for manufacturing chalk for use by his teachers on the blackboards, when Lancaster found the import of chalks prohibited. In the 1816 Inquiry, Josiah Wedgwood stated that he had his own day school and paid the teacher.

As the Government (through its factory legislation) raised the age of child labour in factories and mines, there soon arose the problem of providing day schools or elementary education for children. This ushered in the battle royal of sectarianism over education, typified by the two rival systems founded by Lancaster and by Bell.

Scriven, the Schools Inspector, in his Report on 'the Education of children in the Potteries' in 1843, put his finger on the cause for the low standard of education and instruction of children and young persons in the Potteries. He stated 'that three-quarters of the children personally examined by him, where the means of instruction are the most abundant, could neither read nor write'. Then he pinpointed the reason for this state of affairs: 'The main cause of this neglect of education is here, as everywhere else, the early age at which children are taken from the school to work, their inability to attend evening school after the labour of the day, and the utter inefficiency of the Sunday Schools to compensate for the loss of the Day Schools.'

Scriven was a keen education enthusiast, and his Report contains one of the strongest pleas for the social and industrial value of education. He reports: 'The most enlightened employer in almost all the districts told me "The better a man is educated the better workman he makes." . . . The managers of the factories concur in expressing an opinion that the extension of education, which the persons engaged in their service have received, is a just measure of their value as workmen. Observation and experience convinces them, not only that their intelligence and other general evidence, but also that their social, moral and religious character, and conduct of the working class as a body, will be raised above its present state, when their education is improved and extended.'

In 1826 a Mechanics' Institute was established. The Marquess of Stafford gave £200, Josiah Wedgwood II gave 100 guineas, and the Duke of Sutherland £100 towards its funds. In 1834, because of the popularity of the institution, a new building was erected, consisting of a lecture room, library, laboratory, committee room and classrooms. It had 1,500 volumes in its library. Ward describes the various educational activities. They included: 'Lectures occasionally delivered either gratuitously by members or friends or else by professional persons, on astronomy, chemistry, geology, botany, or other brands of natural or experimental philosophy. The arts of drawing and design, so intimately connected with the china manufacturers, as well as chemistry in its application to local purposes are the most important studies promoted by the institution.'

However fast the teaching at Sunday Schools and the formal instruction and education at factory and other day schools developed, its full result could only be really effective in a generation or two after our period. The meagre grant of £20,000 from the Government in 1833 was not adequate, however much the voluntary principle operated by Church, Chapel and owners of factories was extended. The quarrels between the religious sects over the curriculum of the elementary education, and the type of teacher, were real stumbling blocks to educational development.

In the widest sense, however, the education of the working class embraced more than formal instruction. The meetings and discussions held in trade-union rooms, the union lodge, the friendly society, and even the oratory of local enthusiasts at street-corner meetings; or the polished lectures and orations by political reformers or radicals, anti-Poor Law speakers, Land Nationalizers, Home Colonizers, Emigrationists, Adult Suffragists, Secularists and what not — all in the long run, in spite of and because of their conflicting views and ideas, helped in their devious ways to enlighten the masses, despite some confusion of thought.

In spite of the Stamp Acts, the period under study was the age of the popular pamphlet and cheap press. Every trade union and political movement had its journal. As we have seen, the pottery workers had their penny weekly *The Potters' Examiner and Workmen's Advocate.*

The Report of the Commissioners sent into the Potteries as late as 1850, emphasizes the influence of literature of this kind. Seymour Tremenheere stated:

There is want of adequate religious and general instruction, hence this state of distrust between men and masters. This distrust is increased by the kind of cheap periodical literature now circulating. Some of them are in the form of penny almanacs, by far the greater part of the matter contained in them being extracts from socialist writers. The Republican and Socialist literature of the Continent is plainly visible in its effect on the tone, language and doctrines of all the English publications. The new feature of the present agitation is the extreme bitterness of spirit and violence of language against all classes, except the lowest, its crusade against wealth and its advocacy of infidelity, and its open adoption of the principles of Socialism.

Here we get a hint of the penetration of Socialist and independent working-class politics into the Potteries, in the decades towards the end of the century, which played such a big part in the creation of a strong Labour Party organization.

Later in the early decades of the twentieth century, all the Parliamentary seats in the Potteries were captured from the pottery manufacturers, and they were replaced on the benches of the House of Commons by trade union leaders from the pottery workers' and miners' unions.

Bibliography

AIKIN, JOHN *A Description of the Country from thirty to forty miles around Manchester* (London, 1795)

ALLBUTT, T. *The Staffordshire Directory* (pub. Hanley)

—— *View of the Staffordshire Potteries* (1818)

ASHTON, T. S. *Iron and Steel in the Industrial Revolution* (Manchester, 1924)

—— (with J. SYKES) *The Coal Industry in the 18th Century* (Manchester, 1929)

BABBAGE, CHARLES *On the Economy of Machinery and Manufactures* (London, 1832)

BAINES, T. *History of the Commerce and Town of Liverpool* (London and Liverpool, 1852)

BARBER, E. ATTLEE *The Pottery and Porcelain of the United States* (New York, 1910)

BOLTON, H. CARRINGTON (ed.) *Scientific Letters of Joseph Priestley*

BOWDEN W. *Industrial Society in England towards the end of the 18th Century* (New York, 1925)

BOYLE, J. Article in *Royal Statistical Society Journal* (Vol. 1, 1839)

—— *Diary, 1834–42* (MSS. Spode Archives)

BRADSHAW *'Railway Guide'* (1847)

BUCHER, CARL *Industrial Evolution* (New York, 1907)

BURTON, WILLIAM *Josiah Wedgwood and His Pottery* (London, 1922)

CHURCH, A. H. *Josiah Wedgwood: Master Potter* (London and New York, 1903)

CLAPHAM J. H. *An Economic History of Modern Britain*, Vols. I & II ('Three vol. edition Cambridge, 1926–38)

DAY, CLIVE *The Distribution of Industrial Occupations in England 1841–1861* (New Haven, 1927)

—— *A History of Commerce* (London, 1909)

DEFOE, DANIEL *Tour of the Whole Island of Great Britain* (Oxford, 1927)

ELY, R. T. *Studies in the Evolution of Industrial Society* (New York, 1910)

EVANS, WILLIAM *The Art and History of the Potting Business*

FALKNER, F. *The Wood Family of Burslem*

FARRER, LADY *Wedgwood-Bentley Correspondence* (Published privately)

FAULKNER, H. V. *Chartism and the Churches*

FONG, H. D. *Triumph of the Factory System in England* (Tientsin, 1930)

FULTON, ROBERT *Treatise on the Improvement of Canal Navigation, etc.* (London, 1796)

FURNIVAL, W. J. *Leadless, Decorative Tiles, etc.* (Stone, Staffs., 1904)

HAMMOND, J. L. AND B. *The Rise of Modern Industry* (London, 1925)
—— *The Town Labourer 1760–1832* (London, 1917)
HARRIS, F. Article on Pottery Machinery *North Staffs Field Club Transactions* (1905)
HAYDEN, A. *Spode and His Successors: A History of the Pottery, Stoke on Trent* (London, 1925)
HELM, E. *Chapters in the History of the Manchester Chamber of Commerce* (London, 1898)
HOME OFFICE PAPERS 1816–20, 1835,6,7 (Public Record Office)

JACKMANN, W. T. *The Development of Transportation in Modern England* (Cambridge, 1916)
JEWITT, LLEWELLYN *The Ceramic Art of Great Britain* (London, 1878)
—— *The Wedgwoods* (London, 1865)

MACPHERSON, D. *Annals of Commerce, Manufactures, Fisheries and Navigation* (London, 1805)
MANTOUX, P. *The Industrial Revolution in the 18th Century* (London, 1929)
MENNELL, R. O. *'Tea, an Historical Sketch'*
METEYARD, ELIZA *The Life of Josiah Wedgwood from his private correspondence and family papers* (London, 1865–66)
—— *A Group of Englishmen, 1795–1816* Records of the Younger Wedgwoods and their Friends: (London, 1871)
MOFFITT, L. *England on the Eve of the Industrial Revolution* (London, 1925)

NEF, J. V. *The Rise of the British Coal Industry* (London, 1932)
NICOLSON, J. S. *History of the English Corn Laws* (London and New York, 1904)

OSBORNE, E. C. AND W. *Guide to the Grand Junction or Birmingham Liverpool and Manchester Railway, etc.* (Birmingham and London, 1838)
OWEN, HAROLD *The Staffordshire Potter* (London, 1901)
OWEN, HUGH *Two Centuries of Ceramic Art in Bristol* (1873)

PARLIAMENTARY PAPERS
   Report of the Inspector of Factories and Mines (1833 and 34)
   Inquiry into the Employment of Children in the Potteries (1816)
   Select Committee Inquiry into the Combination Laws (1824–25)
   Report of the Commissioners to the Potteries (1843)
   House of Commons Journal (1763 and 66)
   Inquiry into the Effects of Power Driven Machinery on the Employment of Children (1834)
PITT, W. *A Topographical History of Staffordshire* (Newcastle-under-Lyme, 1817)
—— *A General View of the Agriculture of the County of Staffordshire* (London, 1794)
PLOT, ROBERT *Topographical Study of Staffordshire* (1686)
'POTTER, THE OLD' *'When I was a child'*
PRATT, E. A. *History of Inland Transport and Communication in England* (London, 1912)

REDFORD, PROF. A. *The Economic History of England* (1760–1860) (London, 1939)

SAINT-FOND, F. de *Travels in England*
SCRIVEN, H. *The Education of Children in the Potteries* (Report, 1843)
SCRIVENOR, H. *The Railways of the United Kingdom* (London, 1849–51)
SHAW, SIMEON *History of the Staffordshire Potteries* (1829)
SMILES, SAMUEL *Lives of the Engineers*, 3 vols. (London, 1861–62) (with special reference to Vol. I on James Brindley)
—— *Josiah Wedgwood: His Personal History* (London, 1894)
SYKES, J. (with T. S. ASHTON) *Coal Industry of the 18th Century* (Manchester, 1929)

TELFORD, THOMAS *A General View of Shropshire*
TUNNICLIFFE, W. *Topographical Survey of the Counties of Staffordshire, Cheshire and Lancashire* (1787)
TURNER, W. *Transfer Printing*

WARBURTON, W. H. *The History of Trade Union Organisation in the North Staffordshire Potteries* (London, 1931)
WEBB, SIDNEY and BEATRICE *The History of Trade Unionism* (London, 1894)
WARD, JOHN *History of Stoke on Trent*
WEDGWOOD, J. C. *Staffordshire Pottery and Its History*
—— *History of the Wedgwood Family*
WEDGWOOD, JULIA *Personal Life of Josiah Wedgwood*
WELCH, C. *History of the Worshipful Company of Pewterers of the City of London* (London, 1902)
WEST, JULIUS *History of the Chartist Movement* (London, 1920)
WILLIAMSON, G. *The Wedgwood Russian Service*
WOODCROFT, B. *List of Patents* (1726–1850)

YOUNG, ARTHUR *Six Months Tour Through the North of England* (London, 1769)

Documents, Private Correspondence, Account Books, etc.

Boulton-Watt Archives. City of Birmingham Library
BOYLE, JOHN. Journal, 1832–42 (Spode Archives MSS.)
BOULTON, WILLIAM. Patent with Joseph Worthington (1863 and 1867)
CARTHEW, JOHN. Clay Lease (1st November 1782)
FOTHERGILL and BOULTON. Correspondence, Assay Office MSS. 1732
General Chamber of Manufacturers. Minutes 1784
Indenture Documents. Aaron Wood to Dr. Thos. Wedgwood, 23 August 1731. Josiah to Thos. Wedgwood, November 11, 1744
MINTON, THOMAS. Archives
MOORE OF HANLEY. Pamphlet (1837) Report of Important meeting of Delegates in the Potteries on behalf of the Potters on December 28,29,30, 1836
North Staffs. Railway Co. History. L.M.S. 1925
OWEN ROBERT. MSS. Collection, Co-operative Union, Manchester
Potters' Chamber of Commerce: Minutes. Pamphlet: The Case of the Manufacturers of China and Earthenware in the Staffordshire Potteries
PROSSER, RICHARD. Patent, 1840 for making tiles, buttons etc.
SPODE-COPELAND. MSS. Collection
WEDGWOOD, JOSEPH. MSS. Collection: Etruria Museum
WHIELDON, THOMAS. Memorandum Book etc., 1749, 1760: Hanley Museum
WRIGHT, SAMUEL. Patent (1830) for Making Tiles

Index

There are four entries which cover the Pottery Industry:
i) Potters: mention of minor potters and the general concerns of master-potters. The major potters are indexed separately by name;
ii) Pottery Industry: general considerations, organisation, numbers, wages etc;
iii) Pottery manufacturing, raw materials and processes;
iv) Trade, methods of selling, exports of pottery and countries involved.